T0330254

The Challenges of Self-Employment in Europe

The Challenges of Self-Employment in Europe

Status, Social Protection and Collective Representation

Edited by

Renata Semenza

Professor of Economic Sociology, University of Milan, Italy

François Pichault

Professor of Human Resource Management, University of Liège, Belgium

Cheltenham, UK • Northampton, MA, USA

Published by
Edward Elgar Publishing Limited
The Lypiatts
15 Lansdown Road
Cheltenham
Glos GL50 2JA
UK

Edward Elgar Publishing, Inc.
William Pratt House
9 Dewey Court
Northampton
Massachusetts 01060
USA

A catalogue record for this book
is available from the British Library

Library of Congress Control Number: 2019930622

This book is available electronically in the **Elgar**online
Social and Political Science subject collection
DOI 10.4337/9781788118453

ISBN 978 1 78811 844 6 (cased)
ISBN 978 1 78811 845 3 (eBook)

Typeset by Servis Filmsetting Ltd, Stockport, Cheshire
Printed by CPI Group (UK) Ltd, Croydon CR0 4YY

Contents

Figures

Tables

Boxes

Contributors

Laura Beuker is a researcher at LENTIC and project officer at MSH (MSH-ULiège). Her previous work has focused on public intermediaries on the labour market in the French-speaking community of Belgium. She has different areas of expertise: the labour market and its evolution, the sociology of public action and labour market intermediaries.

Paolo Borghi is a researcher at the Work and Employment Relations Division, University of Leeds, UK. He is a member of the ERC Starting Grant project SHARE (Seizing the Hybrid Areas of work by Re-presenting self-Employment).

Marie-Christine Bureau is a research sociologist at LISE-CNAM-CNRS in Paris, France. Her work focuses on changes in work and social protection, as well as emerging forms of cooperation. Recent publications include *Un salariat au-delà du salariat?* with A. Corsani (PUN, 2012), 'Le progrès social: quoi de neuf depuis la Tour Eiffel?' (*Dores et déjà*, 2015) and *Makers: Enquête sur les laboratoires du changement social*, with I. Berrebi-Hoffmann and M. Lallement (Seuil, 2018).

Antonella Corsani is an economist and sociologist, currently Associate Professor at University Paris 1 Panthéon Sorbonne. She is a member of the research laboratory IDHES UMR 8533. She works on changes in work and labour relations, especially on the grey zone of labour relationships. She also works on the hypothesis of cognitive capitalism and neoliberalism.

Bernard Gazier is Emeritus Professor of Economics at the Université Paris 1 Panthéon Sorbonne and specializes in labour economics. Most of his work focuses on labour market transitions management and the role of the public policies shaping them. He has edited two Edward Elgar books: G. Schmid and B. Gazier (eds) 2002, *The Dynamics of Full Employment: Social Integration through Transitional Labour Markets* and B. Gazier and F. Bruggeman, 2008, *Restructuring Work and Employment in Europe: Managing Change in an Era of Globalisation.*

Alejandro Godino is a researcher at the Sociological Research Centre on Everyday Life and Work (QUIT) of the Autonomous University of Barcelona (UAB). Previous work has involved the analysis of job quality in outsourced services. He is currently participating in the coordination of European projects focused on changes in the labour market, employment relations and organizations. In addition, he participates as a correspondent with the European Foundation for the Improvement of Living and Working Conditions (EUROFOUND).

Bas Koene is Associate Professor at Rotterdam School of Management in the Netherlands and director of the RSM Case Development Centre. His research interests lie in the area of human agency in processes of institutional change and the evolving organization of work and management of employment. He has published in journals such as *Leadership Quarterly*, *Journal of Management Studies*, *Human Resource Management Journal*, *Journal of Organizational Change Management* and *Human Relations*.

Antonio Martín-Artiles is Full Professor of Industrial Relations and Sociology of Work and director of the Institut d'Estudis del Treball (IET) at the Autonomous University of Barcelona (UAB). He has published in reviews such as the *Journal of Industrial Relations, Transfer: European Review of Labour and Research, Revista Española de Sociología, Política y Sociedad* and *Cuadernos de Relaciones Laborales*.

Oscar Molina is Associate Professor in the Department of Sociology and researcher at the Centre d'Estudis QUIT/Institute for Labour Studies, Autonomous University of Barcelona and has a backgound in social and political science at the European University Institute (EUI-Florence). After working as a research assistant at the Robert Schuman Centre, he spent some time at the Industrial Relations and Human Resources Group, University College Dublin (2005–07). He has taught courses on globalization and industrial relations, industrial relations in Europe and sociology of work.

Anna Mori is a researcher at the University of Milan. Specializing in labour studies, she worked as a research assistant at the Warwick Business School. She has held visiting positions at King's College London and the FAOS, University of Copenhagen. Her research focuses on employment relations and trade union strategies from a comparative perspective, with a specific interest in the public sector. She has published in the *European Journal of Industrial Relations* and *Transfer: European Review of Labour and Research*.

Frédéric Naedenoen specialized in finance at the Graduate School of Liège and in corporate management at the University of Liège. A researcher at LENTIC since 2003, he is a specialist in change management, new employment forms and organizational restructuring. He also studies socio-organizational change in private and public organizations. Since 2014, Frédéric has also been a lecturer at HEC Liège, and since 2015, at the University of Namur, teaching HRM and social dialogue.

Maria Norbäck is a researcher and senior lecturer at the School of Business, Economics and Law at Gothenburg University, Sweden. She studies how media companies and media work is organized. She is especially interested in how freelance work is organized in the media field, how digitalization and social media are changing the media industry, and how the media labour market is transforming.

François Pichault is Full Professor at HEC-Liège (Belgium). He chairs, at the University of Liège, an action-research centre (LENTIC) focused on human and organizational aspects of change processes and new work arrangements on the labour market (see http://www.lentic.ulg.ac.be/). He has authored or co-authored numerous books, book chapters and scientific papers in peer-reviewed journals, on strategic HRM, change management and flexible work arrangements. He currently holds at the University of Liège the Securex professorship on New Opportunities for Organizations, People & Employment Intermediaries in a Changing Labour Market.

Manuela Samek Lodovici is a labour economist, currently president of the Istituto per la Ricerca Sociale (IRS) and director of the IRS Labour Market and Productive Activities Research Unit. She teaches public economics at the University of Castellanza and labour economics at the Catholic University of Milan. She specializes in the evaluation of labour market trends and policies, gender equality policies, socio-economic analysis, industrial relations, and regional and cohesion policy. She has long-standing experience in the direction and coordination of European comparative studies and evaluations for European and national institutions.

Renata Semenza is Professor of Economic Sociology at the University of Milan and Coordinator of the European Master in Labour Studies (MEST-EMLS); principal investigator of the EU project I-WIRE (Independent Workers and Industrial Relations in Europe) and responsible for Horizon 2020–INCASI (International Network of Comparative Analysis on Social Inequalities). Her recent publications include 'Self-Employed Professionals in the European Labour Market: A Comparison between Italy, Germany and the UK' with A. Mori and P. Borghi (2018); 'The Migration of Women in the Light of the Backward and Forward Linkages' (2017); and 'Ensuring Labour Justice in Global Manufacturing: New Actors for Revitalizing Industrial Relations' with I. Hossein (2017).

Elena Sinibaldi has a background in analysis and evaluations of public policies (University of Pavia). Since 2008 she has been working as a freelance social researcher. Her main areas of interest are labour market policies and regional development in rural areas. She is a member of ACTA, the Italian Association of Freelancers.

Klemen Širok is Associate Professor at the University of Primorska, faculty of management, lecturing on human resource management, the sociology of work, organizational behaviour, employee resourcing and career management, and business communication. He has also taught courses on quality management in education, the labour market and management of cross-cultural differences. His research interests include evaluation studies within the labour market and quality assurance in education.

Anna Soru is a researcher in economics and a freelancer. Her main areas of interest are the labour market, highly skilled work, entrepreneurship, self-employment and professional self-employment. In 2004 she founded and is president of ACTA, the Italian Association of Freelancers.

Maylin Stanic attended Rotterdam School of Management and Bocconi University, with a focus on management, specifically Human Resource Management (at RSM) and International Management (at Bocconi). She also worked as a research assistant at Rotterdam School of Management. She currently works as a business consultant with a focus on change management at BearingPoint.

Lars Walter is Associate Professor at the School of Business, Economics and Law at Gothenburg University, Sweden. His research interests include organizing practice in the healthcare sector and the organization of labour markets.

Cristina Zanni has worked in research, training and guidance since 1993. Her main areas of interest are the high-skills market, entrepreneurship, self-employment and independent workers, and labour market evaluation. She is a founding member of ACTA—the Italian Association of Freelancers.

Abbreviations

ACTA	Associazione Consulenti Terziario Avanzato
AFD	Alliance Française des Designers
AJP	Association of Professional Journalists
ATA	Asociación de trabajadores autónomos
BDÜ	Federal Association of Interpreters and Translators [Germany]
BEC	business and employment cooperative
CEPYME	Confederación *Española* de la Pequeña y Mediana Empresa
CESA	Contrat d'entrepreneur-salarié associé
CESE	Conseil économique, social et environnemental
CFDT	Confédération française démocratique du travail
CGIL	Confederazione generale Italiana del lavoro
CGT	Confédération nationale du travail
CIAE	Confederación Intersectoral de Autónomos del
CISL	Confederazione Italiana sindacati lavoratori
CLAP	Camere del Lavoro Autonomo e Precario
CNV	Christelijk Nationaal Vakverbond
CPA	Compte personnel d'activité
CSC	Christian Trade Union [Belgium]
CTAC	Confederation of Autonomous Workers of Catalonia
DBA	*Wet deregulering beoordeling arbeidsrelaties*
DIS-COLL	Indennità di disoccupazione per i lavoratori con rapporto di collaborazione coordinata e continuativa
EAS	Enterprise Allowance Scheme
EFIP	European Federation of Independent Professionals
ERA	Employment Relationship Act
ESPN	European Social Policies Network
Eurostat	Statistical Office of the European Communities
EWCS	European Working Conditions Survey
FEDAE	Federation of Auto-Entrepreneurs [France]
FNV	Federatie Nederlandse Vakbeweging
GLOSA	Union of Culture and Nature of Slovenia
HMRC	Her Majesty's Revenue and Customs [UK]
ICT	information communication technology
IG-Metall	Industriegewerkschaft Metall

INPS	Istituto Nazionale di Previdenza Sociale
INSEE	Institut National de la Statistique et des Etudes Economiques
IoT	Internet of Things
IPs/IPros	independent professionals
IPSE	Association of Independent Professionals and the Self-Employed
ISCO	International Standard Classification of Occupations
I-WIRE	Independent Workers and Industrial Relations, European Research Project
JU	Journalist Union [Sweden]
KSK	*Künstlersozialkasse*
LETA	Ley del Estatuto del Trabajo Autónomo
LMIs	labour market intermediaries
MISSOC	Mutual Information System on Social Protection
MU	Musicians' Union [UK]
NIPs	new independent professionals
OECD	Organisation for Economic Co-operation and Development
OLI	Online Labour Index
PAYE	Pay As You Earn
PIMEC	Pequeña y Mediana empresa de Cataluña
PZO-ZZP	Platform for Independent Entrepreneurs [Netherlands]
REC	Recruitment and Employment Confederation
RETA	*Régimen Especial de Trabajadores Autónomos*
RSI	Régime social des indépendants
Smart	Société Mutuelle pour ARTistes
SUKI	Union Association of Autonomous Creators in the Fields of Culture and Information of Slovenia
TRADE	Trabajadores autónomos dependientes económicamente
TUs	trade unions
UATAE	Unión de Asociaciones de Trabajadores Autónomos y Emprendedores
UC	umbrella company
UCC	union of executives cadres
UPTA	Unión de Profesionales y Trabajadores Autónomos
VAR	*Verklaring Arbeidsrelatie*
VAT	Value Added Tax
VCP	Verenigde Communistische Partij
Ver.di	*Vereinte Dienstleistungsgewerkschaft*—United Services Union
ZSSS	Association of Free Trade Unions of Slovenia
ZZP	Zelfstandige Zonder Personeel

Foreword

David Marsden

It is 20 years since the publication of the Supiot Report, *Au delà de l'emploi*, and the call by a distinguished group of European legal and employment scholars to re-think employment law. How should employment rights adapt to emerging organizational practices of businesses and changing patterns of households. 'Fordist' employment practices of large firms were giving way to more flexible patterns among smaller firms, often working in networks and on a project basis, and driven by changes in technology and product market competition. On the household side, employment and social protection law, modelled on the 'male breadwinner model', was leaving increasing numbers of workers with inappropriate protection. Twenty years on, the rise in the numbers of self-employed, particularly among the highly qualified, and the increased variety and complexity of the tasks they undertake, accentuate the need to adapt the modes of employment and social protection, and the style of representation.

This multi-country study traces out the new opportunities for self-employed professionals. These relate mainly to greater opportunities for autonomous work, being one's own boss, and how global platforms have expanded the market for their services. This has also brought greater flexibility regarding the time and location of their work, and potentially improved work-life balance. Nevertheless, the study also shows how these advantages have come with the risk of greater job insecurity, gaps between projects, lower incomes, and lesser social protection. While the long-established Fordist model of employment, with relatively stable long-term jobs, had a clear demarcation between 'insiders' and 'outsiders', in the sectors of independent professionals, these lines are being redrawn. Although these 'i-Pros' often cluster into communities of practice, which provide a source of job information and reputational control, to become a recognized member may require a long period low paid and insecure work as extended entry tournaments have come to replace established entry paths into employment.

When considering new forms of legislation to improve the employment rights and social protection of workers in self-employment and in the large grey area between that and employee status, one needs a good map of current practice. Above all one needs to know more about the individual and collective strategies that these workers develop in order to ensure a fair bargain. Employment law was long dominated by the 'gold standard' of full-time, long-term, employment as this had emerged from the demands of large-scale capitalist employers and the aspirations of workers and their unions. Although they had conflicting demands over distribution, they frequently shared a common interest in productivity and real wage growth. As Sumner Slichter showed in his classic studies of the rise of collective bargaining in the US economy, large-scale employers shared an interest in stabilizing employment and developing skills, and the norm of full-time long-term jobs provided a contractual framework that suited the interests of both parties.

The chapters in this study illustrate how much the systems of production and service provision have changed over recent decades. The employment law reforms of the mid-twentieth century did not invent what has become known as 'the standard employment contract'. Rather, they sought to build on the employment norms that had evolved out of the interests of labour and employers of their day. Their aim was to consolidate these, and limit abuses. The challenge in the new environment is to identify the emerging patterns and norms of the penumbra that has grown around this contractual form. Then we can begin to consider what practices facilitate new modes of exchange, and what are the abuses that need to be controlled. As Fritz Scharpf observed in *the Games real actors play*, employment rules need not be a source of rigidity. Very often they facilitate cooperation by reassuring the parties concerned that what he calls 'worst case scenarios' have been ruled out, or at least made less likely. In real life prisoners' dilemmas, cooperation is difficult to achieve because the other party has a stronger incentive to defect than to cooperate. But well-designed institutions can make this less likely, so the fruits of cooperation can be enjoyed.

It is hard to conceive such practices in the abstract. One of the values of this study, is that it complements information on the 'top-down' initiatives by established representative institutions, with an account of the 'bottom-up' self-organizing activities. Both are important. The top-down approach can help resolve collective action problems. In contrast, the bottom-up approach is often closer to the immediate dilemmas faced by these workers to balance the flexibility needed to expand their activities with the need for protection from the risks of disloyal behaviour by their contracting partners. By studying these, one can form a picture of the forms of disloyal behaviour to which freelancers and the self-employed themselves know they are exposed, as well as the solutions they have sought to develop. For many self-employed professionals, the cost of production of their service is great, whereas its reproduction is relatively cheap, so that intellectual and artistic property are major concerns. Thus, the British Musicians Union has adapted special norms to regulate recordings in order to protect their members from theft. Likewise, the Writers' Union provides a service to lodge manuscripts in case of disputes over originality. Lacking the workplace as a location of organization, some of these workers have developed new forms of connectivity, exploiting the same platform technologies that have displaced the firm as an employing organization. Exploring these devices provides clues to the development of functional equivalents to the protections that characterize the standard employment relationship. With such protections, these independent professionals can more confidently expand their services, and society benefits. They also provide valuable clues as to the paths for collective action and new forms of employment legislation.

More generally, the findings of this study call for a rethink of the theory of the firm as an employing organisation. The classic works on the modern firm, of Chester Barnard, Ronald Coase and Herbert Simon, derive from the period when 'managerial capitalism' was consolidating its hold. They contrasted the exchange of labour services governed by an open market 'sales contract' with the employment contract governed by an authority relationship. Historically, this made sense as the old contract system was being displaced by the spread of the employment relationship. The growing importance today of hybrid forms of employment and their diversity, as documented in this study, highlight the need to re-think not just employment, but also the nature of employing organisations.

David Marsden
Professor of Industrial Relations
London School of Economics

1. Introduction: self-employed professionals in a comparative perspective

François Pichault and Renata Semenza

The aim of this volume is to explain the variance in legal status, working conditions, social protection and collective representation of self-employed professionals[1] across Europe. The Introduction contextualizes self-employment in a comparative perspective, explaining the economic and technological reasons that support in particular the growth of self-employed professionals, who offer highly qualified and specialized skills that perfectly respond to the needs of contemporary capitalism. The proliferation of these occupations, functional to the services economy, which deviate from the traditional employment relationship, pose challenges to the systems of institutional regulation of labour, welfare and collective representation. The chapter deals with the individual dimensions of autonomy at work (work legal status, work content and working conditions) and addresses the issue of how employment autonomy is governed in different European national contexts. It emphasizes the importance of understanding in which institutional settings professionals develop their activity and may find policy responses to emerging needs for social protection and collective representation. The last part of the Introduction describes the structure of the book, giving a summary of the content of each chapter.

Virtually all capitalist economies deal with the challenges of transition to an on-demand service economy, supported by unprecedented technological developments and the digital revolution that has modified traditional professions and generated new ones, fostering the growth of a body of highly qualified professionals. Since the 1990s, they have played a key role in satisfying the growing demand for flexible, skill-based and

---

[1] We will use this term to cover various concrete individual situations of knowledge-based workers, sometimes with self-employed status, sometimes not, whose activities are neither regulated by the state (via laws) nor by professional bodies and which are often labelled differently: freelancers, independent professionals (IPros), autonomous workers, solo entrepreneurs, etc.

hyper-specialized competences. These project-based forms of occupations produce new job opportunities, but also new risks that demand a revision of the regulatory and social protection framework in European countries. However, at first glance, both institutional regulation and representation seem unequal and remain fragmentary: different countries have adopted different types of legal arrangements, social protection schemes vary in scope and the development of collective organizations differs within each nation. Apparently, common economic pressures, such as global competition and socio-economic change, do not translate into convergent policy responses among European nations.

The spread of individual bargaining is strictly connected to the individualization process of working conditions that has taken place in every industrialized country. The process is ambiguous: it offers more autonomy and self-determination but, on the other hand, workers are subject to facing all the risks associated with their chosen activity. This ambiguity is clearly visible in professional self-employment, largely concentrated in the advanced service sector, comprising a heterogeneous group of workers with both intellectual and technical skills, various types of contract relations and very unequal income levels. Moreover, the demand for collective representation is challenging traditional industrial relations institutions. Given the high diversity of contractual situations, the traditional industrial regulation model based on collective bargaining cannot be applied as such to growing sectors and new forms of work (Eurofound 2015). During the last two decades, innovative experiences have been supported by new forms of association, such as 'quasi-unions' (Heckscher and Carré 2006; Sullivan 2010), and labour market intermediaries (LMIs) (Autor 2008; Bonet et al. 2013; Lorquet et al. 2018; Vinodrai 2015). Consideration of these new scenarios in socio-economic research has been scarce, the focus being mainly on union revitalization strategies (Benassi and Dorigatti 2015; Gumbrell-McCormick and Hyman 2013; Murray 2017). This scarcity is probably also a reaction to the decline of unionization rates and to the loss of centrality of traditional industrial relations models and collective bargaining (Burawoy 2008; Tattersall 2010) that reflects also the sectoral change of the economy. Even less explored is the relationship and coordination between these different forms of workers' organizations and institutional regulation. In particular, there are very few studies on the coordination between unions, quasi-unions and LMIs—either at national or international level—that could be crucial in generating new social dialogue initiatives and supporting the efforts of governments, employers and workers' organizations to manage change and achieve economic and social aims.

The growth of new self-employed professionals—related to the transition to the service economy and the innovative power of digital technologies—can be contrasted to other employment conditions, such as overall numbers of self-employed and employees, which have remained relatively stable over time with perhaps a slight decline in the latter group at the head. What do statistical data tell us?

Firstly, that there is a relevant increase of self-employed professionals involved in knowledge/skill-based activities within the service sectors, especially in non-regulated professions, such as consultants, trainers, interim managers, interpreters, information communication technology (ICT) specialists, artists, creative workers, and so on. Secondly, that it is a structural trend: with a growth rate of 45 per cent in the USA, the UK and Europe during the last decade, it is quite clear that the numbers will continue to grow. Thirdly, contrary to what was long thought, few of them must be considered as false (or bogus) self-employed, that is to say sharing the same working conditions as employees and working for one single client; conversely, the majority are authentically self-employed and work for a plurality of customers on an intermittent basis and short- or mid-term contracts, which matches the needs of contemporary capitalism.

Despite this rise under way in most European countries, especially in the area of non-regulated professions, awareness about the working life experiences of the self-employed is still lacking, both in the political sphere and in academia. In the official discourse of many policymakers, it is a workforce associated with innovation, economic growth and future prosperity. It is also a workforce which can represent a challenge to the traditional organizational and social structures of the workplace, particularly as the intellectual rather than manual nature of their work makes it difficult to apply traditional bureaucratic control over what they do (Thompson et al. 2009; Wynn 2016). Rapelli (2012), Leighton and McKeown (2015), or again Nye and Jenkins (2016) use the term independent professionals (IPros) to capture this population. Their research highlights how uncomfortable they feel with standard employment relationships usually associated with bureaucratic systems and stressful working conditions. In theory, no IPros should be considered as 'failed employees' pushed into self-employment as they have no other choice: many of them have made a conscious choice to work this way (Leighton and Brown 2013) and actively seek independence, autonomy and choice in the workplace (McKeown 2015). However, the legal status adopted by these professionals does not always result from individual choices: it can be imposed, lead to economic dependency and be associated with precariousness as shown in numerous studies (Bergvall-Kåreborn and Howcroft 2013; Casale 2011; de Peuter 2011; Popma 2013; Standing 2011). Thus, while some individuals voluntarily opt-in (Wynn 2016) or act in response to socially embedded practices in their occupation or industry (Bögenhold and Klinglmair 2016; McKeown et al. 2011), others are involuntarily pushed (McKeown 2015). This tension in the push and pull of self-employed professional work suggests that the notion of autonomy at work must be considered carefully.

On the academic side, the literature on flexibility, neo-liberal reforms and labour market changes have focused mainly on temporary and contingent workers, on which most policymakers direct their attention (Koene et al. 2014). Much less attention has been given to other workers with alternative employment arrangements, including independent contract relations (direct contracts for particular services with limited benefits), such as freelancers, self-employed professionals, solo entrepreneurs, and so on, 'whose work is wrapped in a wider context set by the client organization hiring them for their expertise' (Leighton 2014) at the head. Furthermore, most work in this field fails to adopt a cross-country viewpoint. This is where the research interest of this book is located.

We present the major re-elaborated findings of a two-year European project, Independent Workers and Industrial Relations in Europe (I-WIRE).[2] The book draws on empirical work carried out in nine European countries, which embody different welfare state regimes and diverse models of labour market and professional regulation systems. More specifically, the study has been conducted at three levels (Table 1.1): a micro level investigation, through a web survey, of the individual experiences of new independent professionals, examining their working conditions and social needs (wages, benefits, training, working time, etc.); a meso level analysis exploring the support offered by traditional and emerging initiatives of collective representation, with twenty-nine case studies of local and regional organizations across European countries; and macro level research considering the institutional framework of legal regulation and social protection for self-employment at the head. The added value of this comparative study was gained by the significant fieldwork involved, which provided original data and information on new features of the labour market and industrial relations.

Given the critical considerations developed earlier and the lack of attention these issues have received, the volume has a threefold goal: (i) to shed light on conceptual definitions of the topic, (ii) to provide new empirical insights and (iii) to outline effective policy recommendations.

---

[2]   The project (VS2016/0149), supported by the European Commission, was coordinated by Renata Semenza, University of Milan, in partnership with Lentic, Liège University; CNRS, Université de Paris I; ACTA; UAB, Universidad Autonoma de Barcelona; IMIT, Göteborg: University of Primorska; Erasmus University, Rotterdam; IRS; and SMARTbe.

Table 1.1   Summary table: levels of analysis and research contributions

Dimensions	Macro	Meso	Micro
Theoretical orientation	Institutional analysis	Organizational analysis	Individual analysis (subjective orientation)
Unit of analysis	National institutional frameworks	Representative organizations and associations	Self-employed professionals
Empirical focus	Self-employment regulation settings in the EU Member States	Structures and strategies of new and traditional collective representation	Working conditions and social needs of self-employed professionals
Methodological approach	Comparative/ cross-country analysis	National case studies on collective organizations and selection of significant practices	Web survey
Major challenges (collective action problems)	How to create a European common framework of legal status, social protection and labour market regulation	How to support coordination (coalition building, reframing of employment relations system)	How to improve working conditions (supportive network for professional improvement and personal development, active labour market policies)
Key concepts	– Legal recognition of status – Social protection – Collective representation	– Quasi-unions – LMIs – Unions – Self-organizations	– Self-employed professionals; broad professions/ multi-task professions – Middle-class position

1.   INDIVIDUAL EXPERIENCES OF AUTONOMY AT WORK

If autonomy at work must be considered as a key feature of new independent professionals' identity, it is important to take into account the various dimensions through which it can be experienced within modern work arrangements. Three aspects at least must be distinguished.

1.1   Autonomy in Work Status

The prevailing definitions of professionals are logically associated with self-employment (Leighton and McKeown 2015; Nye and Jenkins 2016; Rapelli 2012). However, the seminal paper of Cappelli and Keller (2012) on nonstandard work provides a more complex analytical framework leading to the differentiation of at least four situations:

1. Purely self-employed, working alone and acting as a solo entrepreneur (head of limited company), with a direct relationship to client organizations.
2. Independent contractors supported by umbrella organizations or other third parties, such as crowd-work platforms acting as administrative facilitators.
3. Workers under employment contract with third parties such as professional employer organizations or temp agencies and leased out to client organizations.
4. Regular employees in a subcontracting firm.

The work status of self-employed professionals has consequences for social protection in terms of sickness, disability or retirement. They can access private systems, enjoy facilitated access to the 'functional equivalents' (Marsden 2004) of some social rights, and experience continuous or discontinuous social protection. The legal status may mask more complex situations once we consider the potential economic dependency on a single principal. New independent professionals may indeed establish business relations with either one or numerous clients, either simultaneously or successively. The economic dependency on one single principal may result from a lack of freedom: workers are then forced to accept the status of self-employed (Kautonen et al. 2010). Conversely, the possibility of choice is presented as a key component of self-employed professionals' identity (Leighton and McKeown 2015).

1.2   Autonomy in Work Content

We will now consider a second dimension of employment autonomy: work content. Building on the contributions of Mintzberg on work coordination mechanisms (1979, 1983), we can associate different levels of autonomy with different kinds of control experienced by workers. It is clear that more hierarchical mechanisms (like direct supervision or standardization of work processes imposed by the client organization) will probably give self-employed professionals less autonomy. Conversely, looser mechanisms (like standardization of norms, mutual adjustment and, to a certain extent, standardization of outcomes) provide self-employed professionals with more autonomy in the way they do their job. In most real-life working situations, however, several coordination mechanisms are combined. We must also keep in mind that project-based work may lead to more subtle and implicit forms of control via the internalization of time and organizational pressures (Cicmil et al. 2016). The quality of support offered when performing the job, as well as the possibility of accessing professional expertise, may be another key differentiator of individual working situations.

1.3 Autonomy in Working Conditions

The working conditions of new independent professionals must also be considered. Four scenarios can be distinguished, ranging from more to less autonomy:

- Working conditions can be entirely under the professional's individual responsibility with no engagement of their business partner in terms of skills development, income flows, or time and space arrangements.
- At a higher level, independent professionals can access training packages, shared facilities, and administrative and financial services from third-party structures.
- They can also negotiate customized training paths, salary packages, flexible time and space arrangements.
- Eventually, they can be submitted to standard training programmes, structured salary grids (usually resulting from collective agreements) and fixed time and space arrangements.

These various dimensions (work status, work content and working conditions) may be combined and vary independently. This is why a better understanding of the complex individual working situations of self-employed professionals is needed. A specific chapter of this book reports the results of a survey on such questions.

2. GOVERNING AUTONOMY: NATIONAL CONTEXTS IN COMPARISON

Furthermore, it is important to understand the institutional context in which self-employed professionals develop their activities. The various contextual dimensions can indeed strongly influence the conditions under which they experience autonomy at work, as shown by Schulze Buschoff and Schmidt (2009). These authors compared national legislations in the UK, the Netherlands and Germany, and the extent to which they tend to enlarge either the scope of labour law or the status of employee to dependent self-employed workers (through paid holidays, sickness pay, coverage by collective agreements, etc.). In the UK, a specific status of 'worker', between dependent employment and self-employment has even been created. In Germany, self-employed workers may access unemployment allowances under certain preconditions, while this remains impossible in the UK. In the Netherlands, the recent Work and Security Act (2015) has altered the balance between 'insiders' (employees with permanent contracts) and 'outsiders' (employees with flexible contracts), making easier the entitlements of outsiders to unemployment benefits and redundancy payments. The different countries may thus be clustered according to specific considerations for self-employed workers in their regulatory frameworks.

The way in which the question of economic dependency is considered in each national context is also crucial. Intensive debates continue to take place among scholars and practitioners about the conditions under which a presumed economic dependency may be qualified as a regular employment relationship (Prassl and Risak 2015). In some countries, this question remains mainly based on court judgements—highly dependent on individual perceptions of judges—while in other countries strict criteria are defined by law.

The union density and the coverage rate of collective bargaining widely vary from one country to another (Visser 2012), which may create a specific set of constraints and opportunities for professionals. In particular it is interesting to explore the links between union density and the degree of specific consideration for self-employed workers in the regulatory framework.

Another important question is the level of social protection offered. The focus on professionals in the nine countries covered by our research is an opportunity to test the validity of well-established theories on the varieties of capitalism and welfare state coverage (Esping-Andersen 1990; Hall and Soskice 2001).

The way in which labour market policies are designed in each European member state may also create differences in terms of voicing the concerns of self-employed professionals. Some countries are characterized by a strong public intervention: any new initiative related to work arrangements originates from legislation, often observed in France for instance (self-entrepreneurship status, wage portage, job secondment, employers' alliances, etc.). Some countries (like Belgium) give a priority to collective bargaining, and state intervention is required when social partners are unable to find agreement: the probability of specific legal rules concerning self-employment may be lower in these conditions. In some other countries (like the UK), professional associations have a strong influence on labour market regulation and policies, so that professionals may benefit from special recognition through their active involvement in such associations.

2.1 Shifting the Boundaries of Collective Representation

Facing the risks of job insecurity, discontinuity of income, lack of skills development, restricted access to social security and exclusion from collective bargaining (Davidov 2004; Havard et al. 2009; Hirsch 2016; Keller and Seifert 2013; Wears and Fisher 2012), most self-employed professionals voice their concerns on an individual basis. They want to 'retain the strongly felt option of independence' (Osnowitz 2010, p. 128) with a spontaneous reluctance vis-à-vis collective action (Wynn 2015). Many of them consider that the peculiarities of their work are not understood by conventional unions (who often see them as 'false' self-employed or 'disguised' employees) and prefer to voice directly their own demands. Moreover, their circumstances often prevent self-employed professionals from developing membership of organizations that could grant them the power of collective bargaining (Berntsen 2016; Heery 2009). However, as suggested by Mironi (2010), new forms of representation and voice must be developed according to the multiple and interacting employment models in contemporary organizations.

The ambition of our book is to scrutinize the conditions under which more inclusive forms of social dialogue might be developed in order to meet, as suggested by Heery et al. (2004), the basic needs of self-employed professionals in terms of security (pensions, insurance packages, financial guarantees in case of late payment or bankruptcy, access to mortgages, etc.), human capital (skills development, exchange of expertise) and job-matching (job vacancies, career opportunities).

Monitoring changes in the nature of work relationships is crucial to understanding the scenario affecting labour markets. In the post-industrial capitalism and neo-liberal labour regime era, we can observe how the role of traditional labour market institutions—such as unions and collective bargaining—is declining or experiencing radical transformation (Baccaro and Howell 2011; Meardi 2014) towards new and unconventional settings of employment relations, with the partial exception of Scandinavian countries. This is due to industrial, economic, political and social changes (Crouch 2014; Regalia 2006; Visser 2016).

Trade unions have become less successful in attracting new workers with different types of employment contracts (e.g. nonstandard jobs, economically dependent self-employed, project-based workers). The decline of the traditional institutions of collective industrial relations mixes with the spread of atypical work and the growth of new independent professionals in the most innovative economic sectors (Crouch 2012; Glassner et al. 2011; Streeck 2009). The traditional role of trade unions has been challenged and collective bargaining cannot be applied to a growing part of the job market (Leighton 2014; Rapelli 2012).

In recent years, trade unions in Europe have tried to extend their representation to new groups of workers, both dependent and self-employed. We call this phenomenon the expansion scenario. They have implemented new strategic and organizational actions in order to satisfy the protection needs of 'non-organized' workers (Benassi and Dorigatti 2015; Gumbrell-McCormick and Hyman 2013; Murray 2017). A critical question here is whether self-employed professionals should be absorbed within existing organizational structures or whether a specific structure should be devoted to them (Kornelakis and Voskeritsian 2016; Wynn 2015).

At the same time, new bottom-up organizations have begun to fill the gap left in the system of representation by the trade unions (Milkman 2013; Oswalt 2016). These organizations (often called 'quasi-unions') do not act according to traditional models based on collective bargaining (Bologna 2018). They have different forms and structures, but the same objective: to give voice to all workers who face risks related to their job on an individual basis. Therefore, they adopt similar network strategies (Blyton and Jenkins 2012; Heckscher and Carré 2006; Heery et al. 2004; Jenkins 2013; Sullivan 2010; Tapia 2013). In Europe, such quasi-unions are frequent among self-employed professionals. Apart from some rare studies (e.g. Charhon and Murphy 2016), they have not been examined thoroughly. Industrial relations studies have focused mainly on community and labour organizing approaches adopted by traditional trade unions (Frege and Kelly 2004; Murray 2017; Sullivan 2010). Moreover, studies on job transformations have not focused on the representation needs of 'new self-employed workers'. In EU countries, very few studies have focused on the coordination between unions and quasi-unions. Finally, these new organizations can also deliver specific services as new LMIs: the relations between such LMIs and quasi-unions are thus very important to consider (Xhauflair et al. 2018).

A third possibility is the development of alternative managerial artefacts securing flexible jobs through a direct participation of workers, on a local basis, without any form of collective action and/or representation on a broader scale. In this perspective, self-employed professionals—often belonging to similar business sectors—create small-scale structures in which they can be directly involved in decision-making processes and daily management. They retain distance from conventional unions and do not want to be represented by any other institutional body. These new forms of industrial democracy are more likely to develop through specific legal structures such as cooperatives (Siapera and Papadopoulou 2016). They may be seen as mutual support organizations, offering employment contracts and a variety of services from bookkeeping and legal help to invoicing and credit control. In some countries, like France, they may benefit from a favourable regulatory framework and appear as levers of institutional innovation (Bureau and Corsani 2015).

Some studies have documented the expansion scenario and some advocacy work emanating from activists and associations of self-employed professionals, but few empirical investigations are available on the various paths towards more inclusive industrial relations for such workers. This volume fills this gap through an in-depth understanding of the solutions developed by unions, quasi-unions or other kinds of LMIs in each European member state.

3. STRUCTURE OF THE BOOK AND MAIN RESULTS

In order to understand how self-employment regulation has developed across countries from a socio-economic perspective, this book outlines a way to clarify three critical dimensions relating to the labour market conditions of self-employed professionals at the head: (i) the contested definition of their legal status and the (ad hoc) regulation adopted in different European countries (Dekker 2010; Heery et al. 2004; Leighton 2014; Rapelli 2012; Schulze Buschoff and Schmidt 2009; Westerveld 2012); (ii) their position in the social protection system (European Social Policies Network, ESPN; Bouget et al. 2017); and (iii) the complexity of collective representation within a context of labour market fragmentation.

Given these three critical dimensions, different questions may be raised. Is there a process of similar (convergent) policy responses among European countries, or does differentiation still prevail? Are there innovative regulation laws, policies and practices—either at the national or regional level—able to match these critical dimensions? To what extent do these collective organizations provide new collective capabilities in terms of income continuity, skills development, access to health protection, retirement and unemployment benefits? Are they mainly based on individual pick-and-choose formulas? Do they replicate the social rights of employees or do they offer 'functional equivalents' to these rights (Marsden 2008)? Do they exploit existing 'holes' in the current regulatory framework or do they breach this framework and develop new devices? Can we predict a new era of collective representation, with the rise of new durable solidarities? The responses to such socio-economic challenges are organized in the book as follows.

Chapter 2 tackles the topic of the new forms of self-employment as a theoretical matter, in the light of their extraordinary increase in European economies. Considering first the drivers of this growth in the majority of countries, it then provides some interpretations on the way in which professional self-employment—halfway between hierarchy and market—is challenging the solid theories of labour market dualization (insider–outsider divide) and the contraposition between dependent and autonomous work. Moreover, the chapter explains why self-employment is becoming the typical work model for the digital economy and how a paradox is occurring between the survival of a model of professionalism, both in markets and companies and, simultaneously, the loss of social status for these professionals. High levels of education and professional specialization are no longer a guarantee of high levels of income and social status, and this has repercussions for class structure. Within this theoretical framework, the second part of the chapter is devoted to considering the multiple institutional dilemmas that the governments and the European Union are called upon to face, with respect to the ambiguity of self-employed professionals' legal status and the weakness of their social protection.

In Chapter 3, after the construction of an empirical basis and some conceptual definitions, within a preliminary quantitative analysis on the total self-employed population (using Eurostat data), the original results of an international web survey are presented, whose aims are to explore the socio-economic characteristics, professional status, expectations and perceived needs of self-employed professionals. 'Snowball sampling', a research technique widely experienced in the social sciences, was used as a way of gathering information about a population without having to measure its entire size. The social needs of new independent professionals strongly differ from those of employees because they usually operate with a high degree of autonomy, they multiply various subordination links and working places, and they may be the owners of their working tools. Therefore, they are submitted to very high risks of precariousness and social exclusion due to their discontinuous access to social rights.

As part of the growth of contingent work, the overall picture that emerges from the data analysis shows a population with clearly identifiable characteristics: urban localization, variable working time and simultaneous engagement in multiple jobs. A strong orientation towards autonomy at work emerges, but the majority of respondents state a low annual income level in all European countries considered. Low pay is one of the three main problems for the self-employed professionals, the others being a perception of vulnerability in respect to social risks (unemployment, future pension benefits, illness, maternity) and a vacuum of collective representation.

Chapter 4 presents an overview of the various regulatory and legal frameworks around self-employed workers, the main institutional arrangements in place and a state-of-the art of the social dialogue in each country's case study. Nine European countries are covered: Belgium, France, Germany, Italy, the Netherlands, Slovenia, Spain, Sweden and the UK. They embody different welfare state regimes and diverse models of labour market and professional regulation. Each country study presents the same structure, and includes an analysis of the institutional framework, of the public policies supporting self-employment, and of the emergent and innovative strategies of collective representation. The picture that emerges from the country studies is small reforms at the margin and great fragmentation of the measures implemented, accompanied by institutional experimentalism and some innovative strategies of collective representation, carried out by new actors in the industrial relations arena.

Chapter 5 provides a transversal analysis of the country studies presented in the previous chapter, with the aim of explaining variances and convergences among European countries, and aspects of continuity or discontinuity with the past. The comparative analysis of national regulation systems includes differences and similarities in the legal recognition of a specific status for self-employed professionals (universal, binary and hybrid approaches). A common cross-country feature is that self-employed workers benefit from weaker social rights than regular employees. The chapter explores if there is any movement towards a better social protection for self-employed workers. In order to reach an appropriate understanding of the complex and fragmented dynamics occurring in the European labour market, it proposes a multidimensional interpretative approach. This means combining structural dimensions (such as regulatory framework, industrial relations system, degree of economic development, cultural openness vis-à-vis new work arrangements or socio-demographic characteristics) with agency factors (e.g. institutional entrepreneurship, strategies emanating from unions, quasi-unions and labour market intermediaries, and political reforms).

Chapter 6 focuses on the new forms of collective representation and organization by which self-employed professionals articulate and defend their interests. This is a specific topic in the broader debate on nonstandard and precarious work. The deep analysis of innovative forms of collective interest representation, based on twenty-nine collective organizations investigated across Europe, provides a picture of the proliferation of new actors, bottom-up organizations, beside (or beyond) traditional unions, aimed at collective representation of this growing unorganized segment of the labour market. More specifically, the chapter focuses on the presence of 'new' forms of organization and self-organization (quasi-unions, LMIs and cooperatives); the organizational and strategic answers coming from the traditional trade unions to include and give voice to new independent professionals; and the rise of new forms of dialogue and cooperative relationship (coordination) between 'old' and 'new' organizations. The chapter explores the conditions under which coordination between trade unions, quasi-unions and LMIs can help social inclusion and meet the heterogeneous representation demands and protection needs arising from new types of professionals. Three main organizational strategies are identified: provision of services, as neo-mutual organizations; advocacy, lobbying and political activities; building coalition and new alliances in order to reinforce their legitimacy. A combination of strategies and capacities to create partnerships characterize each national context or cluster of countries. These organizations have gradually institutionalized, becoming relevant interlocutors in the public debate and policy making.

Chapter 7 takes up the most relevant results that emerge from the various contributions of the book and underlines that the growing part of self-employed professionals has not yet been accompanied by a structural revision of the regulatory framework. There is a lack of a comprehensive reform design regarding legal recognition and regulation, social protection and industrial relation models, which still need to be adapted to unanswered demands. Are we currently facing a transition from a prevalent 'legal-regulatory paradigm' towards a 'representative paradigm' of qualified self-employment in Europe? We can expect that new forms of collective representation will have an impact on both legal and professional status and state regulation, in terms of eligibility to social protection. The challenges posed by new employment trends ask for new tailored and focused policy responses to support the equal treatment of workers, whatever their status. Among many options assessed in the recent debate, the adoption of a universal rights approach, whatever the status and employment relationship, appears the most appropriate to address current and future trends in employment patterns. Fair work and payment conditions, standardized access to social rights (maternity and parental leave, health insurance, safety at work, etc.), professional recognition and lifelong learning should transcend employment status and relationships with particular employers.

Finally, the Afterword explores the possibility that a new era of social dialogue is currently emerging in Europe. Self-employed professionals represent a key stake, because they are skilled, they are mere workers and do not possess the traditional capital and assets of entrepreneurs. Since the beginning of the twenty-first century, they have been the most dynamic segment of the labour market. They represent, in a context of enduring unemployment and precariousness in the European Union, a central way of developing employment and diversifying careers. However, they do not fit into the classical processes of social dialogue, which were devised and implemented for salaried workers many years ago. Beginning with a traditional definition of social dialogue, and briefly showing the trends and challenges affecting it in the European Union, the Afterword considers the specific needs of these new workers connected to the rich resources they can provide.

The main findings of our book show a mixed picture, with shared challenges and partly divergent responses that denote, however, signals of change with the potential to overcome the insider–outsider labour market divide. Firstly, throughout all aspects explored during this research, we found many common trends among the EU countries investigated. However, facing similar challenges, each country shapes its own responses in terms of social sustainability. Secondly, three strategic models of collective representation and mobilization may be observed across different national contexts: servicing, lobbying and coalition-building. Each national context is characterized by a specific combination of strategies depending upon the local capacity of partnership and coalition. Thirdly, an increasing number of self-employed professionals are involved in digital platforms as one of the tools of their main employers/users/customers/business partners. Self-employed professionals are, in fact, among the principal recipients of platform capitalism, which has accelerated and exasperated all the perverse effects of labour market deregulation. Regulation in this sector of the economy is lagging behind the reality. Beyond legal re-regulation, other urgent challenges have emerged: (i) the potential extension of social protection to minimal and universal social protection schemes (versus selective and fragmented protection); (ii) the potential implementation of active labour market policies to support and promote sustainable self-employment; and (iii) the potential strengthening of bottom-up organizations (quasi-unions, LMIs, etc.) extending the collective representation of new independent professionals within a renewed social dialogue. Are we witnessing a defensive wave in society against market excesses, leading to the reinvention of new solidarity links according to the current evolution of work arrangements?[3]

---

[3] This study was completed with the financial support of the European Union (DG Employment and Social Affairs VS/2016/0149); the content of this publication is the sole responsibility of the authors and the European Union is not liable for the views expressed by the authors not at the head.

The editors would like to thank France Bierbaum (Liège University) for the revision of references.

REFERENCES

Autor, D. H. (2008), *The Economics of Labor Market Intermediation: An Analytic Framework*, Working Paper 14348, National Bureau of Economic Research, September, accessed at http://www.nber.org/papers/w14348.

Baccaro, L. and C. Howell (2011), 'A Common Neoliberal Trajectory: The Transformation of Industrial Relations in Advanced Capitalism', *Politics & Society*, **39** (4), 521–63.

Benassi, C. and L. Dorigatti (2015), 'Straight to the Core—Explaining Union Responses to the Casualization of Work: The IG Metall Campaign for Agency Workers', *British Journal of Industrial Relations*, **53** (3), 533–55.

Bergvall-Kåreborn, B. and D. Howcroft (2013), '"The Future's Bright, the Future's Mobile": A Study of Apple and Google Mobile Application Developers', *Work, Employment and Society*, **27** (6), 964–81.

Berntsen, L. (2016), 'Reworking Labour Practices: On the Agency of Unorganized Mobile Migrant Construction Workers', *Work, Employment and Society*, **30** (3), 472–88.

Blyton, P. and J. Jenkins (2012), 'Mobilizing Resistance: The Burberry Workers' Campaign against Factory Closure', *The Sociological Review*, **60** (1), 25–45.

Bögenhold, D. and A. Klinglmair (2016), 'Independent Work, Modern Organizations and Entrepreneurial Labor: Diversity and Hybridity of Freelancers and Self-Employment', *Journal of Management & Organization*, **22** (6), 843–58.

Bologna, S. (2018), *The Rise of the European Self-Employed Workforce*, Milan: Mimesis International.

Bonet, R., P. Cappelli and M. Hamori (2013), 'Labor Market Intermediaries and the New Paradigm for Human Resources', *Academy of Management Annals*, **7** (1), 341–92.

Bouget, D., D. Ghailani, S. Spasova and B. Vanhercke (2017), *Access to Social Protection for People Working on Non-Standard Contracts and as Self-Employed in Europe: A Study of National Policies*, Luxembourg: Publication Office of the European Union.

Burawoy, M. (2008), 'The Public Turn: From Labor Process to Labor Movement', *Work and Occupations*, **35** (4), 371–87.

Bureau, M.-C. and A. Corsani (2015), 'Les coopératives d'activité et d'emploi : pratiques d'innovation institutionnelle' [Business and Employment Co-Operatives: The Practices of Institutional Innovation], *Revue Française de Socio-Économie*, **1** (15), 213–31.

Cappelli, P. and J. Keller (2012), 'Classifying Work in the New Economy', *Academy of Management Review*, **38** (4), 575–96.

Casale, G. (ed.) (2011), *The Employment Relationship: A Comparative Overview*, Oxford: Hart; Geneva: International Labour Office.

Charhon, P. and D. Murphy (2016), *The Future of Work in the Media, Arts & Entertainment Sector: Meeting the Challenge of Atypical Working*, accessed at https://www.fim-musicians.org/wp-content/uploads/atypical-work-handbook-en.pdf.

Cicmil, S., M. Lindgren and J. Packendorff (2016), 'The Project (Management) Discourse and its Consequences: On Vulnerability and Unsustainability in Project-Based Work', *New Technology, Work and Employment*, **31** (1), 58–76.

Crouch, C. (2012), 'Employment, Consumption, Debt, and European Industrial Relations Systems', *Industrial Relations: A Journal of Economy and Society*, **51** (s1), 389–412.

Crouch, C. (2014), 'Putting Neoliberalism in its Place', *The Political Quarterly*, **85** (2), 114–21.

Davidov, G. (2004), 'Joint Employer Status in Triangular Employment Relationships', *British Journal of Industrial Relations*, **42** (4), 727–46.

de Peuter, G. (2011), 'Creative Economy and Labor Precarity: A Contested Convergence', *Journal of Communication Inquiry*, **35** (4), 417–25.

Dekker, F. (2010), 'Labour Flexibility, Risks and the Welfare State', *Economic and Industrial Democracy*, **31** (4), 593–611.

Esping-Andersen, G. (1990), *The Three Worlds of Welfare Capitalism*, Princeton, NJ: Princeton University Press.

Eurofound (2015), *New Forms of Employment*, Publications Office of the European Union, accessed at https://www.eurofound.europa.eu/fr/publications/report/2015/working-conditions-labour-market/new-forms-of-employment.

Frege, C. M. and J. E. Kelly (eds) (2004), *Varieties of Unionism: Strategies for Union Revitalization in a Globalizing Economy*, Oxford and New York: Oxford University Press.

Glassner, V., M. Keune and P. Marginson (2011), 'Collective Bargaining in a Time of Crisis: Developments in the Private Sector in Europe', *Transfer: European Review of Labour and Research*, **17** (3), 303–22.

Gumbrell-McCormick, R. and R. Hyman (2013), *Trade Unions in Western Europe: Hard Times, Hard Choices*, Oxford and New York: Oxford University Press.

Hall, P. A. and D. W. Soskice (eds) (2001), *Varieties of Capitalism: The Institutional Foundations of Comparative Advantage*, Oxford and New York: Oxford University Press.

Havard, C., B. Rorive and A. Sobczak (2009), 'Client, Employer and Employee: Mapping a Complex Triangulation', *European Journal of Industrial Relations*, **15** (3), 257–76.

Heckscher, C. and F. Carré (2006), 'Strength in Networks: Employment Rights Organizations and the Problem of Co-Ordination', *British Journal of Industrial Relations*, **44** (4), 605–28.

Heery, E. (2009), 'Trade Unions and Contingent Labour: Scale and Method', *Cambridge Journal of Regions, Economy and Society*, **2** (3), 429–42.

Heery, E., H. Conley, R. Delbridge and P. Stewart (2004), 'Beyond the Enterprise: Trade Union Representation of Freelances in the UK', *Human Resource Management Journal*, **14** (2), 20–35.

Hirsch, B. (2016), 'Dual Labor Markets at Work: The Impact of Employers' Use of Temporary Agency Work on Regular Workers' Job Stability', *ILR Review*, **69** (5), 1191–215.

Jenkins, J. (2013), 'Organizing "Spaces of Hope": Union Formation by Indian Garment Workers', *British Journal of Industrial Relations*, **51** (3), 623–43.

Kautonen, T., S. Down, F. Welter, P. Vainio, J. Palmroos, K. Althoff and S. Kolb (2010), '"Involuntary Self-Employment" as a Public Policy Issue: A Cross-Country European Review', *International Journal of Entrepreneurial Behaviour & Research*, **16**, 112–29.

Keller, B. and H. Seifert (2013), 'Atypical Employment in Germany: Forms, Development, Patterns', *Transfer: European Review of Labour and Research*, **19** (4), 457–74.

Koene, B. A. S., N. Galais and C. Garsten (eds) (2014), *Management and Organization of Temporary Agency Work*, New York: Routledge.

Kornelakis, A. and H. Voskeritsian (2016), 'Getting Together or Breaking Apart? Trade Union Strategies, Restructuring and Contingent Workers in Southern Europe', *Economic and Industrial Democracy*, available at https://doi. org/10.1177/0143831X15627500.

Leighton, P. (2014), 'The Rise of Europe's Independent Professionals: But Why the Reluctance to Embrace Them?', *Business Law Review*, **35** (3), 84–92.

Leighton, P. and D. Brown (2013), *Future Working: The Rise of Europe's Independent Professionals (IPRos)*, EFIP.

Leighton, P. and T. McKeown (2015), 'The Rise of Independent Professionals: Their Challenge for Management', *Small Enterprise Research*, **22** (2–3), 119–30.

Lorquet, N., J.-F. Orianne and F. Pichault (2018), 'Who Takes Care of Non-Standard Career Paths? The Role of Labour Market Intermediaries', *European Journal of Industrial* Relations, **24** (3), 279–295.

Marsden, D. (2004), 'The "Network Economy" and Models of the Employment Contract', *British Journal of Industrial Relations*, **42** (4), 659–84.

Marsden, D. (2008), '"Project-Based Employment" and Models of the Employment Contract', in P. Ester, R. Muffels, J. Schippers and T. Wilthagen (eds), *Innovating European Labour Markets: Dynamics and Perspectives*, Cheltenham: Edward Elgar Publishing, pp. 133–62.

McKeown, T. (2015), 'What's in a Name? The Value of "Entrepreneurs" Compared to "Self-Employed"', in A. Burke (ed.), *The Handbook of Research on Freelancing and Self-Employment*, Dublin: Senate Hall Academic Publishing, pp. 121–34.

McKeown, T., M. Bryant and R. Cochrane (2011), 'The Role of Emotions in Supporting Independent Professionals', in C. E. J. Härtel, N. M. Ashkanasy and W. J. Zerbe (eds), *What Have We Learned? Ten Years On: Research on Emotion in Organizations*, Bingley: Emerald, vol. 7, pp. 133–47.

Meardi, G. (2014), 'The (Claimed) Growing Irrelevance of Employment Relations', *Journal of Industrial Relations*, **56** (4), 594–605.

Milkman, R. (2013), 'Back to the Future? US Labour in the New Gilded Age', *British Journal of Industrial Relations*, **51** (4), 645–65.

Mintzberg, H. (1979), *The Structuring of Organizations: A Synthesis of the Research*, Englewood Cliffs, NJ: Prentice-Hall.

Mintzberg, H. (1983), *Power In and Around Organisations*, Englewood Cliffs, NJ: Prentice-Hall.

Mironi, M. (2010), 'Reframing the Representation Debate: Going beyond Union and Non-Union Options', *ILR Review*, **63** (3), 367–83.

Murray, G. (2017), 'Union Renewal: What Can We Learn from Three Decades of Research?', *Transfer: European Review of Labour and Research*, **23** (1), 9–29.

Nye, L. and K. Jenkins (2016), *Understanding Independent Professionals in the EU 2015*, London: IPSE, June, accessed at http://www.crse.co.uk/research/understanding-independent-professionals-eu-2015.

Osnowitz, D. (2010), *Freelancing Expertise: Contract Professionals in the New Economy*, Ithaca, NY: Cornell University/ILR Press.

Oswalt, M. M. (2016), 'Improvisational Unionism', *California Law Review*, **104** (3), 597–670.

Popma, J. (2013), *The Janus Face of the 'New Ways of Work': Rise, Risks and Regulation of Nomadic Work*, Working Paper 2013.07, Brussels: ETUI, p. 45.

Prassl, J. and M. Risak (2015), 'Uber, Taskrabbit, and Co.: Platforms as Employers—Rethinking the Legal Analysis of Crowdwork', *Comparative Labor Law & Policy Journal*, **37** (3), 619–52.

Rapelli, S. (2012), *European I-Pros: A Study*, London: Professional Contractors Group Ltd.

Regalia, I. (ed.) (2006), *Regulating New Forms of Employment: Local Experiments and Social Innovation in Europe*, Abingdon and New York: Routledge.

Schulze Buschoff, K. and C. Schmidt (2009), 'Adapting Labour Law and Social Security to the Needs of the "New Self-Employed"—Comparing the UK, Germany and the Netherlands', *Journal of European Social Policy*, **19** (2), 147–59.

Siapera, E. and L. Papadopoulou (2016), 'Entrepreneurialism or Cooperativism? An Exploration of Cooperative Journalistic Enterprises', *Journalism Practice*, **10** (2), 178–95.

Standing, G. (2011), *The Precariat: The New Dangerous Class*, London and New York: Bloomsbury.

Streeck, W. (2009), *Re-Forming Capitalism: Institutional Change in the German Political Economy*, Oxford and New York: Oxford University Press.

Sullivan, R. (2010), 'Organizing Workers in the Space between Unions: Union-Centric Labor Revitalization and the Role of Community-Based Organizations', *Critical Sociology*, **36** (6), 793–819.

Tapia, M. (2013), 'Marching to Different Tunes: Commitment and Culture as Mobilizing Mechanisms of Trade Unions and Community Organizations', *British Journal of Industrial Relations*, **51** (4), 666–88.

Tattersall, A. (2010), *Power in Coalition: Strategies for Strong Unions and Social Change*, Ithaca, NY: Cornell University Press.

Thompson, P., M. Jones and C. Warhurst (2009), 'From Conception to Consumption: Creativity and the Managerial Missing Link', in A. McKinlay and C. Smith (eds), *Creative Labour: Working in the Creative Industries*, Basingstoke: Palgrave Macmillan, pp. 51–71.

Vinodrai, T. (2015), 'Constructing the Creative Economy: Design, Intermediaries and Institutions in Toronto and Copenhagen', *Regional Studies*, **49** (3), 418–32.

Visser, J. (2012), 'The Rise and Fall of Industrial Unionism', *Transfer: European Review of Labour and Research*, **18** (2), 129–41.

Visser, J. (2016), *ICTWSS Data Base: Version 5.1*, Amsterdam: Amsterdam Institute for Advanced Labour Studies (AIAS), University of Amsterdam, September, accessed at http://uva-aias.net/en/ictwss.

Wears, K. H. and S. L. Fisher (2012), 'Who is an Employer in the Triangular Employment Relationship? Sorting Through the Definitional Confusion', *Employee Responsibilities and Rights Journal*, **24** (3), 159–76.

Westerveld, M. (2012), 'The "New" Self-Employed: An Issue for Social Policy?', *European Journal of Social Security*, **14** (3), 156–73.

Wynn, M. T. (2015), 'Organising Freelancers: A Hard Case or a New Opportunity?', *International Review of Entrepreneurship*, **13** (2), 93–102.

Wynn, M. T. (2016), 'Chameleons at Large: Entrepreneurs, Employees and Firms— the Changing Context of Employment Relationships', *Journal of Management & Organization*, **22** (6), 826–42.

Xhauflair, V., B. Huybrechts and F. Pichault (2018), 'How Can New Players Establish Themselves in Highly Institutionalized Labour Markets? A Belgian Case Study in the Area of Project-Based Work', *British Journal of Industrial Relations*, **56** (2), 370–94.

2. New self-employment as a theoretical matter

Renata Semenza and Anna Mori

As noted in Chapter 1, this book aims to update the comparative knowledge of self-employment in technical and intellectual professions, in the light of its extraordinary increase in European economies.[1] The expansion of self-employment is relevant not just from a quantitative aspect, but also for the change in its internal composition and for the growing relevance it is taking as a contractual form of work, whose nature and characteristics are functional to new knowledge-intensive areas of the economy. At an analytical level, the study of this segment of the labour market has the advantage of representing—as a unit of analysis—an identified category (though heterogeneous) composed of independent highly skilled workers, concentrated in the advanced tertiary sectors of the economy.

Thus, a first crucial question concerns the driving forces of such growth. The main reasons are certainly to be found in the processes of transformation of the economy and in the organizational change of production, but a comprehensive explanation has also to take into account those individual motivations linked to new lifestyles and new social aspirations experienced by self-employed workers. Accordingly, analysis of the drivers underpinning the development of this phenomenon has to focus on changes in the demand and the supply, and on the way in which the division of labour between industrial and service sectors is taking shape. Furthermore, the increasing interplay between internal and external labour markets is relevant, considering elements of competition and iniquity between the so-called insider and outsider workers. This chapter provides some insights from literature that will explain the causes and the consequences of these new labour market configurations.

---

[1]   The analysis of trends in self-employment in Europe, as we will see in Chapter 3, shows that between 2008 and 2016 the increase in the number of self-employed professionals peaked at +24.8 per cent, while the number of employees increased by 11.1 per cent and the number of non-professional self-employed decreased by 0.9 per cent (Eurostat 2017).

1. DRIVERS OF NEW SELF-EMPLOYMENT GROWTH

The dynamism of the new self-employment is due to the process of economic transformation that has marked the shift from industrial manufacture to a service economy. This change is strictly intertwined with technological evolution, which has radically changed the organizational models of services production, in particular in the tertiary sector through socio-technical transformation processes (Dolata 2011).

Advanced capitalist societies have, in fact, experienced a gradual overcoming of mass production processes, replaced by the post-Fordism organization of production. Organizational studies on post-Fordism have focused on the 'network enterprise' model (Butera 1990), which posits a central productive nucleus surrounded by a myriad of smaller entities, including single professionals and collaborators, functional to core production. On the other hand, contrasting scholarship has investigated the concept of flexible production (Regini 1987): the search for increasing flexibility in the production chain has in fact put major pressure on firms, which as a response started to outsource a growing number of activities and tasks. Restructuring practices towards outsourcing led to a widening of the labour supply, increasingly comprised of autonomous workers offering their skills and professionalism in the labour market (Stanworth and Stanworth 1995). Moreover, under mounting international pressures, firms started to downsize their directly employed workforce and replace it with an autonomous external labour force. Following such transformations, the post-Fordism paradigm affirmed itself, requiring a new reserve army of independent workers. From a sociological posture, this segment of the self-employed increasingly bears out Sennett's (1998) notion of the flexible person, characterized by the lack of any tie to a company as a community, and by a remarkable availability to all kinds of temporal, spatial, and even existential flexibility.

Since the 1990s, the socio-economic debate has treated labour market flexibility as an organizational solution that allows firms to adapt more easily to market fluctuations, increasing their performance through a reduction of labour hoarding. However, from an empirical point of view, the nature of the relation between flexibility and productivity remains under scrutiny (Malgarini et al. 2013). On the one hand, the literature has highlighted a positive effect of nonstandard contracts on firm performance, due to a reduction in labour costs and an increase in companies' ability to innovate and compete in global markets. On the other hand, a negative effect of flexibility has been pointed out, due to a decrease in human capital investment and, hence, in performance and competitiveness in the long term.

Moreover, current trends towards restructuring and vertical disintegration of work within global value chains (i.e. organizations with 'weak' rather than 'strong' links between segments, modules and work phases, where the latter are distinct and dispersed globally) are turning work into a variable highly dependent (much more so than in the past) on market cycles. Hence, this model of work organization has been accorded an increasingly important role to self-employed professionals, given that companies entrust them with wide-ranging types of activities and tasks, including planning, design, advertising, marketing and markets exploration, thus exploiting and at the same time fostering the reproduction of a new generation of self-employed workers.

A further driver of the growth of self-employment can be found in transformations of the socio-economic system over recent decades, which has required a strong expansion of the services functional to businesses (as intermediate services) and to people (final services) and accordingly a larger and 'far more diverse workforce incorporating high earning and highly skilled workers who serve a dynamic role for businesses, mainly working as complements to employees and frequently undertaking innovation' (Burke 2015, p. iii).

Hence, such process of tertiarization of advanced economies has further contributed to the demand for independent professional workers (Wright 1997), functional to newly developed economic sectors like intermediation, financial activities, consultancy and information sharing. More recently, new research streams are shedding light on the linkages between independent workers and the new economies, including the platform economy (Drahokoupil and Fabo 2016), the collaborative economy (European Commission 2016) and the gig economy (McKinsey Global Institute et al. 2016). Despite these economic segments still involving limited numbers of an employed workforce,[2] they have opened new reflections on the development of work in the digital labour market, characterized by poorly regulated, segmented or even unregulated working conditions for freelancers offering services online.

---

[2] The relevance of digital labour markets is very difficult to quantify and sources usually comprise aggregated administrative data provided by large platforms or ad hoc surveys, often of little significance. McKinsey Global Institute et al. (2016) has estimated self-employed enrolment at 64.5 million workers; a second report (Codagnone et al. 2016) estimated a figure of 52.2 million. These are either underestimations because they consider only large platforms, or overestimations because the same individual could have been counted several times if he/she was registered on more than one platform. Recently, the Oxford Internet Institute has developed the Online Labour Index (OLI) (https://www.oii.ox.ac.uk/blog/tag/online-labour-index/), an economic indicator providing statistics on the digital labour market, relating to the five major English language platforms, intercepting both job demand and supply (Kässi and Lehdonvirta 2016).

A further aspect to be considered is the change in workers' individual preferences about lifestyle and the need to find alternative access to employment, due to the lack of standard employment contracts. Independent work might in fact represent a response to the search for alternative and innovative contractual arrangements that ensure hourly flexibility, high mobility and commitments to multiple employers (Benz and Frey 2008). Since the 1970s, European and American sociologists have attributed the surge in the population of self-employed to a sort of spontaneous and liberating uprising of the new generations of workers, attracted by lifestyles providing an alternative to the status of an employee, tied to the constraints set by companies (Bureau and Corsani 2014). Hence these workers have been stimulated by the desire for higher autonomy, flexibility, discretion in the management of working time and place, and the possibility of grasping opportunities offered by societal innovations. These go hand in hand with the opportunity for freelancers to establish their own rules, as opposed to experiencing a hetero-direct existence (Hakim 1988; Leighton 1982).

It follows that adhering to the post-Fordism paradigm implies that the proliferation of a population of self-employed workers cannot be considered either a cyclical effect of the employment crisis (Steinmetz and Wright 1989) or simply a phenomenon limited to false self-employment. Other observers have partly attributed the revival of self-employment to the decline of employment opportunities in the salaried economy (Bögenhold and Staber 1991). It is hence symptomatic of labour market deficiencies, rather than the result of fundamental changes in the 'advanced economies that made self-employment more attractive and/or competitive' (Blau 1987, p. 447). Accordingly, the rise in self-employment has to be seen as a structural phenomenon, which responds to the contemporary socio-economic needs.

This topic has been explored also through the theoretical lens of cognitive capitalism which postulates a further transition of advanced economies from the post-Fordism era to a cultural-cognitive one (Colletis and Paulré 2008). In this context, self-employment has undergone a relevant transformation, sustained by the novel nature of work. In fact, the content of work has profoundly changed: production and control of knowledge has replaced the production of goods—material goods have been substituted by intangible and intellectual ones. In this perspective, the capitalist process of accumulation involves new immaterial goods such as knowledge, relationships, networks, and the control of space in both geographical as well as virtual terms (Negri and Vercellone 2007), productive factors that are crucial in sectors such as high-technology industry, financial services, personal services, the media, and graphic cultural industries. With a high degree of flexibility, an elevated educational background and a remarkable capacity to network and develop virtual relationships, the independent worker is immediately fitted for the requirements of the cognitive economy.

More than twenty years after the seminal work *The Second Generation of Self-Employment*, in which Bologna and Fumagalli (1997) traced the origins of the proliferation of self-employed workers back to the deep transformations that had occurred in work organization, the ICT sphere, and in the lifestyle preferences expressed by workers, we can say that the new and revolutionary factors that account for such transformations are technological advancement and processes of digitalization. The contemporary socio-economic debate is, once again, the relationship between technology and labour, and the potentiality of technologies to create new professional profiles, new skills and new work models (Balliester and Elsheikhi 2018).

2. CRITICAL DIMENSIONS IN THE SOCIOLOGICAL DEBATE

Having disentangled the driving forces underpinning the growth of highly skilled self-employment in modern economies, the next questions that arise are why the study of professional work is relevant today in the debate and what theoretical framework supports the empirical content of this book.

First, the new and expanding form of professional self-employment is different from other types of contractual arrangements characterized by nonstandard contracts, even if they share common employment-related characteristics, such as a temporary or limited work relationship and a deficit of social protection. As explained in Chapter 1, what clearly distinguishes self-employment from other nonstandard contracts is the component of autonomy, chosen to a large extent by workers themselves, as witnessed by several international research reports[3] and confirmed by the survey presented in Chapter 3. These dimensions of autonomy and entrepreneurship characterizing freelance activities reflect their needs for independence and self-rule. Consequently, sociologists have clustered the new self-employed workers as being opposed to bureaucracy and hierarchical organizations.

---

[3]   The sixth European Working Conditions Survey (EWCS Eurofound 2015)—which identifies and maps various features of self-employed workers in Europe—finds that among the 'self-employed with employees' (comparable to entrepreneurs), a higher proportion of individuals voluntarily choose self-employment (71%), than among the 'self-employed without employees' (54%), a third of whom (24%) claim to have chosen self-employment because there were no alternative types of work available.

However, unlike traditional liberal professionals working in the market and protected to a different degree by associations or professional orders depending on the traditions of each country (Feltrin 2012), new professional self-employed workers can be located halfway between market and hierarchy, between practices of human capital internalization and outsourcing. This is corroborated by the fact that in the majority of European countries an intermediate or hybrid legal status has been regulated between autonomy and subordination, as will be discussed in Chapter 5.

2.1 Challenges to Labour Market Dualization Theory

The expansion of self-employed professionals provides useful insights from a labour market perspective and challenges some foundations of the dualization theory. As we know, labour segmentation as a global trend depends mostly on the economic system, namely the division of labour among activity sectors, affecting employment characteristics and the labour market structure. However, heterodox theories on labour market segmentation (Doeringer and Piore 1985; Reich et al. 1973; Rubery 1978; Wilkinson 1981) include other complementary aspects. First, labour institutions and public policies are considered, since they can compensate for inequalities but also perpetuate them by reinforcing employment divisions. Second, on the demand side, they consider economic and commercial strategies, and business ideologies and practices, in particular labour flexibility practices and outsourcing. Third, the characteristics of the labour force, such as education, qualification, age, gender and nationality, can lead to different conditions within the labour market, explaining differentials in working conditions. Overall these theories assume that there is not a unique labour market but, conversely, different segments characterized by diverse hierarchical positions corresponding to specific occupational profiles among workers.

This issue is part of the wider socio-economic debate on inequality generated by the processes of workforce ranking and sorting, which allocate workers into positions inside or outside the boundaries of firms, but also in between (Granovetter and Tilly 1988). More specifically, since the 1970s theoretical contributions falling under 'labour market segmentation theories' have contested the unity of the labour market. The (neo-) institutional approach of labour market dualism and the insider–outsider divide (Doeringer and Piore 1985) have highlighted a dichotomy between a primary sector of workers with higher salaries and employment stability, and a secondary sector of workers characterized by lower wages and job instability.

An internal labour market exists when employers regularly fill vacancies for certain jobs by utilizing their own workforce, rather than by external recruitment and, in this way, they can retain more control over job structures, which could be expected to vary considerably among industries and occupations. According to Doeringer and Piore (1985), three major factors underpinned the initial generation of internal labour markets: skill specificity, on-the-job training and customary law, the latter referring to an unwritten set of rules largely based upon past practices. Workers in internal markets enjoyed mobility between jobs within the same firm, high wages, benefits and a career based on seniority, in exchange for a deep engagement in the longevity of the firm, and cooperative industrial relations where collective bargaining coordinated the interests of both managers and workers within a unionized productive sector.

This analytical framework influenced the subsequent neo-institutional debate, developed in particular by the Cambridge School that emphasized the interaction between internal and external labour markets (Cappelli 1995; Rubery and Wilkinson 1994). Studies on internal labour market transformations (Cappelli et al. 1997; Grimshaw and Rubery 1998) high-lighted that job and pay hierarchies, permanent contracts and training provisions were adopted not only to meet organizational needs (e.g. worker's commitment, a certain level of job stability and seniority schemes, in order to regain on-the-job training costs and avoiding staff turnover), but they were also related to some particular exogenous conditions, such as strong trade unions, low unemployment and steady economic growth (Grimshaw et al. 2001).

However, the internal labour market – as a structured approach in managing the workforce – is becoming less relevant and applicable today, in light of the increase of low-quality jobs and employment precariousness (Kalleberg and Dunn 2016). Firms are increasingly expanding into the more competitive external labour market, making less investment in labour force training and training on-the-job, considering that they can find specific skills and qualifications directly in the labour market, thus avoiding the costs of recruiting, hiring and training their own workforce. Accordingly, this productive model has started to question the division between internal and external labour markets and the insider–outsider divide which, considering their increasingly blurred and ambiguous boundaries, has turned out to be overestimated (Emmenegger 2009). Work is actually more fluid and dynamic than in the past: workers perform multiple jobs that are often casual, short-term and ancillary. In a nutshell the so-called 'secondary sector' of the labour market is losing part of its expected peculiarities, namely that of being peripheral, contingent, unqualified, lower-paid and belonging to specific social groups, resulting in challenges to the insider–outsider theoretical framework.

From this perspective a further telling example is represented by the large and growing segment of professional self-employed workers (such as advertisers, designers, analysts, accountants, artists, consultants), who are neither assimilated to traditional craft workers, nor exactly to liberal professionals. One might observe highly qualified/specialized profiles combined with working and individual conditions that are very far from those rules and values on which internal labour markets were built. As our study demonstrates, self-employed professionals are increasingly experiencing jobs with low salaries, insecurity in customer payments, lack of funds for training, intermittent jobs and instability. The insider–outsider division is still fully relevant—considering that labour market risks are increasingly unequally distributed between insider and outsider groups (Emmenegger et al. 2012; Palier and Thelen 2010; Rueda 2007), the dynamics of the self-employed professionals worker segment indicates that labour market vulnerability has spread well into the more educated sectors of the workforce (Häusermann et al. 2015).

To sum up, the growth of professional self-employment in the labour market accompanied by poor working conditions and limited social protection challenges the theoretical infrastructure of the labour market dualization. In fact, it blurs the boundaries between internal and external labour markets, overcoming the long-standing sharp division in terms of skills specificity, job protection and relevance within the core firm.

2.1.1 Self-employment in the digital economy: a standard working model

As anticipated, the relevance for this growing segment of the labour market is strongly linked to the new digital technologies and to the development of the intermediation of platforms,[4] topics at the centre of a wide and flourishing debate. We are in fact assisting in the development of a new conception of collaborative economy that exploits technological platforms as a new way to share and exchange goods, services and knowledge, thanks to the virtual intermediation of social relations. The expansion

---

[4] Digital platforms are a heterogeneous archipelago, both for their characteristics and the impact they have on work. In this regard Srnicek (2017) outlines five types of platforms (industrial, advertising, cloud, product and slim), of which the last type operate through hyper-outsourcing (of workers, fixed assets, costs, maintenance and training). The slim digital platforms, which allow a match between supply and demand of work and the exchange of labour intensive services, are those that pose more problems of legal regulation, referring both to classification of the employment relationship between employees and self-employed (De Stefano 2016) and to the functional classification of the employer (Prassl and Risak 2015). Labour control takes place through a reputation-based system; evaluation systems are generally one-sided, that is, the client can evaluate the worker but not vice versa.

of the platform economy calls into question the very foundations of the labour market and of the company—meant as productive locus—with transformative effects linked to various dimensions: a drastic reduction in transaction costs; the large-scale potential that exploits availability through digital connection devices; an efficient demand–supply match thanks to the use of sophisticated algorithms and extensive bilateral information on customers and providers, with marginal costs close to zero.

What is relevant in this context is that self-employed workers turn out to be the main recipients and users of these new labour opportunities made available by digital technologies. Self-employed workers, providers of both physical and online services, represent the main actors of this socio-technic process of change. Although the debate on the employment status of platform workers is fully underway, many observers agree upon the autonomous nature of contractual arrangements on the platforms (European Commission 2016; Valenduc and Vendramin 2016). Despite some research that shows a certain variability in terms of size, geographical scope, services offered and business models among countries beyond some technical differences, the main common characteristic of this kind of worker is their status as independent contractor (Fabo et al. 2017).

A large study on the so-called gig economy (Mckinsey Global Institute et al. 2016) has shown that the activities related to platforms are growing rapidly in both the USA and the EU, with positive effects on the activity rates, employment and productivity of both capital and labour. According to the Online Labour Index (OLI), measuring the trend of digital labour markets online, between 2016 and 2017 these markets grew by 26 per cent (Kässi and Lehdonvirta 2016). Hence, countries with persistently high unemployment and low participation in the labour market, such as Greece, Spain and Italy, could potentially benefit the most from new employment opportunities offered by the platforms (McKinsey Global Institute et al. 2016), which can make the labour markets more inclusive (Eurofound 2015).

However, such developments have also triggered negative effects, in particular concerning the working conditions of the workers involved in the platforms: if individual flexibility is often cited as one of the most important perks of working on the online platforms (Abadie et al. 2016), it is also generally associated with a high degree of uncertainty regarding pay and working hours. The virtual platforms create globalized marketplaces where workers from all over the world are potentially in competition, hence triggering a downward trend in terms of pay rates. Hence, the new forms of work organization, typical of platform capitalism, have broken the ties that traditionally bound businesses, workers and local environments, and which lay at the basis of twentieth-century economic and social systems

(Parsons and Smelser 1956). The old model, built on the exchange of work for social and family security, has been lost. While the new knowledge and platform economies have created new employment opportunities for a skilled workforce, at the same time the career paths of these workers, often self-employed, are associated with job insecurity, income volatility and very limited access to social security systems (Davidov 2004).

Thus, we can expect that self-employed workers involved in the new economy based on platforms and the new technologies will present, in the immediate future, increasing claims for higher labour standards and major protection against social risks. There are in fact some typical aspects that have so far concerned only dependent work, but which will necessarily have to be extended or adjusted also to independent work (e.g. access to unemployment benefits, insurance for sickness and accidents at work, and training).

2.1.2 Self-employment between professionalism and downward status: a social paradox

The debate on self-employment has also focused on the contradictory relationship between the ideology of professionalism and the risk of downward social mobility. We are witnessing in fact a tension between two theoretically opposite trends: the still relevant 'professionalism' as a reference social model, and the loss of status of modern professionals combined with greater social vulnerability.

The notion of 'professionalism' as described in the seminal work of Bledstein (1976), who undertakes a historical reconstruction of professionalism in America, refers primarily to the concept of specialism. Bledstein's notion of specialism includes a combination of skills, knowledge and expertise, with an emphasis on ethical codes. More radically, the Weberian concept of profession (illustrated in his famous 1917 conference, *Wissenschaft als Beruf*) consists also in the notion of vocation (denoted by the depth of the word *Beruf*): an individual who embarks on a professional path should be aware that it implies compliance with the values and the moral conditions of such profession.

The debate on professionalism in contemporary society, from historical (Abbott 1983; Bologna 2018), juridical (Beaton 2010) and socio-economic perspectives (Perkin 1989), agrees in considering its growing relevance in an increasingly professionalized society. In contrast to pre-industrial and industrial societies, a professional society is based on human capital creation through education and on specialized knowledge which has become far more accessible for the modern professions (Perkin 1989). In *The Rise of Professional Society* Perkin also claims that expanding professionalization is permeating all levels of society, in a way in which the more traditional liberal professions were not able to do.

More recently, an interesting comparative study on the transformation of professions in Europe[5] (Feltrin 2012) showed a generalized tendency towards 'a professionalization': a growing number of non-regulated occupations, both traditional and new, tend to adopt internal rules typical of the regulated professions as they emerged in the twentieth century. Another typical trait of these emerging professional figures is the overlapping of competences between different professions that have traditionally always been sharply demarcated. This process recalls what Abbott (1988) explained in his *System of Professions* about the role of professions in modern society, namely that the social structure of professions was characterized by continuous adjustments and internal changes as it adapted to various market pressures.

In light of these transformations in intellectual professions (e.g. those not belonging to the typical liberal professions of lawyer, architect, and medical professional), 'professionalism' has persisted as a sort of reference model for the whole world of the highly specialized self-employed. Professionalism, in fact, can respond to the need for recognition through professional associations, to the need for ethical codes and to the exigence to control access to the profession in order to reduce market competition by limiting the supply of professionals. Thus, 'the ideology of professionalism did not go away' (Bologna 2018, p. 188), even if something else might explain it in the current post-industrial age.

During the twentieth century, sociological studies on social stratification have considered professionals, both self-employed and subordinated, as the expression of the middle class, since they were treated not only as highly qualified workers but also as belonging to higher social and economic classes. Hence, originally, professionals came from the elitist part of society and have for long continued to belong to it, representing the main component of the middle class. These studies conventionally identify the diverse classes through occupational classifications, namely clusters of workers based on classes of employment (Crompton 2010), including information about the status of the worker as employee or self-employed (see ISCO-8 2012). Accordingly, each occupation represents

---

[5]   The report highlighted the presence of differentiated professional systems in European countries, although they share the strong expansion of services to businesses and families since the 1980s. Hence, some basic general tendencies are similar in all countries, but they do not produce an immediate institutional convergence in the ways in which the regulation of status, social protection and forms of collective representation are structured, starting from the definitions adopted. Great differences remain linked to associative systems and contractual models.

the framework of the correspondent socio-economic, cultural and welfare background, including dimensions such as income level, educational attainment and entitlement to social protection at the head. In the case of the new self-employment, the employment-derived class is still questioned. In fact, starting from the 1990s, professionals underwent a contradictory transformation within the capitalist economic system: despite increases in demand for specialized independent professionals, their economic conditions worsened, a dynamic further exacerbated by the 2008 financial crisis. So, if on the one hand we witness the consolidation of a 'professional work model' that, sustained by a growing demand for specialization, identifies with a high social status and new and more complex technical competences, on the other hand these professionals are experiencing downward mobility and a growing exposure to employment and social risks. They are in fact increasingly characterized by high levels of social risk and greater income volatility due to the intermittent nature of work. Furthermore, despite that inter-professional mobility and multiple skills are necessary ingredients for professional survival, since they facilitate shifts between diverse project-based commitments, it contrasts with the corporative attitude of professional bodies in monitoring the degree of qualification required that accordingly restricts access to professions. Interestingly, research also points out the combination and accumulation, not only of professional competences, but also of different jobs, which can be extremely diversified and not always consistent with one's professional profile and area of education.

Accordingly, a lower return on education and a growing income volatility (for further detail refer to Chapter 3) are major factors responsible for inconsistency in the status of the skilled self-employed, who are downgrading from a standard middle-class position to social precariousness. Such a shift contributes to confirmation that the middle class is losing its central position in processes of social transformation (Bagnasco 2016) reversing Perkin's (1989) theoretical expectation that workers who gain specialized knowledge and expertise are in privileged positions and can obtain greater status, favourable working conditions, higher salaries and other rewards for their professionalism.

What has been said so far has an inevitable impact on the model of social organization, with possible effects on work regulation, on the construction of new forms of unionism and an extension of social protection in a universalistic sense. As discussed, is it possible that individual needs do anticipate a level of collectivity as theorized by Simmel (1890)?

2.2   Multiple Institutional Dilemmas

The transformation of post-industrial economies described so far has not always been followed by a congruent adaptation of the institutional and regulatory frameworks within which these changes took place. The rise of professional self-employment as a new form of work in economic sectors traditionally dominated by a subordinated workforce, with its tangible effects on workers' professional paths and careers, embodies a clear example calling for an assessment of their compatibility with existing social and labour institutions and regulatory systems in which they operate as professionals.

In fact, such a numerical surge has not drawn the attention expected in the political sphere. In the public debate, national policymakers across European countries have slowly started to acknowledge the increasing relevance of the phenomenon and to address the emerging demands of the new professional self-employed in the labour market and within national systems of social security and the welfare state. Recently, at a European level, the issue has been put on the political agenda of member states. The European Parliament (2014) has in fact approved the resolution *Social Protection for All, Including Self-Employed Workers* (2013/2111(INI)-14/01/2014). This resolution invited member states to guarantee social protection for all workers, including the self-employed; to provide mutual assistance to cover accidents, illnesses and pensions; to guarantee continuous training for all workers; and to oppose 'bogus' self-employed workers. Specific reference to the category of self-employed in the supranational regulatory framework represents a significant step towards recognition of the peculiar identity of the independent worker, whose legal status is still debated and ambiguous.

However, the picture at country level still features the necessity of updating legislative frameworks and social protection systems to new emerging demands. The rise in the share of independent workers has not been accompanied by a congruent definition of the regulatory framework to fill the gap between high-skilled professionalism and its attached low social status. As pinpointed also by international bodies such as the Organisation for Economic Co-operation and Development (OECD), 'concerns have been expressed over the working conditions, training, security and incomes of some self-employed' (OECD 2000, p. 155). Specifically, three main gaps can be identified concerning the condition of professional self-employed workers: namely a recognition gap, a social protection gap and a representation gap (Grimshaw et al. 2016).

The recognition gap concerns the suitability of legislative frameworks that regulate the legal status and the attached rights and duties for self-employed workers within different European national contexts and cross-nationally. The regulatory dimension is in fact further complicated by professional careers that are increasingly oriented towards an international dimension and involve transnational mobility, while the configuration of their legislative recognition is still defined by national laws.

The social protection gap, or access/entitlement to benefits, is strictly connected to the regulatory configuration of the self-employed's status. The eligibility criteria for admission to social protection institutions, designed and calibrated to meet the needs of a subordinated workforce, are often not applicable in the case of self-employment, as the latter is often intermittent and involves the provision of services to a multiplicity of clients with whom employees do not share risks on a collective basis. Thus, the transformation of the labour markets has generated new challenges for European social regulatory systems, whose traditional institutions for labour regulation and social protection are weakened and unable to exercise control over working conditions for a growing segment of workers who share a lack of protection with other categories of non-standard workers.

Since the 2010s, the visibility of professional self-employed workers in public and union debates has increased significantly, partly through initiatives launched by the self-employed themselves and their newly created freelance organizations. This effort has shed light on critical issues and areas for potential change, and on some occasions has led to important policy results, thereby improving the representation gap. What new forms of collective representation are emerging for the interests of self-employed workers, characterized by highly individualized employment relationships? The transition from a labour market primarily grounded on a salaried dependent workforce towards a society where the demand and supply of labour are increasingly dominated by independent workers sheds light on the inefficacy and the incongruity of the traditional model of collective representation. Such a shift in fact triggers a profound redefinition of employment relations, which calls for a revitalization of the strategies and organizational forms to collectively represent workers' interests, while a number of scholars agree on the concern of integrating the increasingly heterogeneous constituencies of independent workers into the union movement (Dølvik and Waddington 2002; Gottschall and Kroos 2003). The difficulty in building a class consciousness within the population of independent workers is recognized, since they have limited personal contact with other workers in similar conditions of employment (Pernicka 2006). In the next section we will briefly disentangle these three critical aspects.

2.2.1 The ambiguous definition of legal status

Despite the diffusion of self-employed work during the 2010s and the gradually mounting resonance the phenomenon is obtaining, there is still a remarkable discrepancy among EU countries in the regulatory definition of the legal status of these workers. It is commonly recognized that self-employment encapsulates multiform categories of workers in terms of occupation, job structure, degree of autonomy and professionalism, and overall the legislative framework is multifaceted and fluid (Finotto 2018). Moreover, from a cross-country comparative perspective, the respective national legislative and institutional frameworks influence the categories of workers to be included in definitional boundaries.

The first challenge to proper recognition of this specific segment of the labour market, which has repercussions also for access to systems of social protection and collective representation, is the methodological fallacy of equating self-employment to small enterprises and entrepreneurship (European Commission 2010; Henrekson 2007): 'This somewhat vague notion refers to the idea of the innovative self-made man who starts out with nothing and becomes a captain of industry' (Rapelli 2012, p. 6). The figure of the self-employed worker is, in fact, erroneously assimilated to the role of the entrepreneur who autonomously establishes and leads his/her own business with entrepreneurial and managerial ambitions often employing dependent personnel. Such a perspective represents a misleading interpretation of the category since it does not conceive the independent work outside the entrepreneurial perspective. In addition, such categorization hides the considerable heterogeneity that is a feature of self-employment.

A second order of problems deals with a false dichotomy we find in some literature between low-skilled manual salaried workers and the highly skilled professional self-employed (Bronzini 1997). Such a misleading conception can be attributed to the dichotomy between professional occupations, characterized by highly skilled and intellectual tasks, generally associated with autonomy, and low-skilled manual jobs, which require a dependent 'more protected' contractual arrangement. As is recognized, however, the category of self-employed workers encompasses a wide and multifaceted array of occupations and professionalisms. Similarly to the dependent salaried worker, independent work can be a contractual configuration for both manual and intellectual jobs. Traditionally, autonomous work developed in agriculture, the retail sector, the manufacturing industry, and in artisanal business, are all inherently manual occupations despite the technical content (Ranci 2012). With the advent of the post-Fordism era and the marked tertiarization of advanced economies, autonomous work has proliferated in several professional labour markets ranging from financial services to the ICT industry, creative sectors, consultancy and intermediation services. Therefore, recognizing that only professional jobs contain an element of independence is not only erroneous but also misrepresentative.

A third set of issues relates to the variety of labels adopted to define the population of self-employed, not fully overlapping and not always referring to the selfsame population: independent professionals (Leighton 2015), autonomous workers or IPros (Rapelli 2012), new self-employed workers (Schulze Buschoff and Schmidt 2009; Westerveld 2012), second-generation autonomous workers (Bologna and Fumagalli 1997), self-employed without employees (Dekker 2010), and freelance (Heery et al. 2004). These definitions describe the same phenomenon only in general terms, each recalling different definitional shades. Moreover, an excursus of the international literature shows how each definition, according to the country, might address different groups of workers reflecting differences in the regulatory and legal frameworks across the EU.

Fourth, the recent changes in the world of work described above have progressively questioned the legal framework defining whether a worker has to be considered as being in an employment relationship or not. Legal status, either as an employee or self-employed is in fact often unclear and the juridical *querelle* regarding this dichotomy has never reached a common position (Zilio Grandi and Biasi 2018). Such demarcation is particularly relevant since belonging to a formal employment relation-ship entitles a worker to an array of protections and rights enshrined by labour laws. The traditional paradigm of standard employment relations characterized by a salaried worker depending upon a full-time open-ended contract with an employer has seen a gradual decline accompanied by the widespread diffusion of self-employed workers. In particular, the growth of a grey area of employment between salaried dependent work and independent employment has called into question the legislative boundaries of employment relations, making it increasingly problematic to establish employment relationships and, accordingly, entitlements to the rights and duties relating to such contractual relationships (Perulli 2003). In fact, in some European countries an intermediate category of dependent self-employed workers (Muehlberger 2007) has spread, namely 'workers who are legally self-employed but [are] in fact wholly dependent on the company' (Pernicka 2006, p. 125). According to some juridical scholarship, a less sharp demarcation between the dichotomous categories of subordinate and independent work might solve such regulatory and definitional uncertainty (Perulli 2018). An intermediate category is even more important in the light of the transformation of the labour market fol-lowing the implementation of new digital technologies. Hence, a growing body of the international literature treats the category of economically dependent self-employed as workers who, although formally regarded as self-employed, 'lack the criterion of economic independence on the market because they are mainly dependent on just one principal for their income' (Schulze Buschoff and Schmidt 2009, p. 151).

Moreover, in addition to overlapping and blurred boundaries between the two categories, attempts are often made to 'disguise the employment relationship or to exploit the inadequacies and gaps that exist in the legal framework or in its interpretation or application' as a way to benefit from an intermediate status between salaried and independent (Casale 2011). Despite potential overlapping in practical implementation and in its repercussions for workers, this kind of self-employment must be clearly distinguished from what has been labelled 'bogus self-employment'. If in the former case dependence on a main employer is primarily economic, in the latter we suggest a deliberate classification of a worker's employment status as self-employed under a civil law framework, even though the quality of his/her working situation meets all the criteria that would qualify an employment relationship as one of dependence.

The literature has paid considerable attention to 'bogus self-employment', otherwise labelled as 'sham', 'disguised' or 'false' self-employment. In this case, the legislative boundaries circumscribing the category of self-employed have been stretched deliberately as a way to exploit its economic and financial advantages. This illegal practice is implemented also through an inappropriate use of the commercial and civil legislative framework instead of the labour law code (European Commission 2006). One issue is that workers are forced into self-employment by employers with the aim of reducing labour costs. Compared to dependent employment, independent work has few, if any, legal protections and fewer social security rights, making the relationship more convenient for the employer/client. In some other cases, workers voluntarily opt for self-employment as a way to lower some fiscal and social insurance contributions (European Parliament 2013). Hence, the growing number of workers whose employment status is not clear is strictly intertwined with the fact that they do not enjoy the social and employment protections normally associated with their employment relationship.

It can be seen that the definitional exercise has a decisive impact on the regulatory regime of self-employment, which can vary significantly in relation to the boundaries set by the definitions adopted. Moreover, starting from the accepted recognition that self-employment embodies a multifaceted and transversal category of workers and whose definition can vary among countries, it is fundamental to take into account the discrepancies and inconsistencies that follow the legal and fiscal framework of reference, in terms of access to the system of social protections, as we will see in the next section.

2.2.2   The weakness of social protection systems

In the international literature on social protection and welfare state systems, independent work is treated as a phenomenon that presents some challenges for social policy systems across the EU. In fact, independent workers embody a social group not easy to position in the class structure. Its inherently intermediate and transversal configuration locates independent workers in a tricky position between social class and social status (Mills 1951). In fact, the generation of professional independent workers in the post-industrial economy is located in diametrically opposite position by class and by status. If, on the one hand, independent workers share a high social status and educational attainment, on the other hand, according to their income rate and occupational position, they look more like the lower class (Ranci 2012). In other words, the proliferation of these figures has widened the misalignment between class and status, reflected in the gap between the high professionalism attached to the occupational position and low social status in terms of social rights and institutional protections, including low income, precarious working conditions and lack of universal welfare protection (D'Amours 2009). A further contradiction characterizes the status of independent worker. Similarly to dependent employees, independent workers rely on selling their labour. But differently from employees, they are generally subject to the civil and commercial legislative framework, and not to labour law, and thus do not enjoy employment protections guaranteed by labour rights (Schulze Buschoff and Schmidt 2009). This difference has led to a rising gap in employment and social rights between independent workers and employees, something that they have to bear with on an individual basis.

In fact, the notable resurgence of independent workers in Europe in many cases, 'was not reflected in any formal overall review of the social security position of self-employed people' (Corden 1999, p. 32). Some preliminary academic contributions at the beginning of the 1990s had already pointed out this issue, observing a 'policy vacuum' and a 'stagnation' of social security policy for the groups of independent workers (Brown 1992). More recent studies have confirmed the lack of an appropriate social security system for independent workers:

> unlike dependent employees, a large proportion of self-employed people are not included in social security systems. Alongside the general protection scheme, which provides a minimal level of security, self-employed people are not or

only partially covered by statutory systems. And even in case of coverage, the statutory social security systems for the self-employed are very heterogeneous. (Fachinger and Frankus 2015, p. 135)

Traditionally, the social protection scheme for independent workers has been characterized by a high degree of voluntarism. Self-employed in fact are, to a certain extent, free to establish the level of protection they are willing to insure themselves against social risks, including invalidity, short- and long-term sickness, widowhood, disability, lack of clients (corresponding to unemployment), and delay in payment (Directorate-General for Employment, Social Affairs and Inclusion, 2014). More specifically, when health insurance is at stake, in most EU member states independent workers are covered by the country-specific national health service, but which generally represents, once again, a basic insurance that does not take into account the specific needs and demands of independent workers. The need to fill in the gaps in the social security entitlements of the independent workers' population thus emerges as a question of legitimate rights and justice (Schulze Buschoff and Schmidt 2009).

Such problematic aspects have raised concerns at European level. The European Commission, in the Green Paper *Modernising Labour Law to Meet the Challenges of the 21st Century* (2006), promotes some forms of 'good practice' which member states are invited to use as a benchmark. A 'targeted approach' is favoured, which gives 'categories of vulnerable workers involved in complex employment relationships [. . .] minimum rights without an extension of the full range of labour law entitlements associated with standard work contracts' (European Commission 2006, p. 12). A more recent study commissioned by the European Parliament set more ambitious and universalistic goals in terms of social protections:

> it is fully consistent with the ambition of the European social model to provide more universal and appropriate social protection for all, notwithstanding different formal types of employment. This implies also extending social protection, and particularly social insurance, to (dependent) self-employed or particular target groups or the creation of specific social security regimes for (dependent) self-employed workers. (European Parliament 2013, p. 11)

Hence, self-employed professionals (as bearers of new social needs) embody, together with other categories of nonstandard workers, the outsiders of the welfare state, since they belong to an area largely abandoned to market forces and without effective regulation. These social needs are both specific to their profession (such as the deductibility of expenditure on training, competition control, adequacy of compensation, payment terms and fiscal treatment)[6], and universalistic (such as maternity benefits, parental benefits, protection for accident and health, social security aspects and pensions). Accordingly, over recent years, this segment of the labour market has gradually, but increasingly, demanded a more systematic, structured and legitimized collective representation in order to try to raise its voice and have ad hoc policies.

2.2.3 The vacuum of collective representation

The growth of self-employed professionals in the European labour market, associated with a decline in working conditions and a lack of social protection, has triggered an unprecedented demand for collective representation by these workers. This segment of workers, in fact, has for long not felt the need to have a recognized and legitimized collective voice in public and political spheres. Their high specialization has traditionally ensured a solid professional career for these workers and strong individual bargaining power in the labour market with their counterpart, their clients. However, the socio-economic factors elucidated in this chapter, including the spreading use of platforms, growing competition in a potentially global labour market and fast developments in digital technologies, have weakened the position of these professionals and their individual bargaining capacity regarding their working conditions. The dynamic of individual negotiation is particularly ambiguous, as it bears both risks and opportunities. On the one hand, it allows more freedom and self-determination, but on the other hand, the worker is forced to face all the risks of his/her activity on an individual basis (Banfi and Bologna 2011). As long as the bargaining power of the worker is high in the labour market, the benefits of this process overcome the risks, but in the current socio-economic landscape, companies and clients increasingly offer pre-defined job positions and the worker can only accept or refuse the offer. Effective bargaining can only take place with 'strong' workers, those who have specialized skills and are in great demand in the market, as was traditionally the case. The current conditions instead have emphasized the risks borne on an individual basis and the triggering of a gradual but increasing demand for collective representation of their specific needs and demands.

---

[6] The recent study *A Broken Social Elevator? How to Promote Social Mobility* (OECD 2018) highlights how taxes and benefits interact in different ways on individual income changes and how the role of taxes and transfers varies across countries. The report shows, as an example, that individuals taking permanent or full-time employment are twice as likely exit low income. One of the drivers explaining income changes triggered by job-to-job transitions is the nature of the contract. Moving from a temporary to a permanent contract goes hand in hand with a large income gain in most countries. Hours worked is another dimension explaining the impact on incomes of a work transition.

As a response, since the late 1990s, trade unions in Europe have tried, more or less successfully, to extend their representation to the new generation of self-employed workers. In some countries, they have implemented new strategic and organizational actions in order to satisfy the protection needs of these workers (Gumbrell-McCormick and Hyman 2013). Some trade unions have offered services, such as legal, fiscal and social security assistance. They have adopted the servicing model, not only for the new professional autonomous workers, but also for all non-standard workers. Other trade unions have adopted innovative strategies by initiating new organizational patterns to promote the direct participation of workers and their collective mobilization. This last model represents a more active approach, because trade unions do not try to attract workers passively but go and look for them (Frege and Kelly 2004). Both servicing and organizing are part of a general strategy to expand trade union representation in new sectors and new labour market segments, traditionally not organized. It has been probably also a reaction to the decline of unionization rates and to the loss of centrality of traditional industrial relations models and central collective bargaining (Burawoy 2008; Tattersall 2010). These strategies have been mainly targeted so far at the lower segment of the labour market.[7]

'Quasi-unions' (Heckscher and Carré 2006) and LMIs (Autor 2008) have vigorously emerged as organizational forms trying to organize the new self-employed workers with medium-high skill levels. Quasi-unions have spread mainly where trade unions have not taken into account the peculiarity of the new generation of professional autonomous workers. The trade unions have often considered them as atypical workers, false employees and/or entrepreneurs and in general they have neither understood nor represented their specific needs, both professionally and socially speaking. In the international literature, these organizations have been defined in different ways: Jenkins (2013) calls them 'pre-union' while Sullivan (2010) defines them as 'proto-union'. Regardless, they have a common target: to increase the vocal capacity of workers who face the risks of their working conditions on an individual basis. They also have similar networking strategies (Blyton and Jenkins 2012; Heckscher and Carré 2006; Heery et al. 2004; Sullivan 2010; Tapia 2013).

To summarize, the transition from a labour market primarily grounded on a salaried dependent workforce towards a society where the demand and supply of labour are dominated by independent workers sheds light

---

[7]   For example, one of the most successful campaigns is 'Justice for Janitors', started in the early 1990s by SEIU (Service Employees International Unions), a North American trade union operating in the low-skilled service sector.

on the inefficacy and the incongruity of the traditional model of collective representation. Such a shift in fact triggers a profound redefinition of employment relations which calls for a revitalization of the strategies and organizational forms to collectively represent workers' interests, while a number of scholars agree on the necessity of integrating increasingly heterogeneous constituencies of independent workers into the union movement (Dølvik and Waddington 2002; Gottschall and Kroos 2003). The difficulty in building a class consciousness within the population of self-employed is recognized, since they have limited personal contact with other workers in similar conditions of employment (Pernicka 2006). This issue will be investigated in depth in Chapter 6, which will provide also empirical examples of the kind of organizations that have emerged, the structures they adopted to collectively organize these workers and the strategies they chose to pursue.

REFERENCES

Abadie, F., F. Biagi, K. Jaksic, S. Jemmotte, S. Marino, G. Piroli and A. Xavier (2016), 'The Labour Market Implications of ICT Developments and Digitalisation', in *Employment and Social Developments in Europe 2016*, European Commission, Directorate-General for Employment, Social Affairs and Inclusion, pp. 149–87.

Abbott, A. (1983), 'Professional Ethics', *American Journal of Sociology*, **88** (5), 855–85.

Abbott, A. D. (1988), *The System of Professions: An Essay on the Division of Expert Labor*, Chicago, IL: University of Chicago Press.

Autor, D. H. (2008), *The Economics of Labor Market Intermediation: An Analytic Framework*, Working Paper 14348, National Bureau of Economic Research, September, accessed at http://www.nber.org/papers/w14348.

Bagnasco, A. (2016), *La questione del ceto medio. Un racconto del cambiamento sociale*, Bologna: Il Mulino.

Balliester, T. and A. Elsheikhi (2018), *The Future of Work: A Literature Review*, Working Paper 29, International Labour Office (ILO), 17 April, accessed at https://www.ilo.org/wcmsp5/groups/public/---dgreports/---inst/documents/publication/wcms_625866.pdf.

Banfi, D. and S. Bologna (2011), *Vita da freelance: i lavoratori della conoscenza e il loro futuro*, Milan: Feltrinelli.

Beaton, G. R. (2010), *Why Professionalism is Still Relevant*, Legal Studies Research Paper No. 445, Melbourne: University of Melbourne, College of Law, 31 January, accessed at https://ssrn.com/abstract=1545509.

Benz, M. and B. S. Frey (2008), 'The Value of Doing What You Like: Evidence from the Self-Employed in 23 Countries', *Journal of Economic Behavior & Organization*, **68** (3–4), 445–55.

Blau, D. M. (1987), 'A Time-Series Analysis of Self-Employment in the United States', *Journal of Political Economy*, **95** (3), 445–67.

Bledstein, B. J. (1976), *The Culture of Professionalism. The Middle Class and the Development of Higher Education in America*, New York: W. W. Norton & Co.

Blyton, P. and J. Jenkins (2012), 'Mobilizing Resistance: The Burberry Workers' Campaign against Factory Closure', *The Sociological Review*, **60** (1), 25–45.

Bögenhold, D. and U. Staber (1991), 'The Decline and Rise of Self-Employment', *Work, Employment & Society*, **5** (2), 223–39.

Bologna, S. (2018), *The Rise of the European Self-Employed Workforce*, Milan: Mimesis International.

Bologna, S. and A. Fumagalli (1997), *Il lavoro autonomo di seconda generazione: Scenari del postfordismo in Italia*, Milan: Feltrinelli.

Bronzini, G. (1997), 'Postfordismo e garanzie: il lavoro autonomo', in S. Bologna and A. Fumagalli (eds), *Il lavoro autonomo di seconda generazione: Scenari del postfordismo in Italia*, Milan: Feltrinelli.

Brown, J. (1992), *A Policy Vacuum: Social Security for the Self-Employed*, York: Joseph Rowntree Foundation.

Burawoy, M. (2008), 'The Public Turn: From Labor Process to Labor Movement', *Work and Occupations*, **35** (4), 371–87.

Bureau, M.-C. and A. Corsani (2014), 'Du désir d'autonomie à l'indépendance. Une perspective sociohistorique', *La nouvelle revue du travail*, (5), 1–17.

Burke, A. E. (ed.) (2015), *The Handbook of Research on Freelancing and Self-Employment*, Foxrock, Dublin: Senate Hall Academic Publishing.

Butera, F. (1990), *Il castello e la rete*, Milan: Franco Angeli.

Cappelli, P. (1995), 'Rethinking Employment', *British Journal of Industrial Relations*, **33** (4), 563–602.

Cappelli, P., L. Bassi, H. Katz, D. Knoke, P. Osterman and M. Useem (1997), *Change at Work*, New York and Oxford: Oxford University Press.

Casale, G. (2011), *The Employment Relationship: A Comparative Overview*, Oxford: Hart; Geneva: International Labour Office.

Codagnone, C., F. Abadie and F. Biagi (2016), *The Future of Work in the 'Sharing Economy': Market Efficiency and Equitable Opportunities or Unfair Precarisation?*, Brussels: Joint Research Center, European Commission.

Colletis, G. and B. Paulré (2008), 'Le capitalisme cognitif et la recomposition du capital', in G. Colletis and B. Paulré (eds), *Les nouveaux horizons du capitalisme*, Economica, pp. 1–20.

Corden, A. (1999), 'Self-Employed People in the United Kingdom: Included or Excluded?', *International Social Security Review*, **52** (1/99), 31–47.

Crompton, R. (2010), 'Class and Employment', *Work, Employment and Society*, **24** (1), 9–26.

D'Amours, M. (2009), 'Non-Standard Employment after Age 50: How Precarious is it?', *Industrial Relations*, **64** (2), 209–29.

Davidov, G. (2004), 'Joint Employer Status in Triangular Employment Relationships', *British Journal of Industrial Relations*, **42** (4), 727–46.

De Stefano, V. (2016), 'The Rise of the "Just-In Time Workforce": On Demand Work, Crowdwork, and Labor Protection in the "Gig Economy"', *Comparative Labor Law and Policy Journal*, **37** (3), 461–71.

Dekker, F. (2010), 'Self-Employed without Employees: Managing Risks in Modern Capitalism', *Politics & Policy*, **38** (4), 765–88.

Directorate-General for Employment, Social Affairs and Inclusion (2014), *Social Protection in the Member States of the European Union, of the European*

Economic Area and in Switzerland. Social Protection of the Self-Employed. Situation on 1 January 2014, Brussels: MISSOC Mutual Information System on Social Protection. European Commission, Directorate-General for Employment, Social Affairs and Inclusion, Unit D/3.

Doeringer, P. B. and M. J. Piore (1985), *Internal Labor Markets and Manpower Analysis*, London: M. E. Sharpe.

Dolata, U. (2011), *Radical Change as Gradual Transformation: Characteristics and Variants of Socio-Technical Transitions*, SOI Discussion Paper 2011–03, Stuttgart: University of Stuttgart, Institute for Social Sciences, Department of Organizational Sociology and Innovation Studies.

Dølvik, J. E. and J. Waddington (2002), 'Private Sector Services: Challenges to European Trade Unions', *Transfer: European Review of Labour and Research*, **3** (2), 356–76.

Drahokoupil, J. and B. Fabo (2016), *The Platform Economy and the Disruption of the Employment Relationship*, ETUI Policy Brief No. 5, Brussels: European Trade Union Institute (ETUI).

Emmenegger, P. (2009), 'Barriers to Entry: Insider/Outsider Politics and the Political Determinants of Job Security Regulations', *Journal of European Social Policy*, **19** (2), 131–46.

Emmenegger, P., S. Häusermann, B. Palier and M. Seeleib-Kaiser (eds) (2012), *The Age of Dualization: The Changing Face of Inequality in Deindustrializing Societies*, Oxford and New York: Oxford University Press.

Eurofound (2015), *New Forms of Employment*, Publications Office of the European Union, accessed at https://www.eurofound.europa.eu/fr/publications/report/2015/working-conditions-labour-market/new-forms-of-employment.

European Commission (2006), *Modernising Labour Law to Meet the Challenges of the 21st Century*, Green Paper, Brussels: European Commission.

European Commission (2010), *Self-Employment in Europe*, European Employment Observatory Review, Luxembourg: Publication Office of the European Union.

European Commission (2016), *A European Agenda for the Collaborative Economy*, Communication from the Commission to the European Parliament, the Council, the European Economic and Social Committee and the Committee of the Regions SWD(2016) 184, Brussels.

European Parliament (2013), *Social Protections Rights of Economically Dependent Self-Employed Workers*, Study IP/A/EMPL/ST/2012-02, Directorate General for Internal Policies, April, accessed at http://www.europarl.europa.eu/Reg Data/etudes/etudes/join/2013/507449/IPOL-EMPL_ET%282013%29507449_EN. pdf.

European Parliament (2014), *Resolution of 14 January 2014 on Social Protection for All, Including Self-Employed Workers (2013/2111(INI))*, P7_TA(2014)0014, Strasbourg, 14 January, accessed at http://www.europarl.europa.eu/sides/getDoc. do?type=TA&reference=P7-TA-2014-0014&language=GA&ring=A7-2013-0 459.

Eurostat (2017), *Labour Force Survey*, accessed 16 January 2017 at https://ec.europa. eu/eurostat/data/database.

Fabo, B., M. Beblavý, Z. Kilhoffer and K. Lenaerts (2017), *An Overview of European Platforms Scope and Business Models*, JRC Science for Policy Report, Luxembourg: Publications Office of the European Union.

Fachinger, U. and A. Frankus (2015), 'Freelancers, Self-Employment and the Insurance against Social Risks', in A. Burke (ed.), *The Handbook on Research on Freelancing and Self-Employment*, Dublin: Senate Hall Academic Publishing, pp. 135–46.

Feltrin, P. (ed.) (2012), *Trasformazioni delle professioni e regolazione in Europa*, Milan: Wolters Kluwer Italia.

Finotto, V. (2018), 'Lavoro autonomo e lavoro agile: una nuova frontiera manageriale', in G. Zilio Grandi and M. Biasi (eds), *Commentario breve allo statuto del lavoro autonomo e del lavoro agile*, Milan: Wolters Kluwer, pp. 27–39.

Frege, C. M. and J. E. Kelly (eds) (2004), *Varieties of Unionism: Strategies for Union Revitalization in a Globalizing Economy*, Oxford and New York: Oxford University Press.

Gottschall, K. and D. Kroos (2003), *Self-Employment in Germany and the UK: Labor Market Regulation, Risk-Management and Gender in Comparative Perspective*, 13/2003, University of Bremen, Centre for Social Policy Research (ZeS).

Granovetter, M. and C. Tilly (1988), 'Inequality and Labor Processes', in N. Smelser (ed.), *Handbook of Sociology*, Newbury Park, CA: Sage Publications, pp. 175–221.

Grimshaw, D., M. Johnson, J. Rubery and A. Keizer (2016), *Reducing Precarious Work: Protective Gaps and the Role of Social Dialogue in Europe*, Report, UK: European Work and Employment Research Centre, University of Manchester.

Grimshaw, D. and J. Rubery (1998), 'Integrating the Internal and External Labour Markets', *Cambridge Journal of Economics*, **22** (2), 199–220.

Grimshaw, D., K. G. Ward, J. Rubery and H. Beynon (2001), 'Organisations and the Transformation of the Internal Labour Market', *Work, Employment and Society*, **15** (1), 25–54.

Gumbrell-McCormick, R. and R. Hyman (2013), *Trade Unions in Western Europe: Hard Times, Hard Choices*, Oxford and New York: Oxford University Press.

Hakim, C. (1988), 'Self-Employment in Britain: Recent Trends and Current Issues', *Work, Employment and Society*, **2** (4), 421–50.

Häusermann, S., T. Kurer and H. Schwander (2015), 'High-Skilled Outsiders? Labor Market Vulnerability, Education and Welfare State Preferences', *Socio-Economic Review*, **13** (2), 235–58.

Heckscher, C. and F. Carré (2006), 'Strength in Networks: Employment Rights Organizations and the Problem of Co-ordination', *British Journal of Industrial Relations*, **44** (4), 605–28.

Heery, E., H. Conley, R. Delbridge and P. Stewart (2004), 'Beyond the Enterprise: Trade Union Representation of Freelances in the UK', *Human Resource Management Journal*, **14** (2), 20–35.

Henrekson, M. (2007), 'Entrepreneurship and Institutions', *Comparative Labor Law and Policy Journal*, **28** (4), 717–42.

ISCO-08 (2012), *International Standard Classification of Occupations*, Geneva: International Labour Office (ILO).

Jenkins, J. (2013), 'Organizing "Spaces of Hope": Union Formation by Indian Garment Workers', *British Journal of Industrial Relations*, **51** (3), 623–43.

Kalleberg, A. L. and M. Dunn (2016), 'Good Jobs, Bad Jobs in the Gig Economy', *Perspective on Work*, **20** (1–2), 10–14.

Kässi, O. and V. Lehdonvirta (2016), *Online Labour Index: Measuring the Online Gig Economy for Policy and Research*, Oxford: Oxford Internet Institute.

Leighton, P. (1982), 'Employment Contracts: A Choice of Relationships', *Employment Gazette*, **90** (10), 433–9.

Leighton, P. (2015), 'Independent Professionals: Legal Issues and Challenges', in

A. Burke (ed.), *The Handbook on Research on Freelancing and Self-Employment*, Dublin: Senate Hall Academic Publishing, pp. 99–110.

McKinsey Global Institute, J. Manyika, S. Lund, J. Bughin, K. Robinson, J. Mischke and D. Mahajan (2016), *Independent Work: Choice, Necessity, and the Gig Economy*, October, available at https://www.mckinsey.com/featured-insights/employment-and-growth/independent-work-choice-necessity-and-the-gig-economy.

Malgarini, M., M. Mancini and L. Pacelli (2013), 'Temporary Hires and Innovative Investments', *Applied Economics*, **45** (17), 2361–70.

Mills, C. W. (1951), *White Collar; the American Middle Classes*, New York: Oxford University Press.

Muehlberger, U. (2007), *Dependent Self-Employment – Workers on the Border between Employment and Self-Employment*, Basingstoke: Palgrave Macmillan.

Negri, A. and C. Vercellone (2007), 'Il rapporto capitale/lavoro nel capitalismo cognitivo', *Posse*, October, 46–56.

OECD (2000), 'Chapter 5: The Partial Renaissance of Self-Employment', in *OECD Employment Outlook*, accessed at http://www.oecd.org/els/employmentoutlook-previouseditions.htm, pp. 155–99.

OECD (ed.) (2018), *A Broken Social Elevator? How to Promote Social Mobility*, Paris: OECD Publishing.

Palier, B. and K. Thelen (2010), 'Institutionalizing Dualism: Complementarities and Change in France and Germany', *Politics & Society*, **38** (1), 119–48.

Parsons, T. and N. J. Smelser (1956), *Economy and Society: A Study in the Integration of Economic and Social Theory*, Glencoe, IL: The Free Press.

Perkin, H. J. (1989), *The Rise of Professional Society: England since 1880*, London: Routledge.

Pernicka, S. (2006), 'Organizing the Self-Employed: Theoretical Considerations and Empirical Findings', *European Journal of Industrial Relations*, **12** (2), 125–42.

Perulli, A. (2003), *Economically Dependent/Quasi-Subordinate (Parasubordinate) Employment: Legal, Social and Economic Aspects*, Brussels: European Commission.

Perulli, A. (2018), 'Il Jobs Act del lavoro autonomo e agile: come cambiano i concetti di subordinazione e autonomia nel diritto del lavoro', in G. Zilio Grandi and M. Biasi (eds), *Commentario breve allo statuto del lavoro autonomo e del lavoro agile*, Milan: Wolters Kluwer.

Prassl, J. and M. Risak (2015), 'Uber, Taskrabbit, and Co.: Platforms as Employers – Rethinking the Legal Analysis of Crowdwork', *Comparative Labor Law & Policy Journal*, **37** (3), 619–52.

Ranci, C. (ed.) (2012), *Partite iva. Il lavoro autonomo nella crisi Italiana*, Bologna: Il Mulino.

Rapelli, S. (2012), *European I-Pros: A Study*, London: Professional Contractors Group Ltd.

Regini, M. (1987), 'Industrial Relations in the Phase of "Flexibility"', *International Journal of Political Economy*, **17** (3), 88–107.

Reich, M., D. M. Gordon and R. C. Edwards (1973), 'A Theory of Labor Market Segmentation', *The American Economic Review*, **63** (2), 359–65.

Rubery, J. (1978), 'Structured Labour Markets, Worker Organisation and Low Pay', *Cambridge Journal of Economics*, **2** (1), 17–36.

Rubery, J. and F. Wilkinson (eds) (1994), *Employer Strategy and the Labour Market*, Oxford and New York: Oxford University Press.

Rueda, D. (2007), *Social Democracy Inside Out: Partisanship and Labor Market Policy in Advanced Industrialized Democracies*, Oxford: Oxford University Press.

Schulze Buschoff, K. and C. Schmidt (2009), 'Adapting Labour Law and Social Security to the Needs of the "New Self-Employed"—Comparing the UK, Germany and the Netherlands', *Journal of European Social Policy*, **19** (2), 147–59.

Sennett, R. (1998), *The Corrosion of Character: The Personal Consequences of Work in the New Capitalism*, New York: W.W. Norton & Company.

Simmel, G. (1890), *Über Sociale Differenzierung. Sociologische und Psychologische Untersuchungen*, Leipzig: Duncker & Humblot.

Srnicek, N. (2017), *Platform Capitalism*, Cambridge: Polity Press.

Stanworth, C. and J. Stanworth (1995), 'The Self-Employed without Employees—Autonomous or Atypical?', *Industrial Relations Journal*, **26** (3), 221–9.

Steinmetz, G. and E. O. Wright (1989), 'The Fall and Rise of the Petty Bourgeoisie: Changing Patterns of Self-Employment in the Postwar United States', *American Journal of Sociology*, **94** (5), 973–1018.

Sullivan, R. (2010), 'Organizing Workers in the Space between Unions: Union-Centric Labor Revitalization and the Role of Community-Based Organizations', *Critical Sociology*, **36** (6), 793–819.

Tapia, M. (2013), 'Marching to Different Tunes: Commitment and Culture as Mobilizing Mechanisms of Trade Unions and Community Organizations', *British Journal of Industrial Relations*, **51** (4), 666–88.

Tattersall, A. (2010), *Power in Coalition: Strategies for Strong Unions and Social Change*, Ithaca, NY: Cornell University Press.

Valenduc, G. and P. Vendramin (2016), *Work in the Digital Economy: Sorting the Old from the New*, Working Paper 2016.03, European Trade Union Institute (ETUI).

Westerveld, M. (2012), 'The "New" Self-Employed: An Issue for Social Policy?', *European Journal of Social Security*, **14** (3), 156–73.

Wilkinson, F. (ed.) (1981), *The Dynamics of Labour Market Segmentation*, 1st edition, Academic Press, London.

Wright, E. O. (1997), *Class Counts: Comparative Studies in Class Analysis*, Cambridge: Cambridge University Press.

Zilio Grandi, G. and M. Biasi (2018), *Commentario Breve Allo Statuto Del Lavoro Autonomo e Del Lavoro Agile*, Milan: Wolters Kluwe.

3. Working conditions and needs: results of a European survey

Anna Soru, Elena Sinibaldi and Cristina Zanni

1. INTRODUCTION

The survey aims to explore the socio-economic characteristics, professional status, expectations and perceived needs of new independent professionals. Since the late 1990s, following tertiarization of the economy and the spread of digital technologies, this professional group has experienced strong growth in all European countries. However, it has remained on the margins of social research for a long time because the nature and articulated internal composition of new independent workers are difficult to identify (Leighton and McKeown 2015), and they engage in many different activities in ICT, media, management events, publishing and arts sectors, design and consulting. In addition, this professional category exhibits a high heterogeneity in income levels and market conditions. Working conditions vary widely between those who, on the one hand, carry out activities fully independently and those who, on the other hand, do not have an effective legal, economic and organizational autonomy. Furthermore, the status of new independent workers varies: some self-employed independent professionals can be registered for VAT, carrying out work activities on their own; others provide services through limited companies, partnerships or other business structures, or use intermediaries, such as umbrella companies; yet others work on the basis of some type of project contract (e.g. occasional collaboration, copyright royalties) often used by both the public and private sector as a low-cost alternative to fixed-term and full-time contracts.

Some scholars have outlined the characteristics of the new autonomous work by comparing differences to the traditional example. In particular, in a pioneering work, Bologna and Fumagalli (1997) showed how the character of this new social group breaks the mould, coining the definition 'second-generation autonomous work': members are engaged in service activities with intellectual or creative content; their autonomy is based on technical-scientific expertise and on communication-related skills, rather than on patrimonial and proprietary bases, as was the case for craftsmen and traders (Bologna 2018).

The lack of a shared definition of professional self-employment and its internal heterogeneity has made the accurate quantification of the aggregate through traditional statistical sources problematic and, consequently, an understanding of the real extent of the phenomenon. This has had a strong impact on the representation of interests and the inclusion of new independent workers in the welfare system.

In light of these considerations, a preliminary conceptual question was necessary to establish the basis of the research: who should be considered a new independent worker?

To answer this question, we proceeded to a systematic comparison of the empirical basis used by other studies through a review of the literature (Section 2). This phase was followed by a data analysis of the total self-employed population, using Eurostat (2015) data. This allowed selection of the social group of independent professionals (IPros) (Section 2.2).[1] Subsequently, the independent professional trend was analysed as part of the growth in contingent work, which includes all outsourced and non-permanent workers hired on a per-project basis (Section 2.3), and a comparative analysis of development dynamics of IPros was carried out in the European context. The analytical choices made at this stage were useful for the design of the international survey (Section 3) that involved, in large part, individuals employed in cognitive and creative professions, highly influenced by new digital technologies. They constitute a subset of IPros that we refer to as new independent professionals (NIPs). The results of the survey are described in a comparative way, using the common characteristics of respondents in different countries (Section 3.1). Finally, claiming that NIPs, as a professional group, pose problems of relevance to work as a whole and, even more pointedly, to the work–citizenship balance, some proposals for the recalibration of public action are elaborated (Section 4).

2.   CONSTRUCTION OF THE EMPIRICAL BASIS

2.1   Conceptual Definitions

The first researchers to carry out empirical analyses were Friedman and Kuznets. In pioneering research, the two scholars defined as *professional*

---

[1]   It should be remembered that, unfortunately, the official statistics do not also allow an estimation of salaried workers who create their own work opportunities and are autonomous in the execution of their work.

those occupations which 'are alike in that all require prolonged and specialized training and involve work that has something of an academic and intellectual flavour—no purely mechanical or commercial pursuit' (Friedman and Kuznets 1945, p. 34).

The authors stress the intellectual content of the activity, observing that there are no precise boundaries, but rather ever-changing ones, and that the level of training required can vary significantly among the different professions:

> Its boundaries are neither precise nor stable. A century ago the 'learned professions' meant medicine, law, and theology; today they include a host of other occupations; and a century hence they will include still others. These occupations are alike in that all require prolonged and specialized training and involve work that has something of an academic and intellectual flavour—no purely mechanical or commercial pursuit can qualify. (Friedman and Kuznets 1945, p. 45)

Finally, they specify that the definition covers both regulated and non-regulated professions: 'While all professions require specialized training, there are sizable differences in the amount of training required and in the extent to which the requirements are formalized.' 'A growing number of professions are restricted to persons "licenced" by the state; and candidates for licensure must ordinarily satisfy minimum educational requirements and demonstrate an acceptable level of competence.' 'In other professions not under state licensure, educational requirements are a matter of custom' (Friedman and Kuznets 1945, p. 47).

Their analysis focuses on independent workers, meaning those who don't receive a salary but payment for services offered. In short, independent professional activities are those that call for extensive, though not necessarily formalized, training, and whose content is intellectual; it can be regulated or unregulated, exercised without ties of subordination and with services performed for a fee.

Even though their definition was decidedly broad and inclusive, Friedman and Kuznets's empirical research only addressed regulated professions, being limited by the type of data available. It was due precisely to the restricted scope of their research that Rapelli (2012) wished to improve on their approach, which he deems to be inadequate, by examining independent professional employment under a new definition.[2] In Rapelli's analysis of the data, independent professionals, whom he refers to as Ipros, consist of all independent workers who either have no employees or engage

---

[2] In reality, as discussed earlier, the shortcomings of Friedman and Kuznets's analyses were due not to the definition utilized, but rather to the scope of the empirical research.

in a service activity and/or intellectual service not in the farming, craft or retail sectors.

This pragmatic definition, though most likely conditioned by which statistical sources were available, has the advantages of being objective, and of permitting trouble-free identification of the category, which also makes possible international comparisons, though, at the same time, it loses characterization based on the cognitive content of the profession. As such, it includes many independent activities (such as hairdressers, beauticians and cobblers) that are more closely related, in terms of problems and practice, to trades rather than intellectual professions. When identified in this manner, the activities do not point to the distinguishing characteristics of the new independent professions.

In this analysis, therefore, it is proposed that the available statistical sources be used for an estimate of professional employment that accepts the conditions of an absence of employees, as posited by Rapelli, in order to distinguish the less structured situations, but that recovers the dimension of cognitive content underlying the classification of Friedman and Kuznets. Such an operation is possible at present because Eurostat, in recent years, has not only kept data on all European Union countries,[3] but has also classified working activities on the basis of professional qualification, using International Standard Classification of Occupations (ISCO) categories. It is worth pointing out that to identify IPros, Rapelli used the data on independent workers who have no employees and provide non-commercial services (NACE,[4] sectors J–S). In identifying those whom we will refer to as independent professionals (IPs), we employ a further restrictive condition, stipulating that they must possess a high professional ranking, such as manager, professional or technician, as identified under the ISCO 100-352 categories.

2.2 Independent Professionals: Data and Trends

Figure 3.1 shows the procedure used to select IPs from the total employed population. In Europe in 2015, there were 23,799,000 active self-employed workers without employees, equal to 10.7 per cent of the total employed,[5] and 7,238,000 IPs, equal to 3.3 per cent of the total employed and 21.9 per cent of the self-employed (Table 3.1). During the period

---

[3] It should be remembered that the data consist of the results of national sampling surveys rendered uniform.

[4] Statistical Classification of Economic Activities in the European Community, commonly referred to as NACE.

[5] Data of self-employed without employees are consistent with Eurofund (2017).

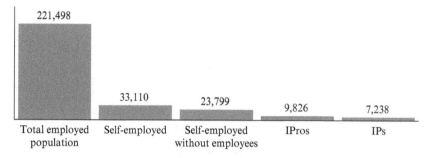

Source: ACTA, analysis of Eurostat microdata.

Figure 3.1   EU-28: from TOTAL employed population to IPs (2015)

Table 3.1   From total employed population to IP in EU-28 (2015)

	EU-28	% of all employed	% of self-employed
Total employed population	221,498	100.0	
Self-employed workers	33,110	14.9	100.0
Self-employed without employees	23,799	10.7	71.9
IPros (NACE, sectors J–S)	9,826	4.4	29.7
IP (ISCO 100-352, managers, professionals and technicians)	7,238	3.3	21.9

Source: ACTA, analysis of Eurostat microdata.

2011–15, although total self-employment (and even self-employment without employees) grew at a lower rate than total employment, the IP growth rate was significantly higher, at +13.1 per cent, just above the average rise for IPros (+12.5 per cent).[6]

Excluding IPs, independent employment fell by 2.4 per cent in the EU-28. The higher IP growth rate is attributable, in part, to rising employment in sectors where IPs are present (services to businesses and social services), compared to sectors where they are not (farming, commerce and manufacturing), signs of the continuing shift of the economy to the tertiary sector. But even if the comparison is limited to non-commercial service sectors, IP growth is almost double that of the rest of the employed population: 13.1 per cent compared to 7.1 per cent.

---

[6]   The IPros are calculated using Rapelli's procedure.

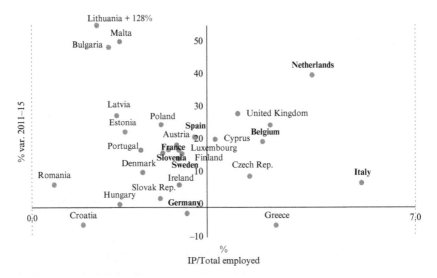

Source: ACTA, analysis of Eurostat microdata.

Figure 3.2   EU countries on the basis of % IP and trend

Countries with the most IPs in absolute terms are the United Kingdom, Italy and Germany, with these three nations accounting for more than half (53.5 per cent) of the IPs of the European Community. In terms of their relative weight out of the total number of employed, the elevated incidences of Italy and the United Kingdom are confirmed, but not that of Germany. Percentages of IPs are also high in the Netherlands and Greece, plus, though slightly behind, Belgium, the Czech Republic and Spain.

Figure 3.2 plots the situations of all the countries, with the y axis showing the IP trends for the period 2011–15 and the x axis the incidence of IPs out of the total employed population. The intersection of the axes constitutes:

(1)   for the y axis (growth trend), 0
(2)   for the x axis (incidence of IPs out of total employed population), the average value for the EU-28, which is 3.3.

The first quadrant (upper right) identifies those countries whose incidence of IPs is high and on the rise. Of these, the Netherlands has the highest growth rate; rates are also strong in Belgium and the United Kingdom, but more modest in Italy, nevertheless shown to be the country with the highest presence of IPs. The second quadrant (lower right), includes only Greece, whose incidence of IPs is high but falling. In the third quadrant (lower left), which combines the conditions of an IP presence lower than the European average and negative growth, we find Germany and Croatia.

Most countries are positioned in the fourth quadrant (upper left) (low presence but positive growth). Some Eastern European countries show strong growth: Lithuania (whose +128 per cent would be off the graph), Bulgaria, Latvia, Poland and Estonia, plus the Scandinavian countries, Spain, France and Austria.

2.3   The Increase in Independent Professionals as Part of the Growth in Contingent Work

The IP trend can be seen as part of the growth in contingent work, which includes all outsourced and non-permanent workers hired on a per-project basis (temporary workers among them). Estimates of the United States (Katz and Krueger 2016) indicate that contingent work accounted for 10.1 per cent of all employment in February 2005 and 15.8 per cent at the end of 2015. The authors hold that all the net growth in jobs in the USA is attributable to contingent workers.[7] The estimates are also consistent with those found in Osborne's (2017) report, which assesses the incidence of contingent work at 20 per cent in 2017, compared to 15 per cent in 2014.

A key contributing factor to the recent growth in the number of contingent workers is technology, not only in terms of increasing the offer of new professional skills on supply, but even more importantly through its effect on demand, seeing that the sum total of new technological developments has revolutionized corporate organizational structures,[8] reducing transaction costs and favouring outsourcing. Thanks to technology, work can be monitored without the need for a physical presence, due in part to the standardization of many activities, while access to elements of reputational evaluation can be accessed, facilitating the selection of skills and know-how.

External constraints, including red tape, can be reduced through outsourcing bureaucratic functions and noteworthy cost savings are possible: no minimum contractual pay levels, no social security costs, lower office and equipment costs, and training becomes the responsibility of the workers themselves. The employment of external workers has become especially attractive in the case of functions that do not play key roles.

---

[7]   There are a number of other estimates that provide very different results but based on data that do not account for occasional workers. One component of the increase in contingent work is the growth of the gig economy, still quite recent, and not very significant (0.5 per cent of all employment, according to Katz and Krueger 2016), but growing strongly.

[8]   Reference is made to the IoT (Internet of Things) and Industry 4.0, meaning the systematic application of technology to optimize production processes on a global scale.

At the same time, the supply of contingent work has increased with the spread of the wish to be independent, to be able to work flexible hours and to be in control of one's own working activities, as is clearly shown by the results of this survey. The move in this direction was heightened by the 2008 economic crisis, when it was seen that even salaried employment was no longer capable of providing security, while a weak job market left increasingly small margins of bargaining power and also narrowed the options for salaried employment.

A portion of this growth is not real, being the outcome of workers classified as independent, whereas they are actually bogus self-employed, but even the increase is the result of a misclassification—the rise of contingent work leads to a lessening of rights, compensation and safeguards. Katz and Krueger (2016) speak of a fissured marketplace, a concept introduced by Weil (2014). In response to competitive pressures, businesses attempt both to reduce turnover with regard to the core group of workers (employed on a stable basis) and to utilize external staff to deal with moments when a greater supply of labour is needed. As Weil sees it, processes of outsourcing (often occurring on various levels, as the company to which the work is outsourced may, for its part, outsource) leave the subcontractor with profit margins that become increasingly smaller the greater the distance from the enterprise actually using the service. Given that cost of labour constitutes a growing component of decentralized business activities, the pressure to save in this area is increasingly strong. Pay and rights are reduced, with empirical examples found mainly in the non-advanced services, although there are also instances in the legal and media activities sectors.

It is interesting to note that many of the trends observed by Katz and Krueger (2016) about contingent workers were also found to hold for independent professionals. In both cases, the following factors were present:

(1) A noteworthy presence of university graduates. According to Osborne's (2017) report, this will be increasingly true, seeing that more recent technological advances will tend to destroy the more routine contingent work focused merely on implementation while creating non-routine, skill-based contingent work.
(2) A high percentage of women.
(3) A significant presence of individuals with more than one job, a development we shall indeed see confirmed by the online survey.
(4) A high incidence of services to businesses, though in recent years there has been greater growth in the education and health sectors.

2.4 The Comparative Data Analysis

The overall picture that emerges from the data analysis shows a population with clearly identifiable characteristics. 'Professional activities' account for 37 per cent of EU IPs, while 16 per cent are employed in the human-health sector. Other sectors of note are ICT, plus education and the arts, each with 10 per cent (Figure 3.3). During the period 2011–15, the sectors with the greatest IP growth were education and real estate (Figure 3.4).

An interesting comparison is that between the growth of IPs and of other employed workers in the same sectors. IP growth is significantly higher than that of other employed workers in education, other services and human health, all sectors where the incidence of IPs is not currently high. In contrast, IP growth is lower than that of other employed workers in the arts and ICT, two sectors with noteworthy levels of IPs. This suggests that the factors behind ongoing IP development are different now than in the past. First, artists, always largely independent, increased significantly in the period considered, but mainly as salaried employees; second, the business service sector, which played a key role in the strong growth of IPs

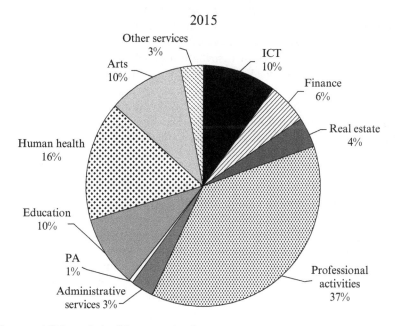

Source: ACTA, analysis of Eurostat microdata.

Figure 3.3   IP sectors in the EU-28

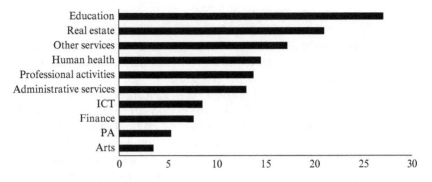

Source: ACTA, analysis of Eurostat microdata.

Figure 3.4   IP trends by sector 2011–15

in the two decades before and after 2000, due to outsourcing by business enterprises, maintained a growth rate of independents well above the average, but with a significantly reduced differential; third, IPs, on the other hand, made a much higher contribution than salaried workers to recent growth in the social services, especially education, as well as services to individuals (included in other services).

Table 3.2 shows the sector distribution of IPs in the leading countries of the European Union. Almost everywhere, the sector with the highest incidence of IPs is professional activities, except in France, where the highest concentration of IPs is to be found in the human-health sector, which is also well represented in Italy, Romania, Slovenia, Sweden and Spain. The UK, France, Germany and the Netherlands have the most widely distributed IP breakdowns.

With regard to socio-demographic characteristics, the EU average for the incidence of women out of all IPs in 2015 is 42.8 per cent, an increase over 2011 (41 per cent). Female participation as IPs is lower with respect to both salaried employment and work not in the professions (IPros not in the professions), while it is higher with respect to employers and independents in the trades, crafts and farming sectors. As always, women account for the majority of those in the caring sectors (education, human health and other services). In contrast, there are far more men in ICT and finance. Women IPs are present in number essentially equal to men in Finland, France and the Baltic Republics, and their number is also decidedly high in Portugal and the countries of Central/Eastern Europe (Hungary, Bulgaria and Romania), falling below 40 per cent only in Ireland, Croatia and Malta. The percentage weight of women IPs is falling in the Netherlands,

Table 3.2 Distribution of IPs by sector in the leading EU countries

	ICT	Finance	Real estate	Professional activities	Administrative services & PA	Education	Human health	Arts	Other services
Austria	**11.8**	4.5	**5.5**	33.6	1.8	7.3	**18.2**	**14.5**	2.7
Belgium	**11.0**	2.6	3.7	37.2	3.7	2.6	**33.0**	4.7	1.6
Bulgaria	4.7	4.7	**7.0**	**44.2**	0.0	0.0	**20.9**	**14.0**	4.7
Czech Republic	**13.9**	**15.4**	**6.5**	**39.8**	2.5	8.5	5.0	7.0	1.5
Germany	**11.3**	5.2	2.8	28.9	**4.8**	**13.1**	16.1	**13.2**	4.6
Denmark	**16.7**	1.9	1.9	**44.4**	3.7	5.6	14.8	9.3	1.9
Spain	8.5	4.5	**7.3**	**46.1**	3.2	8.6	11.7	8.6	1.5
Finland	8.8	4.4	**4.4**	**42.6**	1.5	4.4	14.7	16.2	2.9
France	6.2	1.5	**5.0**	25.4	2.1	9.1	**36.6**	11.8	2.4
Greece	3.1	6.2	1.2	**53.7**	1.9	6.8	22.8	3.7	0.6
Hungary	10.3	**10.3**	1.5	**41.2**	**5.9**	5.9	10.3	11.8	2.9
Ireland	**15.1**	5.7	1.9	34.0	1.9	9.4	11.3	17.0	3.8
Italy	7.4	6.4	3.9	**51.6**	2.1	5.6	14.8	6.1	2.1
Netherlands	10.8	3.5	2.1	35.2	**5.4**	**12.0**	15.7	12.7	2.6
Poland	**12.8**	**10.7**	**4.5**	**38.2**	2.4	6.3	**18.1**	5.0	2.1
Portugal	6.6	7.7	**6.6**	**44.0**	2.2	**11.0**	11.0	8.8	2.2
Romania	8.6	2.9	2.9	**48.6**	0.0	2.9	**20.0**	11.4	2.9
Sweden	**15.4**	1.5	2.3	46.9	2.3	4.6	6.9	15.4	4.6
Slovenia	**17.4**	4.3	0.0	**47.8**	**4.3**	4.3	4.3	13.0	4.3
Slovak Republic	**14.0**	**15.8**	3.5	**40.4**	**5.3**	5.3	5.3	7.0	3.5
United Kingdom	**12.6**	5.3	3.8	29.1	**6.1**	**15.0**	9.7	13.6	4.8
EU-28	10.1	5.5	4.0	37.5	3.7	9.6	16.1	10.4	3.1

Source: ACTA, analysis of Eurostat microdata.

57

Denmark and many Eastern European countries (Slovenia, the Slovak Republic, Croatia, Estonia, Lithuania and Bulgaria).

IPs are most prevalent in middle age groups, especially 40–49 years. The older age groups are growing. There are few over the age of 60, and even fewer young people under 30. Of course, initiating a professional activity generally calls for a higher level of instruction and a certain amount of working experience. Indeed, the presence of young people among IPs is decidedly lower than among salaried employees, although it is higher than among entrepreneurs and the self-employed in traditional sectors. The participation of young people is noteworthy in the ICT, arts and education sectors. Table 3.2 shows young people playing an especially significant role in Eastern European countries.

The level of education among IPs is very high: 70.5 per cent have attained advanced level, while only 3.8 per cent have a low level and women are slightly better educated than men. There is no mistaking the difference with the other IPros, confirming that the definition used effectively takes in professions calling for higher qualifications. Advanced levels of education are possessed by 70.7 per cent of IPs, as opposed to 21.6 per cent of IPros not in professions. The advanced level of education among IPs is also corroborated by a comparison with other categories of workers, including employers. Levels of education are particularly high in the human-health sector and the professions, for which a university degree is more often required by law, and lower in real estate and finance, although even in these sectors the incidence of the highly educated is elevated, approaching 50 per cent. Taking the average of all the countries, at least 50 per cent of IPs are highly educated. The lowest levels are found in the Slovak Republic and Denmark, and the highest in Greece and Belgium. The higher level of participation of IPs in courses of lifelong learning is also confirmed. The propensity of IPs to engage in ongoing instruction is higher in the Scandinavian countries and in Luxembourg and France.

IPs are a typically urban population: they are highly concentrated in densely populated areas, which is where more than half the professionals live. In recent years, however, the incidence of IPs has also increased in less populated areas, especially those of medium density. Thanks to new technologies, remote work is increasingly possible, and so the place of residence can be chosen without reference to where clients are located.

Working hours vary considerably, depending on the type of worker. Although the term 'part-time work' is generally used in reference to salaried employees, it is actually more widespread among IPros not in professions and IPs (37.1 per cent and 34 per cent, respectively). A large number of employers and the self-employed in the farming, craft or retail sectors work more than 40 hours a week (59.8 per cent and 47.3 per cent, respectively), while salaried employees, as was to be expected, have more standard work weeks, generally between 31 and 40 hours. Growth in part-time work is especially strong among IPs. Part-time work is not always voluntary, as over one third of part-time workers would like to work more hours, with this holding true for IPs as well.

Among IPs, part-time work was found to be more frequent for women (40.2 per cent, as opposed to 22.8 per cent for men) and for the lower and upper age groups: one third of workers younger than 30 are part-time, as are more than half of those aged 60 or older, while the figure in the central age groups is 23 per cent. The sectors in which part-time work is most frequent are education and other services, social and personal, while it is rare in finance. Part-time is used most frequently in the Netherlands and Austria but is rare in Eastern Europe and Greece.

Finally, the data show the emergence of the phenomenon of multiple jobs. An ever-increasing number of independent workers have more than one job. This is particularly true of IPs, 7 per cent of whom have a second job. It is increasingly women who hold second jobs (7.7 per cent among IPs, compared to 6.5 per cent of men) and workers of medium-high age (7.4 per cent in their forties and 8.4 per cent in their fifties); while it is rare among the over sixties. As in the case of part-time work, multiple jobs are most frequent in education and less frequent in finance. In contrast to part-time, multiple jobs are also relatively frequent in the arts. Second jobs are most frequent in the Netherlands, Luxembourg and Sweden. In 53.5 per cent of cases, the second job is an independent one, but it is in a different sector from the first job. There is a high level of correlation between part-time work and multiple jobs, demonstrating that the decision to work a second job is often motivated by the need to supplement the first (Figure 3.5). An analysis by country confirms that the increase of part-time work is accompanied by an increase in multiple jobs.

3.   THE INTERNATIONAL SURVEY: SAMPLE AND METHOD

In this section, the main results of the online survey will be described from a comparative perspective and are summarized in Table 3.3. It should be stressed that the sample groups in the different countries involved suffer from bias caused by the self-selection of the respondents. However, an international comparative analysis points to shared characteristics that, corroborated by the Eurostat (2015) data, make it possible to draw up a credible profile of the professional group and its problems.

In large part, the respondents are individuals employed in cognitive and

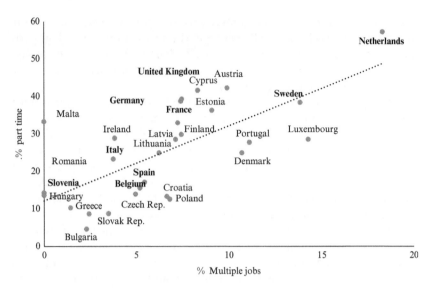

Source: ACTA, analysis of Eurostat microdata.

Figure 3.5   IP: part-time and multiple jobs in EU countries

creative professions, highly influenced by the new digital technologies.[9] They constitute a subset of independent professionals (IPs) that we refer to as new independent professionals (NIPs). The NIP group is actually a difficult population to reach, according to the taxonomy proposed by Kish (1991). A number of methodological considerations, already illustrated in the presentation of the research, follow accordingly. First, the use of a non-probabilistic snowball sampling (Vogt 1999) allowed us to involve a good number of respondents and, leveraging on their social ties, to gradually widen the sample.[10] The snowball sampling provides that the social networks are activated to recruit other sample units, starting from an initial number of subjects belonging to the group to study (seeds). Second, the questionnaire was uploaded onto the Google Forms platform and was spread by associations of freelancers and union organizations.

---

[9]   Even though the survey was meant for all IPs, it failed to reach professionals in the areas of medicine and finance and, in general, those engaged in activities governed by professional orders.

[10]   The questionnaire, meant to highlight the socio-economic characteristics, the professional condition, the expectations and the perceived needs of such workers, consisted of 66 questions divided into six sections: description of the profession and the sector, perceived working conditions, a description of the market conditions, relations with union and quasi-union organizations, and socio-demographic data.

Table 3.3   NIPs: a summary of the main findings

Features of the sample	Countries							
	Italy	France	Belgium	Germany	Netherlands	Spain	Sweden	Slovenia
Number of questionnaires	907 (with weighting)	153	236	231	237 (with weighting)	91	46	31
Main employment status	Mostly NIP and VAT (95%)	Mostly salaried entrepreneurs (72%)	Mostly salaried employees (45%) and members of a coop (25%)	Mostly NIP and VAT, publishing and translation	Mostly sole-entrepreneur (87.5%)	Mostly NIP and VAT, publishing	Mostly NIP VAT publishing	Mostly sole-entrepreneur translators
Level of education (university degree)	81.3%	92%	88%	85%	95%	97%	89%	89%
Multiple jobs	20% → 1 activity	30% → 1 activity	21% → 1 activity	29% → 1 activity	32.5 → 1 activity	24% → 1 activity	23% → 1 activity	31% → 1 activity
Level of independence: objective criteria/ subjective perception	54% → 6 criteria AS → 7.9	Around 76% → 6 criteria AS → 7.9	48% → 6 criteria AS → 7.8	77% → 6 criteria AS → 8.7	64% → 6 criteria AS → 9.1	67% → 6 criteria AS → 7.4	64% → 4/5 criteria AS → 4.5	85% → 4/5 criteria AS → 8.3
Workplace and main market	At home National	At home National	At home and client's working space National	At home National	At home and in own office National	At home National	At home National	At home National and foreign markets
Income	75% <30,000 22%	87% <30,000 27%	81% <30,000 38%	68% <30,000 42%	49% <30,000 57%	56% <30,000 ++81.3%	72% <30,000 22.7%	86% <30,000 48.3%
Online platforms to sell or buy professional services								

Table 3.3 (continued)

Features of the sample	Countries							
	Italy	France	Belgium	Germany	Netherlands	Spain	Sweden	Slovenia
Three biggest problems perceived	Tax burden; unfair competition; low compensation	Tax burden; unfair competition; low compensation	Tax burden; unfair competition; low compensation	Low compensation; tax burden; unfair competition	Unfair competition; low compensation; shortage of assignments	Unfair competition; low compensation; shortage of assignments	Low compensation; shortage of assignments; tax burden	Unfair compensation; competition; low compensation; shortage of assignments
Reasons for satisfaction	Independence and the work itself	Independence and the work itself	Independence and the work itself	Independence and the work itself	Independence and the work itself	Independence and the work itself	Independence and the work itself	Independence and the work itself
Perceived social protection	Low	Quite high	Quite low	Low	High except for unemployment benefits	Low	Low	Low
Representation, mostly members of:	Multi-sectorial associations	LMI/UC	Trade unions, LMI and professional associations (NIP)	Professional associations	Professional associations	Trade unions	Trade unions	Any associations

Note: AS = average score.

Source: ACTA, I-WIRE Survey.

The communication of the survey was relaunched through main social media sites. As is known, however, this sampling technique does not allow generalization of the results to the reference population of interest.[11] Once the collection phase was completed, it was found that the majority of the questionnaires came from professionals not organized into professional orders, as well as from journalists and artists, while there were almost no respondents who belonged to professional orders or worked in finance.

Apart from being difficult, the distribution of the questionnaire proved to be varied in terms of:

(1)   The number of questionnaires gathered, which ranged from 20 in the UK to more than 900 in Italy, a diversity not always explained by the different economic structures of the countries involved or by their respective levels of freelance workers.

(2)   The distribution channels utilized, with associations being the primary channel everywhere, although the target groups reached through such organizations presented noteworthy differences in terms of professional categories, types of employment contracts and the economic force of the respondents.

(3)   The types of professional activities and working arrangements of the respondents.

3.1   Primary Common Results of the Survey

For the reasons illustrated in Section 2.4, it was decided not to pool the country-level data, but rather, after a specific analysis for each country, to compare the countries only in a descriptive way. The dimensions of the factors utilized in the comparison are summarized in Table 3.3, which also includes the countries with fewer than one hundred respondents (Spain, Sweden and Slovenia). As noted, the sample groups were distorted by the self-selection of the respondents. The data collected for Italy and the Netherlands were consistent, on the whole, with those for the sum total of the NIPs, and so weighting operations were carried out to take into account the known variables of the reference universe (Istat 2016 data for Italy and Eurostat 2015 data for the Netherlands), with the objective of reducing the principal distortions.

More precisely, the results are biased in terms of:

---

[11]   Between June and September 2017, a total of 2,054 questionnaires were collected.

(1)   Personal characteristics: many old people in the Netherlands, many women in Italy.
(2)   Professional activities: respondents are mostly in publishing and journalism in Sweden and Germany.
(3)   Types of contracts: in most of the countries involved in the research, the respondents are professionals registered for VAT or work as individual/small businesses (Italy, France, Belgium, Germany, the Netherlands, Spain, Sweden and Slovenia), but the great majority of the respondents (72 per cent) work as salaried employees in France, and 45 per cent of Belgian respondents work through LMIs or umbrella companies (UCs).

Despite these differences, it is interesting to note that all countries have the following common factors: a high level of education, relevance of multiple jobs, high independence, low income, insufficient welfare provision and difficultly in group representation. Each of these factors is now examined briefly.

3.1.1   High qualification

The data confirm the high qualification of the professional group, often identified with 'knowledge workers'. The respondents are highly educated and skilled (Figure 3.6): in Germany and Spain, for example, more than three quarters of the respondents have university degrees, while around 14 per cent have a PhD; in the Netherlands, 51 per cent have bachelor's degrees and 43.7 per cent have a master's. This is consistent with the Eurostat (2015) data, which show that 70.7 per cent of IPs hold a university degree, a figure significantly higher than that for salaried employees (38.6 per cent) or other categories of professionals.

3.1.2   Multiple jobs

The survey sample shows the strong diffusion of multiple jobs. The respondents are active in a wide range of knowledge-based sectors and almost all of

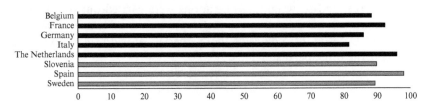

Source: ACTA, I-WIRE survey, analysis of data.

Figure 3.6   Level of education of respondents

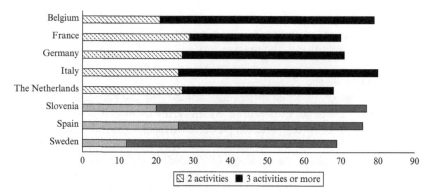

Source: ACTA, I-WIRE survey, analysis of data.

Figure 3.7 Multiple jobs

them practise more than one profession. In fact, in practically all of the countries involved in the research (with the sole exception of Spain), the majority of the respondents state that they work at more than one profession, ranging from 67 per cent of Swedish NIPs to 80 per cent of those in Italy (Figure 3.7). A significant portion of those interviewed even declare that they have four or more jobs (from 20 per cent of NIPs interviewed in Germany and France to 39 per cent of those in Belgium). The Eurostat (2015) figures show that multiple jobs are particularly widespread with NIPs being tied to part-time work, this being especially true in the education and arts sectors.

In the United States, the term 'slash worker generation' was coined to describe this increasingly common condition.[12] The rise of slash workers is traceable to a variety of factors, in particular the development of new professional activities in and around different sectors and/or complementary sectors, a situation most frequently found when digital technology is involved. In other instances, professionals carry out projects for private clients or small businesses based on limited budgets, assignments that often call for solutions of little sophistication, but still require several skills. In other cases, economic difficulties oblige NIPs to supplement their main activity with other, decidedly different pursuits in other sectors, such as sales or crafts. Similar situations present both opportunities and risks: on the one hand, they can increase the ability of NIPs to respond rapidly to new market demands, but at the same time they can gradually undermine levels of specialization, as some freelancers, due in part to a lack of

---

[12]   The term was coined by Marci Alboher (2007) to describe the 'slash' in the job title of someone who is an X/Y/Z, or journalist/web editor/PR, for example.

economic resources for further professional training, could wind up with skills that are overly fragmented or not specialized enough to allow them to remain competitive in the market.

3.1.3   Independence

Given the choice, in all countries the majority of the respondents would prefer to be independent (Figure 3.8). In terms of operational independence, the majority of respondents perceive themselves as independent with regard to both the objective criteria considered (the standard parameters used internationally to gauge levels of subordination/para-subordination) and their self-evaluations. More specifically, the online survey assessed the following parameters to determine respondents' levels of independence or subordination: ability to choose the place of work, working hours, work content, free time and working tools. Along with these elements, consideration was also given to the number of clients.

The majority of respondents in the different countries present a high level of independence: in Germany, for example, almost all of the respondents (91.3 per cent) met between five and six of the criteria that define independence, while three quarters satisfy all six conditions. Self-assessment of independence, judged on a scale of 1 to 10, shows a high average score. In contrast, the estimated percentage of the bogus self-employed, meaning respondents who met fewer than four of the criteria of independence, is not high: from a maximum of 17 per cent in Belgium to a minimum of 4.1 per cent in the Netherlands (Figure 3.9).

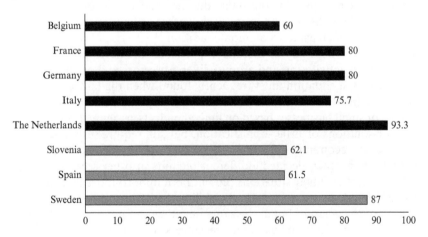

Source: ACTA, I-WIRE survey, analysis of data.

Figure 3.8   Percentage of IPs that want to be independent

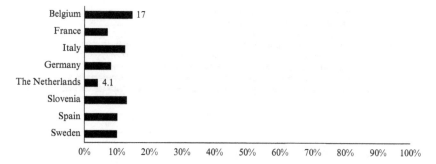

Source: ACTA, I-WIRE survey, analysis of data.

Figure 3.9 Percentage risk of bogus self-employed (<4 parameters)

The primary reasons for satisfaction have to do with independence, content of work and flexible working procedures that make it possible to reconcile professional and family lives. In other words, professional independence stands as a value and a benefit that NIPs are not willing to do without, whereas the levels of pay and social safeguards associated with such employment do not prove to be equally satisfying.

3.1.4 Low income

The survey sample presents an interesting picture of the economic situation of those who deal alone with the labour market and makes it possible to dispel some myths. The majority of the respondents in the different countries earn less than €30,000 per year. In Italy, three quarters of those interviewed have a pre-tax income of less than €30,000, while 23.4 per cent do not earn more than €10,000 per year. In France, Belgium and Slovenia, those with incomes of more than €30,000 are in the minority, at between 12.5 per cent and 18.8 per cent of the respondents. In Belgium and France, there is a disproportionately high presence of artists, workers who use LMIs/UCs as intermediaries, and salaried entrepreneurs in this income bracket (<€30,000 per year). The Netherlands is an exception among the countries involved, with most Dutch respondents (51 per cent) earning more than €30,000, while 15.2 per cent have annual incomes of more than €100,000 (Figure 3.10).

Even when additional income from work or other sources (e.g. pension, rent income, gig employment) is considered, a large number of the respondents state that their overall income is not enough to meet their day-to-day expenses. To cope with this trying economic situation, the majority of respondents are aided primarily by income from a partner or their family of origin. In the case of Germany, there is no mistaking that the primary

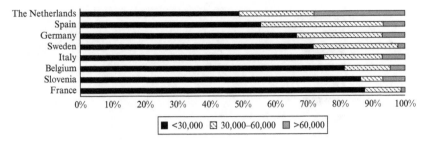

Source: ACTA, I-WIRE survey, analysis of data.

Figure 3.10   Annual income (2016)

approach is a dual-earner strategy. Low incomes are often tied to discontinuous employment and low pay, links that prove particularly evident in the cases of Italy and Belgium. In Slovenia, Italy, Germany and France, respondents who work on a continuous basis account for roughly half, or slightly more than half, of the total. The situation is especially difficult in Belgium, where more than one quarter of those interviewed work less than six months of the year, attributable to the elevated percentage of artists.

In all the countries involved, respondents identified low pay as one of their three main problems. Research on the situation in the United States also shows a shift in pay, as well as a decrease in measures safeguarding workers, accompanying the increase in contingent workers. Lower pay is tied to intense competitive pressure in markets that often present an overabundance of supply. In fact, recurring responses for the three main problems include harmful competition (in seven of eight countries: Belgium, France, Germany, Italy, the Netherlands, Slovenia and Spain) and a shortage of work assignments (France, Germany, the Netherlands, Slovenia and Sweden).

Another problem reported as worthy of note is the high social security/tax payment burden, especially in Belgium, France, Germany, Italy and Sweden. In Italy and Slovenia, these charges are perceived as excessive even by NIPs who benefit from favourable tax rates.

The problems identified in the different countries represent possible vulnerabilities for NIPs, threatening to produce a significant imbalance in incomes in the central portion of the social ladder, as confirmed by a recent research effort in Italy.[13]

---

[13]   A longitudinal study (1994–2014) on the distribution of wealth in Italy points to an income gap within the Italian middle class between salaried employees and independent professionals. During the period 1994–2014, the inequality level was relatively low and

3.1.5 Welfare

With regard to welfare protection, the research sample group perceives a low level of safeguards to protect them against the main risks: unemployment, future pension benefits, illness and maternity. Despite the large-scale changes that have affected the labour market since the early 1990s, the system of guarantees in the majority of the countries involved is still tied to the job as opposed to the worker. A telling example is the case of Germany, where independent professionals enjoy only limited rights compared to salaried employees when it comes to a series of social safeguards. In 2006, for example, obligatory medical insurance was extended to include all residents and independent workers, although the latter, unlike salaried employees and other sectors of the population, must meet the monthly costs themselves, placing those with limited incomes, or who find themselves momentarily unemployed, in serious difficulty. As for unemployment benefits, it was decided, once again from 2006 on, that only independent workers who have previously worked as salaried employees are entitled to remain in the insurance system that covers periods of unemployment, paying into it on a voluntary basis (Borghi 2018). In Belgium and France as well, there is a clear-cut discrepancy between insiders and outsiders: the subset of those interviewed who work through LMIs or UCs, or as salaried entrepreneurs, and who thus benefit from the standard safeguards afforded to salaried employees, consider themselves to be protected by the welfare system, unlike sole entrepreneurs, who feel excluded from the welfare safeguards.

3.1.6 Representation

Problems tied to difficulties in the marketplace and a lack of social safeguards naturally ushers in the subject of how the interests of independent workers are represented, and their resulting capacity to influence public policy. The online survey shows that various approaches to representation are on offer in the different countries, ranging from professional associations to horizontal organizations ('quasi-unions') that take in a number of different sectors, plus umbrella companies and traditional unions. In Italy, horizontal associations are the most widespread approach, while in Germany the great majority of the sample group belongs to a professional association, with membership in traditional unions also being relatively significant. In France, the type of association preferred by the respondents

---

stable among middle-class salaried employees, while it was higher and growing among the self-employed. Among the self-employed, the hardest hit were young professionals who are highly skilled and involved in volatile markets such as the services sector and the knowledge economy (Dagnes et al. 2018).

was the umbrella organization, to be expected, seeing that the respondents were largely reached through such organizations. Membership in unions, on the other hand, was low, even though a large part of the workers opting for this approach were classified as salaried employees.

The variety of different forms of representation observed by the survey would appear to translate into a splintering of union initiatives, a situation that, in turn, weakens the professional group's ability to obtain a hearing for its collective voice. The respondents are aware of this weakness, suggesting that it be remedied through network strategies. Cooperative efforts involving unions and professional associations, or self-organized associations could prove more effective in dealing with complex problems, such as the general reduction in pay, the lack of adequate welfare safeguards and the risk of indigence in old age.

4. PRIMARY FINDINGS ON LABOUR MARKET CHANGE

4.1 New Independent Professionals as Emblematic of a Changing Labour Market

As already noted, despite the distortion caused by self-selection in the online survey sample group, its distinguishing features were still consistent with the reference population, as shown by the Eurostat (2015) data. The profile of the respondents, as described in previous chapters, is characterized by a high level of education, a high degree of operational/professional independence, and a noteworthy level of flexibility and personal engagement. At the same time, their employment situation is characterized by individual exposure to risk and unstable ties with labour organizations.[14]

In other words, NIPs possess the characteristics that today's labour market is looking for (skills and flexibility), and which represent key ingredients in the competitive strength of businesses and the economy as a whole, but they are also subject to 'uncertain' and 'individualised' working conditions (Bauman 2001), and without the support of adequate social safeguards or union representation. If these constituent elements of the NIP 'identity' (as well as that of the IPs, as shown by the Eurostat (2015) data) is viewed within a broader context, it can be observed that this professional group expresses the same tensions to be found in all types of

---

[14] Specifically, there are three main categories of risk: (a) risk tied to economic stability; (b) risk tied to maintaining professional capabilities by updating skills and know-how; (c) risk resulting from exclusion from the system of social protection.

employment (whether independent or salaried) since the business model that had guaranteed lifelong employment and protection from the risk of unemployment for thirty years following the Second World War began to lose its validity.

A number of considerations in support of our reflection can be summarized as follows.

In industrial societies, two categories found at opposite ends of the social hierarchy are exposed to risk: (a) at the top, business owners, (b) at the bottom, marginalized groups that live outside institutionalized rules. Salaried employees are exempt from risk, being safeguarded by a labour market designed according to the model of a large-scale company that ensures virtually full employment on a permanent basis and at an adequate salary. This type of labour market works in combination with a social security system based on the figure of the adult, male head of the family, or the so-called male breadwinner. In other words, the system of social protection safeguards the head of the family by protecting his job.

The advent of the post-industrial model brought on a crisis for the two pillars that had upheld security in the previous society (the labour market and the welfare state). Under the new approach to organizing production, flexibility has become the key element in working relations: types of employment have gradually strayed from the standard 'mould' of salaried employment (as a full-time, permanent salaried worker). With the spread of atypical forms of employment, situations of insecurity have also become more common, as risk began to climb the social ladder (from bottom to top), with significant repercussions for those found 'in the middle' (the middle class), as insecurity became the new 'norm' for certain sectors of salaried employees as well.

To deal with transformations on the labour market, the northern European countries tried out the flex-security approach (Wilthagen and Tros 2004),[15] which has been imitated in the rest of Europe in the years since, though in the form of less all-encompassing initiatives. Under this approach, the welfare system includes non-standard workers, but only those with contracts of salaried employment. The self-employed, being considered on the same footing as businesses, generally remain outside guarantees regarding income (minimum salaries set under law and collective bargaining), as well as social safeguards, and in particular protection against unemployment. An in-depth examination of the case of Sweden

---

[15] 'A policy strategy that attempts, synchronically and in a deliberate way, to enhance the flexibility of labour markets, work organizations and labour relations—on the one hand— and to enhance security (employment security and social security) notably for weaker groups in and outside the labour market—on the other hand' (Wilthagen and Tros 2004).

(Norbäck et al. 2018) shows that the self-employed lack protection against unemployment, once again provided only to salaried workers, and that not all of them are able to pay for pension coverage.

During the 2010s, the economic crisis has exerted a downward pressure on pay, bringing to light, on the one hand, the lack of bargaining power of the self-employed when dealing with client enterprises, and on the other hand, the obsolete nature of the old Fordism model that saw independent workers as being able to cope with times of difficulty on their own, thanks to their savings. Independent workers, whose numbers have grown at a very rapid pace in the meantime, now have incomes that are, on average, lower than those of salaried employees, meaning that they are no longer able to set aside sufficient resources.

In light of the above considerations, we hold that the NIPs, as a professional group, pose problems of relevance to work as a whole and, even more to the point, the work–citizen equilibrium. These issues amount to 'wicked problems', or complex, multi-dimensional, stratified questions that cannot be dealt with under an exclusively technical approach, as the political sphere must take responsibility for whatever arises as well. Specifically, the primary problems posed by IPs are: (a) the transformation of social welfare and (b) market regulation in terms of pay and income.

4.2   Social Welfare for a Changing Working World

The topic of the changing working world and the resulting inadequacy of its systems of social welfare have been a focus of public debate throughout Europe and the United States for at least two reasons: the growing percentage of workers excluded from social safeguards, or included only marginally, and the increasingly fluid nature of work, along with the growing practice of holding multiple jobs, which has led to cracks in systems of social protection designed for the standard model of salaried employment. The topic, though it has entered the public realm, has only been dealt with in part by decision-makers, seeing that, as is the case with all wicked problems, it casts doubt on the validity of the very architecture of current welfare systems. What is called for is a well-thought-out political consensus, given that, at least over the short term, someone must *lose* something.

The measures tried out to date, as confirmed by national case studies and the survey, present a number of distinguishing characteristics: they maintain the social welfare model of insurance for salaried employment, they contemplate 'market-based' solutions and they regard only a portion of the self-employed. In practical terms, the solutions identified are: (a) efforts to eliminate misclassification, (b) establishment of a 'tertium genus' (or third category), (c) assimilation of the self-employed into the category of salaried employment (regardless of their effective degree of subordination, as in the case of entertainment-industry workers in Belgium and France), and (d) classification of independent workers on the same footing as salaried employees through an intermediate structure that acts in liaison with the client (referred to by the generic term umbrella company). It should be noted that in certain countries this mode of intermediation is subject to strict regulations, being allowed only if the organization of intermediation presents specific features that ensure participation of the workers in the governance of the enterprise (Belgium and France).

The following are more thorough descriptions of these four possible solutions:

(1)   In the majority of countries involved in the survey, criteria have been established for identifying 'bogus' self-employed workers and bringing them back under the category of salaried workers. The underlying concept is that only the 'fake' self-employed should be protected. As is noted in the transversal analysis developed by Beuker and Pichault (Chapter 5 in this volume): 'Sometimes the qualification of the working relationships remains mainly based on court judgements; in others there is prevalence of the law on judgements, with strict predetermined criteria.' In this last case, however, the effectiveness of the criteria employed under legal doctrine (and by the survey) appear increasingly unable to keep pace with technological transformations, seeing that the development of the technology of the Internet of Things (IoT) has led to the creation of new monitoring systems that eliminate the need to define space and time. Such transformations make it more difficult to identify 'bogus' self-employed workers. Nor is it a simple matter to take action without damaging the interests of the workers themselves, in terms of relations with their clients. Many companies could deem it advantageous to deal with service enterprises, so as to avoid the risk of taking upon themselves the expense and obligations of a salaried employee.

(2)   The establishment of a 'third category', meaning a hybrid of a salaried employee and an independent worker. This would ensure that independent workers who are economically dependent benefit from certain safeguards for which the client is responsible, though without the workers being subject to contracts of fully fledged subordination. This approach has been taken in some countries and in an emblematic way in Spain, which has introduced the contractual figure of the Trabajadores autónomos económicamente dependientes (TRADE) in its legal system, and a similar proposal by Harris and

Krueger (2015)[16] has reached an advanced stage of development for the United States, in addition to receiving subsequent mention in Taylor's (2017) report[17] for the United Kingdom and in the Ichino legislative proposal in Italy (2017).[18] Still, this remains a decidedly low-cost approach, lending itself, as such, to widespread use in situations where workers possess little bargaining power. As shown by the experience in Spain, while there are those who hold that TRADE has helped reduce the divergence between salaried employees and independent workers, others see it simply as a way to legalize the figure of the bogus self-employed worker, opening the way for further abuses.

4.3   Choosing the 'High Road' to Competitiveness

Collective bargaining is the primary tool for protecting salaried employees who find themselves in an asymmetric employment relationship, but independent workers cannot use it because, being considered on an equal footing with businesses, they are subject to antitrust regulations that exclude any form of collective bargaining or setting of minimum salaries or fees. Under this scenario, IPs pay the price for the failure to recognize them as 'independent workers', meaning that professional figures are employed in a labour market that is no longer polarized between salaried employment and self-employment. So once again, the IPs wind up crushed between two extremes: (a) companies, which stress business considerations at the expense of labour factors and (b) atypical employment, which classifies IPs as economically dependent workers.

In reality, contractual safeguards and rules amount to an uninterrupted continuum, meaning that no clear-cut distinction can be made between salaried workers who deserve to be protected and independent professionals whose bargaining power is so high as to constitute a threat to competition. Work is not just another type of merchandise whose price can be left to market forces, regardless of whether the worker is a salaried employee

---

[16]   Harris and Krueger propose legal recognition of an intermediate figure between the traditional salaried employee and the self-employed worker, suggesting that the term 'independent worker' be used.

[17]   Taylor's (2017) report proposes the identification of 'an intermediate category covering casual, independent relationships, with a more limited set of key employment rights applying', under the name of 'dependent contractors'.

[18]   The proposal presented by Senator Ichino P.– October of 2017 is Legislative Bill no. 2934, accessed 10 February 2018 at http://www.senato.it/japp/bgt/showdoc/17/DDLPRES/1059435/index.html.

or self-employed. It follows that the implementation of regulation is the course to take.

The survey shows that one problem affecting IPs in all sectors, and in all the countries involved, is low pay, followed by harmful competition. These problems are serious and perceived as such. Furthermore, in a market where the 'low road' to competitiveness holds sway (price cutting, scarce quality and innovation) everyone suffers (lose–lose): poorly paid professionals, clients receiving low-quality services, and the countries whose economies are unable to grow.

One tool for examining this state of affairs would be the establishment of parameters to define fair compensation for services performed. Similar parameters would be binding on public administration and provide guidelines for private enterprises and for the professionals as well, especially newcomers, who are not always aware of the need to insist on receiving adequate pay to avoid further encouraging a downward price spiral. But this measure alone would not be adequate or even fair. In a labour market where abundant free labour is available, it would cure the symptoms instead of the illness. This is why it should be accompanied by intensive efforts to counter the illicit growth of contingent work (Artiles et al. 2018) and free work.

REFERENCES

Alboher, M. (2007), *One Person/Multiple Careers: A New Model for Work/Life Success*, 1st edn, New York: Warner Business Books.
Artiles, A. M., Ó. Molina and A. Godino (2018), *Country Case Study: Spain*, accessed 5 March 2018 at http://www.i-wire.eu/wp-content/uploads/2018/02/i-wire_WP3_D3.1_country-case_spain.pdf.
Bauman, Z. (2001), *Liquid Modernity*, Cambridge: Polity Press.
Bologna, S. (2018), *The Rise of the European Self-Employed Workforce*, Milan: Mimesis International.
Bologna, S. and A. Fumagalli (1997), *Il lavoro autonomo di seconda generazione: Scenari del postfordismo in Italia*, Milan: Feltrinelli.
Borghi, P. (2018), *Country Case Study: Germany*, accessed 26 February 2018 at http://www.i-wire.eu/wp-content/uploads/2018/02/i-wire_WP3_D3.1_countryca se_germany.pdf.
Dagnes, J., M. Filandri and L. Storti (2018), 'Social Class and Wealth Inequality in Italy Over 20 Years, 1993–2014', *Journal of Modern Italian Studies*, **23** (2), 176–98.
Eurofound (2017), *Exploring Self-Employment in the European Union*, Luxembourg: Publications Office of the European Union.
Eurostat (2015), *European Union Labour Force Survey*, accessed at https://ec.euro pa.eu/eurostat/web/microdata/european-union-labour-force-survey.
Friedman, M. and S. Kuznets (1945), *Income from Independent Professional Practice*, New York: National Bureau of Economic Research.

Harris, S. D. and A. B. Krueger (2015), *A Proposal for Modernizing Labour Laws for Twenty-First-Century Work: The Independent Work*, discussion paper 2015-10, The Hamilton Project, December, accessed at http://www.hamiltonproject.org/assets/files/modernizing_labor_laws_for_twenty_first_century_work_krue ger_harris.pdf.

Istat (2016), *Rilevazione sulle forze di lavoro*, Rome: Istituto Nazionale di Statistica.

Katz, L. F. and A. B. Krueger (2016), *The Rise and Nature of Alternative Work Arrangements in the United States, 1995–2015*, NBER Working Paper 22667, National Bureau of Economic Research, Inc., September, accessed 20 February 2018 at https://ideas.repec.org/p/nbr/nberwo/22667.html.

Kish, L. (1991), 'Taxonomy of Elusive Populations', *Journal of Official Statistics*, **7** (3), 339–47.

Leighton, P. and T. McKeown (2015), 'The Rise of Independent Professionals: Their Challenge for Management', *Small Enterprise Research*, **22** (2–3), 119–30.

Norbäck, M., L. Walter and E. Raviola (2018), *Country Case Study: Sweden*, accessed 2 March 2018 at http://www.i-wire.eu/wp-content/uploads/2018/02/i-wire_WP3_D3.1_sweden.pdf.

Osborne, C. (2017), *The Future of Work, Contingent Workers and New Employment Models*, accessed 22 February 2018 at www.osborneclarke.com/wp-content/uploads/2017/11/OC-The-Future-of-Work-Contingent-workers-8pp-A4-36099 747-SOFT.pdf.

Rapelli, S. (2012), *European I-Pros: A Study*, London: Professional Contractors Group Ltd.

Taylor, M. (2017), *Good Work: The Taylor Review of Modern Working Practices*, accessed 4 March 2018 at https://assets.publishing.service.gov.uk/government/uploads/system/uploads/attachment_data/file/627671/good-work-taylor-review-modern-working-practices-rg.pdf.

Vogt, W. P. (1999), *Dictionary of Statistics & Methodology: A Nontechnical Guide for the Social Sciences*, 2nd edn, Thousand Oaks, CA: Sage Publications.

Weil, D. (2014), *The Fissured Workplace: Why Work Became So Bad for So Many and What Can Be Done to Improve It*, Cambridge, MA: Harvard University Press.

Wilthagen, T. and F. Tros (2004), 'The Concept of "Flexicurity": A New Approach to Regulating Employment and Labour Markets', *Transfer: European Review of Labour and Research*, **10** (2), 166–86.

4. The place of self-employment in the European context. Evidence from nine country case studies: Belgium, France, Germany, Italy, the Netherlands, Slovenia, Spain, Sweden and the United Kingdom

**Laura Beuker, Paolo Borghi,
Marie-Christine Bureau, Antonella Corsani,
Bernard Gazier, Alejandro Godino, Bas Koene,
Antonio Martín-Artiles, Oscar Molina,
Anna Mori, Frédéric Naedenoen,
Maria Norbäck, Klemen Širok, Maylin Stanic
and Lars Walter**

INTRODUCTION

This chapter presents an overview of the various regulatory and legal frameworks around self-employed workers, the main institutional arrangements and a state of the art examination of the social dialogue in each country case study. The nine countries selected, distributed throughout Northern, continental, Eastern and Southern Europe, are representative of different welfare state regimes and embody diverse models of labour markets and regulation of professions.

In light of the results of the survey (presented in Chapter 3) on identities, working conditions and needs of self-employed workers—both in terms of universal social protection and specific measures for supporting professional development—the aim of the country case studies is twofold: to describe the variety of institutional structures present in Europe and to highlight the lines of the national debate around the emergence of a new social dialogue.

Each of the country case studies reported in this chapter, arranged in alphabetical order, has a similar structure. After a brief introduction on national characteristics, the study describes the status of self-employed workers from a legal and contractual point of view, in light of recent developments in national regulations, and then analyses the existing social protection system, tax policies and incentives for self-employment. Each study then addresses the issue of collective representation, framing it among elements of continuity with traditional union policies and factors of discontinuity, favoured by the presence of new actors and innovative bottom-up strategies. Case studies conclude with a brief synthesis.

The picture emerging from the country case studies shows a high variety of institutional configurations and a different degree of political aware-ness of the challenges that the rise of new self-employment poses to the labour market and more generally to the organization of society. What are the national answers to challenges linked to the growth of demand for intellectual, specialized and flexible workforces, and outsourcing practices, within the advanced services sectors? At first glance it would seem that continental European countries (Belgium, France and Germany) place great attention on new configurations of industrial relations systems, while in Southern (Italy and Spain) and Eastern countries (Slovenia), the more controversial issues revolve around the need for an expansion of social protection to counterbalance the growing precariousness of self-employed professionals. In the case of Northern Europe, particularly the Netherlands, the focus is on the prerogatives of self-employed workers (as solo-entrepreneurs) and on their representation rights. Finally, in the case of the UK, a country where professionals have increased in number the most since the late 2000s, self-employment is particularly encouraged, mainly as an antidote to unemployment but with far less social protection than is available to employed workers.

4.1.   BELGIUM: TOWARDS THE END OF THE NEO-CORPORATIST MODEL?

Laura Beuker and Frédéric Naedenoen

Introduction

Although the Belgian social security system is considered as well developed (ESPN 2017), the current national regulatory framework continues to protect standard jobs and careers rather than taking into account the 'grey zone' situated between self-employment and classical employment status.

Project-based autonomous workers represent, in addition, a very heterogeneous category, making definition and quantification of their group difficult. In Belgium, only the classical figures of salaried or self-employed workers are registered in official statistics.

The Belgian Labour Relations Act lays out the legal characterization of working relationships. This law is grafted onto the principle of autonomy of the parties involved stating that: 'the parties should freely choose the way they want to collaborate'. Incompatible elements that question the nature of working relationships, the nature of relations and the corresponding social security scheme, can be refined. Compared to the regular employee's scheme, social rights of self-employed workers are lower: self-employed workers have no entitlement to unemployment benefits, no allowances during the first month of occupational accident or illness, fewer weeks provision in the case of maternity leave, and lower pension allowances.

Moreover, the current regulatory framework remains constrained for self-employed workers: the provision of staff or the 'wage portage' (i.e. workers salaried by an umbrella company) is actually possible, but only under very specific conditions. For this reason it is particularly relevant to explore the emerging initiatives taken by labour market intermediaries (LMIs) and quasi-unions (e.g. Smart, Tentoo, Dies, Pro-Unity) to secure professional paths in the Belgian labour market are (e.g. business or employment cooperatives, employee sharing and umbrella organizations).

The Federal Minister of Employment recently launched a legislative attempt to adapt social regulation to new work arrangements. One of the devices under discussion was the creation of a new hybrid status, located between that of employee and self-employed. This new status would have provided the benefit of equal access to social protection that is available to regular employees. However, this process was abandoned in 2018 due to vetoes by both trade unions and employers' associations.

In Belgium, where the union membership rate is very high (Faniel and Vandaele 2012) social and economic regulation is traditionally the sole prerogative of social partners, the state taking the lead only in cases of major obstacles to progress. This principle is called 'the neo-corporatist regime'. This arrangement gives both employers' and workers' unions considerable power within the Belgian model of collective bargaining and social regulation. However, until recently, trade unions have paid little attention to project-based autonomous workers, partly because their status is often considered the result of individual choice, and employer unions have treated them as if they were classical self-employed workers. The ability of classical unions to represent those workers is thus a real challenge, offering room for the emergence of recent quasi-union initiatives and allowing the government to take initiatives in the regulation in these atypical work arrangements (Léonard and Pichault 2016).

Legal Statuses and Institutional Frameworks in the Belgian Labour Market

Belgium recognizes three employment statuses: self-employment, salaried work, and in the public sector, civil servant. Until the Labour Relations Act was promulgated in 2007,[1] the legal characterization of working relationships had been governed for many years by the sole jurisprudence principle ('the indices method').[2] The 2007 Act had a double objective: to provide more legal stability in the appreciation of labour relations and to tackle the issue of bogus self-employment; it also confirmed the principle of autonomy of the parties involved, Article 332 providing for definitions of working relationships, redefinition of working relationships and appropriate social security schemes.[3] The qualification of the working relation by the parties involved will always take precedence, if it is not incompatible with the real-life situation.

The Labour Relations Act comprises four general criteria that are applicable to all types of working relationships and which qualify the nature of the relation:

- The autonomy of the parties involved;
- Personal freedom to organize working time;
- Freedom in the organization of work;
- The possibility of exercising hierarchical control.

Specific criteria, common to some sectors or professions, must be used as a complement to general criteria. In addition, neutral criteria can constitute hints to qualify the working relation. Nevertheless, this law has been criticized by many parties for its unclear text, its poor wording and for the fact that the authority criterion[4] seems no longer relevant (with respect to the current economic and social context) to qualifying the very nature of labour relations (CGG, 2016/01). A new law in 2012 (25 August 2012, M.B. 11 September 2012) partially changed the existing legal framework and created an administrative commission for the qualification of working relationships (Federal Public Service of Social Security).

---

[1] Title XIII of the programme act of 27 December 2006.
[2] Composed of factual, economic and legal elements.
[3] Comité Général de Gestion pour le statut social des travailleurs indépendants, rapport 2016/01, la Loi sur la nature des relations de travail, p. 13.
[4] Defined as 'to direct, to monitor, to control the worker and to check the way he/she is doing his/her work': Report 2016/01, Law on the nature of work relations, p. 14.

At ground level, public authorities may organize targeted control actions regarding the phenomenon of bogus self-employed. Even though this has been a political priority since the early 2000s, the number of controls remains very low—165 cases in 2014 for a population of one million self-employed workers—despite evidence of a growing proportion of workers situated in the grey zone between salaried and self-employed status.[5]

Furthermore, several local LMI initiatives have emerged for the benefit of non-standard workers: business or employment cooperatives, employee sharing pools, umbrella organizations, and so on. Staff provisions and wage portage (i.e. persons salaried by an umbrella company) are subject to strict conditions and are therefore highly regulated.

Public Policies for Self-Employed Workers

The social security system in Belgium is divided into two parts: social security and social assistance,[6] and has three schemes according to professional status: salaried work, self-employment, and a specific scheme for civil servants. The social security system allows people to obtain replacement income (in the case of loss of wages) or additional income (in the case of social charges).

The financing of these schemes is based on the solidarity principle, between employers and employees, active employees and retired workers, healthy and sick persons, salaried persons and people without resources, family and childfree persons, and so on.[7] It means that everybody contributes to the sustainability of the system by paying social contributions.

In the employees' scheme, both parties—employers and employees—must pay social contributions to the ONSS/RSZ (National Office of Social Security). Social contributions are directly charged on salaries and are proportional to income (30 per cent for employer contributions and 13.07 per cent for personal contributions).

The national office funds the seven branches of social security according to their specific needs, through a series of public agencies: retirement pension or survivor's pension (ONP/RVP), unemployment benefits (ONEm/RVA), insurance schemes for occupational accidents (FAT/FAO) or diseases (FMP/FBZ), family allowances (FAMIFED), care insurance (INAMI/RIZIV) and annual vacations (ONVA/RJV).

---

[5]   e.g. +25% of multiple job holders between 2004 and 2016 (Eurostat, EWCS); +39% of self-employed in a secondary occupation between 2004 and 2015 (INASTI/RSVZ).

[6]   Also called 'residual scheme'. This includes integration revenues, guaranteed incomes for the elderly, family allowances and disabled adults' allowances.

[7]   Social Security Federal Department (2015): 'La sécurité sociale, tout ce que vous avez toujours voulu savoir', p. 8.

In the self-employment scheme, each independent worker must pay quarterly social contributions to the specific social security fund called INASTI/RSVZ. The amount is calculated on the basis of the level of income: 20.5 per cent up to €57,415.67 and 14.16 per cent from €57,415.68 to €84,612.53. Above this ceiling, a maximum contribution of €4,141.19 is due, which renders this status very attractive for workers with high incomes. Self-employed workers are insured for five branches of social security: healthcare, work incapacity or disability; maternity insurance; family allowances; pensions; and bankruptcy.

Compared to the regular employee's scheme, social rights of self-employed workers are lower even if the Belgian scheme may be viewed as well developed compared to other EU countries.[8]

New Legislation to Embrace the Development of the Digital Economy

On 1 March 2017, the Belgian government decided to introduce a specific taxation regime for the digital economy. The incomes generated by individuals are now subject to a unique taxation rate of 10 per cent, collected directly by the collaborative platform. This favourable rate—taxes for this kind of activity are usually set at 33 per cent—is limited to additional revenues below €5,000. Above that amount, individuals are considered as professionals and are subject to the classical self-employed tax regime.

Moreover, a broader law 'concerning feasible and manageable work' is another governmental initiative to adapt legislation to better face societal evolution. The law introduces more working time flexibility, yearly training obligations and tax exemption for part time 'flexi-jobs'. These laws are clearly a way of promoting small-scale entrepreneurial activities in the digital economy. However, we can observe that they encourage workers to develop their business activities without imposing any specific work status. Therefore, the informal way may be chosen, being neither employee, nor self-employed, which paves the way to an increasing black market. Furthermore, even if the fiscal support may contribute to the growth of business activities, it does not offer any social protection to such workers.

---

[8] ESPN thematic report on access to social protection of people working as self-employed or on non-standard contracts, 2017, p. 4.

Collective Representation and Social Dialogue

In Belgium, there are three main workers' unions, which are, in increasing size, the Liberal Union (CGSLB/ACLVB), the Socialist Union (FGTB/ABVV) and the Christian Union (CSC/ACV). The very high membership rates—partly explained by the fact that unions manage unemployment allowances—give them considerable power within the Belgian model of collective bargaining. According to Faniel and Vandaele (2012), Belgium is the only Western country with a high and still growing level of unionization, reaching 74.47 per cent in 2009. However, self-employed workers cannot be affiliated to a trade union and are supposed to be represented on the employer side in the (inter-)sectorial social dialogue. Formerly, unions paid little attention to these: they are not supposed to look for collective representation, are often seen as employers, and are supposed to be represented by employer unions.

Nevertheless, trade unions in general, and their research centres in particular, closely follow the current evolutions of the labour market. They observe a decreased number of 'classical' independent workers (liberal professions, small local independent traders, company owners, etc.) and a consequent increase of 'new' independent workers, often without the responsibility of employees. According to the unions, a large part of the latter are bogus self-employed workers, forced by their 'employer' to adopt this status in order to get a flexible workforce at a reduced social cost.

Several anonymous sources among union members are concerned about a risk of cannibalization, threatening the current membership. Therefore, they are currently considering the opportunity to affiliate these new types of workers. Their plan is not only to offer them access to classical union services (e.g. collective and individual representation, legal advices, collective bargaining) but also to offer them new services likely to answer their specific needs. This strategy would allow unions to increase their membership, therefore gaining more weight in the social dialogue and counterbalance employers' strategies to divide workers on the basis of their status.

Business sector federations, grouped within the Belgian Federation of Enterprises, must be considered as employers unions. According to the project-based autonomous workers interviewed during the I-WIRE project, such organizations seem rather unattractive because they represent the 'classical' independent workers from whom they feel very distant, due to the intellectual nature of their work, or because they do not want to hire workers, or because they consider themselves as being 'on the worker side'.

Conclusion

Despite a rather well-developed system of social protection compared to other EU countries, self-employed workers benefit from weaker social rights than regular employees. Although recent initiatives have been launched at federal level in order to create a new status (between self-employed and employee) the processes have been abandoned due to fierce resistances from both sides of the social dialogue.

Conventional unions take little interest in self-employed workers, even though they closely follow the increase of these 'new' autonomous workers. The trade unions actually fear a risk of cannibalization, likely to reduce their current membership rate. On the other hand, professional unions remain unattractive for new autonomous professionals because they mainly represent 'classical' self-employed workers.

For all these reasons, various initiatives have emerged in order to help those self-employed workers: quasi-union initiatives have started to collectively organize and represent such workers, and LMIs offer them pragmatic solutions so they can behave 'as if' they were employees in order to secure social protection and guarantee continuity of their incomes (Lorquet et al. 2017). Such initiatives (e.g. umbrella companies, employer's alliances, cooperatives) attempt to provide self-employed workers with better protection against the risks and disadvantages of their status.

Federal government is currently proposing new legislation in order to embrace the challenges of the digital economy: a specific taxation regime for platform workers, new laws concerning feasible and manageable work, and so on. However, by acting before any social bargaining has taken place, the Belgian government has opened a breach in the prevailing neo-corporatist regime, thus weakening the capacity of unions and other traditional actors to support emerging categories of project-based professionals.

4.2   FRANCE: A PARTIAL SUCCESS STORY

Marie-Christine Bureau, Antonella Corsani and Bernard Gazier

National Framework on New Autonomous Workers

There is no positive definition of self-employed workers or autonomous workers in French labour law. Self-employed workers are defined by what they are not: neither employee nor agricultural worker. In fact, the French government has refused to create a third status, intermediate between self-employed and salaried worker. The situation in France is characterized first by a large variety of specific situations which extend the scope of employee rights (e.g. presumption of employment, assimilated salaried), and second by the recent regime of auto-entrepreneurs (a microsocial regime for self-employed workers pursuing small-scale activities). This dual characteristic explains the 'partial success story': while most auto-entrepreneurs live in a precarious situation, the deemed employees and assimilated salaried benefit from a certain security.

According to the INSEE (2015), at the end of 2011, 2.8 million persons in France were engaged in a self-employed activity, whether as a main occupation or as a complement to a salaried activity. Between 2006 and 2011, excluding agriculture, the number of non-salaried people has increased by 26 per cent, and even more in some services: management consulting, design, computing, artistic and recreational activities, and education, in particular. This vitality is partly tied to the success of the auto-entrepreneur status. In 2015, more than one million auto-entrepreneurs were administratively registered and 619,000 were economically active (Acoss 2016). The recent study from France stratégie, *Salarié ou indépendant? Une question de métiers* (September 2017) brings a dynamic perspective and explicitly introduces 'freelancers' among different types of employment statuses. The study first highlights the complexity of the link between employment status and the type of trade. From 1984 until 2014, some professions created both salaried work *and* self-employment, while having a self-employment rate above the average, especially in the healthcare and culture-related professions or the information and training trades. At the same time, the rate of salaried employment increased for some traditional self-employed workers (e.g. farmers, liberal professions, child minders). Second, the study highlights the revival of independent work, among which freelancers are counted.

According to the INSEE's survey, 'traditional' non-salaried people earn an average of €3,100 per month. Trade (except for stores), arts and entertainment, hairdressing, taxi driving and education are less profitable sectors, while average incomes are highest in the legal and health professions and the pharmaceutical trade. Inequalities appear to be higher among non-salaried people than among employees in the private sector: 10 per cent of the most well-remunerated self-employed workers account for 41 per cent of the revenues (against 33 per cent for salaried people). However, auto-entrepreneurs earn an average of €460 per month, with little variation between the different sectors.

According to the Inserm's survey (2011), the major psychosocial issues encountered by self-employed workers in their everyday life are: a tendency to work extremely long or short hours; difficulty in balancing work and family lives; uncertainty in levels of monthly revenue; and feelings of loneliness (no colleagues to help in cases of difficulty).

Legal and Institutional Framework

Historically, we can find two main justifications for workers' protection: economic dependency and legal subordination. In France, case law has enshrined the second of these since the 1930s: subordination, not economic dependency, is the major criterion in classifying a work relationship as a salaried one. The qualification by the judge is based on effective working conditions: the employee performs paid work while the employer has the authority to give orders, monitor the work's implementation and sanction any failings. Nevertheless, the legislator has taken into account the situation of economic dependence in several specific cases. Hence, the Labour Code (Book 7) provides specific arrangements for several occupations. Since 1957 homeworkers are deemed employees, without the need to investigate the subordination relationship. There is also a presumption of salaried status for occupational activities, such as journalists, performing artists and models, sales representatives, or janitors and building caretakers. The notion of 'intermittent performing art workers' is specific to the French institutional social system and refers to an exception: according to the law, every contract between an artist and an enterprise of the entertainment sector is presumed an employment contract.

On the other hand, since 1994 (Madelin law), and then 2003 (law for economic initiative), there has been a presumption of independent work for physical persons listed in the commercial register (Registre du commerce), the craft/profession list (Répertoire des métiers) and other company registers. In these cases, however, the work relationship may be reclassified as an employment contract if a relationship of subordination can be proved. As a result, there are many cases in contention, especially in the situations of franchising, provision of services and sales agency.

The regime of the auto-entrepreneurs, introduced by the law of 4 August 2008, can be summarized as the right, for certain self-employed workers, to benefit from simplified tax returns and social security contributions, subject to a maximum turnover. Auto-entrepreneurs enjoy the same security coverage as other self-employed workers and don't benefit from unemployment insurance in the event of a cessation of activity.

The French case is also characterized by a long list of specific measures, creating hybrid situations. Regarding self-employed managers of food retail branches, disputes between companies and self-employed managers fall within the scope of commercial courts if the matter concerns the commercial terms of branch operations, but they fall within the scope of labour courts if the matter concerns the working conditions of self-employed managers. Even though they are non-salaried, these managers are also represented by trade unions in sectoral collective bargaining.

Wage portage or *Portage salarial* in France with an umbrella company (UC) is a system which allows a person to work as a freelancer for a client. The person works as an independent contractor using the services of the *Portage salarial* company. S/he is relieved of administrative burdens, such as invoicing and recovery of payments. Most importantly, the system allows the person to benefit from the social welfare advantages of employee status.

The term 'salaried-entrepreneurs' refers to a new group of workers, independent in their activity but employed by a business and employment cooperative (BEC). In order to include this situation in the Labour Code, the Hamon Law created a new contract, the CESA (contrat d'entrepreneur-salarié associé).

Lastly, the Commercial Code provides other specific protections for economically dependent professionals like sales representatives, independent door-to-door vendors and representative managers, for example a minimum guaranteed commission or severance pay if the contract is terminated (Articles L146-3 and L146-4 of the Commercial Code).

Overall, one can observe, in the Labour Code and Commercial Code, numerous legislative ad hoc measures, depending on negotiations and on balances of power, which concern self-employed workers and assimilated salaried.

Regarding digital platforms, if the expression 'uberization of the workplace' is a success, the platforms and the forms of work they generate are very diverse. As there is no status in France for economically dependent workers, French judges have been tempted to classify situations of economic dependency as employment contracts, by pretending they reveal a relationship of subordination. Nowadays, the legislator hesitates between fostering new forms of employment in a context of high unemployment and protecting workers who often claim their own independence. At the moment, the legislator has suppressed activities like Uberpop, but this was done in the name of the competition law, and the Constitutional Court had nothing to say about it. Nevertheless, Article 60 of the *Loi Travail* introduces in the Labour Code the principle of the platforms' social responsibility, in order to take into account the specific situation of 'workers using an online platform'. It creates three rights for these workers: payment by the platform of insurance contributions covering the risk of accidents in the workplace; other payments by the platform as a contribution to professional training; and the right of concerted refusal to provide services (i.e. a right to strike), without incurring any penalty.

Public Policy to Support Self-Employed Workers

In France, the broadening of social welfare coverage was not achieved by the development of a unique regime, but rather by juxtaposition of multiple different regimes. The family branch, which provides in particular family allowances, is the sole branch featuring universality and full national solidarity.

After strong opposition from non-salaried professions to the 1946 law on old age insurance, the social security scheme for self-employed workers was built separately from the general scheme. Although basic coverage between the two is largely harmonized, significant differences remain, concerning contribution rates and the protections afforded. In particular, there is no compulsory system that covers the risk of accident in the workplace or the risk of unemployment.

The RSI (Régime social des indépendants) was founded in 2005, gathering several funds for sickness and mandatory retirement insurance. But the system ran into a serious credibility problem as a consequence of failures after the financial crash of 2008. Moreover, the old opposition of some self-employed workers to social security affiliation is taking new forms, provoking in 2015 several protest demonstrations against the RSI. In 2017, Emmanuel Macron decided to suppress this regime and to reintegrate it into the General Régime (with a separate management) providing for a transitional period of two years.

We can observe a continuous extension of the general scheme, based on two criteria: economic dependency and business creation. The list of the famous Article L. 311-3 of the French Social Security Code has been expanded including, on the one hand, professionals for whom economic dependency is more obvious than legal subordination, and on the other hand, company founders (support contract for business setting up). As a result, there are a lot of situations where an autonomous professional (e.g. a consultant) may arbitrate between different possibilities and decide which status is better for carrying out his/her activities.

Although one can observe a move to harmonization of social protection schemes, there is a persistent gap between the costs of contributions and the coverages of social risks. We can note the particular situation of workers in the entertainment and audiovisual industries, who benefit from a very specific unemployment insurance system (Régime des intermittents du spectacle), as a result of the occasional nature of their work. This regime of social welfare allows the limitation of living precariousness in a context of discontinuity of labour relations: under certain conditions artists and entertainment workers receive unemployment benefits every day off. At the end of 1970s, the reform of the social welfare system (obtained by trade

Table 4.1   Risk considerations for a new social protection scheme

Options	Problems
To maintain the distinction between employment and self-employed work, while broadening the scope of salaried work and improving transition security	What are the limits to broadening? How to finance the extension of unemployment insurance? How to make a distinction between professionals and amateurs?
To create a third status for economically dependent self-employed	How to specify the thresholds for economic dependency and avoid the threshold effects? What is the contribution of contractors? What consequences are there for other workers?
To go beyond the distinction between employment and self-employed work, while establishing a unique worker's status	How to specify the different stages of protection? What is the perimeter of professional activity? What is the level of universal protection?

unions) started indeed a massive socialization of resources: intermittent performing arts workers could, in this way, achieve their own artistic projects and regain power over their work choices, especially whether or not to make commitments, according to their judgement not only about working conditions but also about quality of artistic and cultural production.

In 2016 France stratégie published a new report, *Nouvelles formes de travail et de la protection des actifs* (*New forms of work and workforce's protection*). It stresses the new risks to consider (fluctuation in revenues for self-employed workers, accidents and illness for freelancers and nomadic workers) and exposes the different options for a new social protection scheme (Table 4.1).

In fact, the option of a third status seems outdated since its rejection following the Antonmattei–Sciberras (2008) report, even if this option is regularly reactivated. The timid launch of the CPA (Compte personnel d'activité) offers the opportunity to reach a new stage in the continuity and personalization of social rights. Providing the portability of several rights, the CPA aims at becoming the key instrument for securing professional career paths and to simplify everyone's access to social rights. It may also help achieve a better balance between professional and personal life, especially in case of family events, such as a child's illness or a parent's dependency. The debate was also relaunched after the election of Emmanuel Macron as president. The CESE (Conseil économique, social et environnemental) (2017) recommends: development of a social dialogue between public authorities, social partners and representative bodies of self-employed; promotion of the responsibility of third parties (e.g. platforms' and BECs' social responsibility, extension of the status of 'entrepreneur-salarié'); the securing of social rights of the new self-employed workers, especially allowing workers on digital platforms to benefit from unemployment insurance in the case of total revenue loss. After election campaign promises to open the unemployment insurance system to everyone, including self-employed workers, the government has taken more modest measures in 2018, proposing a lump-sum grant of €800 per month for six months for entrepreneurs who go through a judicial liquidation.

Collective Representation and Social Dialogue

In France, until recently, union membership was not possible for the self-employed, due to the strength (in the functioning of labour institutions), of the legal distinction between employees and self-employed workers, and to a widespread feeling that the best technique for protecting self-employed workers was to provide employee-like regimes (such as *intermittents* and *Portage salarial*). Nevertheless, the law organized collective bargaining for some categories of self-employed workers who perform their activities under economic dependency, particularly the assimilated employees specified in Book 7 of the Labour Law (e.g. general insurance agents). In professional markets, regulation is ensured by organizations focused on a specific trade. Otherwise, self-employed workers remain poorly represented, even if collectives are developing. In fact, the situation is evolving rapidly, due to new political orientations (e.g. the CPA, opening up of the unemployment insurance system), but also due to attempts at revitalization by the trade unions and by new initiatives at self-organizing by the self-employed themselves. Using the grid proposed by Martine D'Amours (2010), different forms of self-employed workers' collective representation in France can be observed.

Business logic is concerned with the defence of the interests of small businesses, while union logic tries to broaden the scope of union membership in two different ways: offering new services and organizing unorganized people. Thus a few initiatives which aim to consider self-employed workers can be mentioned. In 2000, the Confédération française démocratique du travail (union of executives) CFDT-Cadres (UCC) created a working group of 'autonomous professionals', in order to defend these professionals regardless of their legal status. The UCC clearly raised the issue: is the union intended to represent workers on the margins of salaried status? Or is that a slippery slope? After discussion, the unionists refused to close the door to non-salaried people. In 2016, the CFDT-F3C (Culture, Consulting, Communication) organized a barcamp in a co-working space in Paris, in order to imagine a new form of union, adapted to the needs of workers in the digital economy. They then launched the platform Union. For their part, some federations of the Confédération nationale du travail (CGT), such as the union SNPEF-CGT (education and training staff in the private sector), facing a dramatic increase of auto-entrepreneurs in its sector, decided to provide them with support, especially in the process of requalification for their contract. The CGT also supports bikers' collectives in the bargaining with digital platforms.

The pooling of resources and mutual aid allows cooperatives' members to benefit from social rights and collective support. A professional logic promotes the interests of 'autonomous professionals', whatever their status. The active role of a recently formed organization should also be mentioned: the network 'Sharers and Workers', which was created in 2015 in France by two research institutions (the Institut de recherches économiques et sociales and the Association travail emploi Europe société). The network includes actors from the French social dialogue sphere, from research and from the collaborative and numeric economy, as well as members from other countries.[9] In sum, French unions are increasingly developing collective action in favour of self-employed workers, together with other actors in the field.

Conclusion

Although the legal distinction between salaried work and independent work is founded in France on the subordination relationship, there are nevertheless a wide range of situations that deviate from this rule: for example, the role of executives has been integrated into the scope of salaried work, whereas some workers undergo both subordination and lack of social rights (Supiot 1999). There is in France an ongoing debate about the opening up of the unemployment insurance scheme to self-employed workers. Either way, whether workers who decide on self-employment have no other way of finding a job, or if it is the case that they are choosing to take control of their professional lives, they are under-represented at this time. Different ways of collective action are emerging to deal with this

---

[9]   See http://sharersandworkers.net/.

situation: the CGT aims to support people who work for digital platforms in order to reclassify their contract, or at least to obtain better prices and better work conditions, whereas the CFDT offers tools and services via a new platform; the federation of auto-entrepreneurs aims at the renewal of independent work while improving the social protection of self-employed workers; some associations defend a non-regulated profession, regardless of the legal status of their members; and finally, some cooperative structures promote mutual aid and pooling of resources between different autonomous professionals. The coalition between these different initiatives is nowadays a major stake.

4.3   GERMANY: BETWEEN INNOVATION AND FRAGMENTATION

Paolo Borghi

Introduction

Since the early 2000s, economic and political interest in German self-employment has intensified along with interest in the strategic role of small and medium enterprises (Volkmann et al. 2010). Self-employment has been considered as a way to reduce the unemployment rate (Hartz Reform II, 1 January 2003). At the same time, self-employment is today the strategic subject in the growing context of innovative start-ups and creative industries.

The growth of the service sector, along with structural changes in work arrangements fostered by new technologies, are challenging the traditional idea of self-employment both among regulated professions and within the non-regulated ones. Moreover, the rise of the platform economy (Kenney and Zysman 2016; Schmidt 2017) is stressing the concept of self-employment itself in Germany as well as in many other countries. The German debate on self-employment involves both trade unions, mainly focused on solo self-employment, and crowd workers and new organizations interested in the complex environment of freelancers and innovative start-ups. At the same time, a relevant role is being played both by professional associations and professional bodies mainly concentrated on corporative lobbying.

One of the main focal points of the German public debate on self-employment concerns the welfare system and its sustainability. On the one hand, the compulsory health insurance introduced in 2009 was considered a necessary measure to include population groups previously excluded, for example a relevant part of the freelance community. On the other hand, the monthly high costs of the compulsory insurance are not objectively sustainable for a significant number of freelancers suffering business discontinuity. A second topical issue is the insurance pension fund. In 2012 the Federal government proposed a mandatory contribution for a pension fund devoted to freelancers. After strong protests the measure was withdrawn but recently the theme is coming back in the public debate promoted by political parties. In addition, during recent years the frontiers of self-employment have been extended to the so-called crowd work, that is, in brief terms, an outsourcing process of micro tasks (both online and offline) mediated by digital platforms. After years of explorative debates on the evolution of the digital and platform economy, now some regulative proposals as well as some attempts at organizing crowd workers are emerging.

The German Framework on New Self-Employed Workers

The number of self-employed in Germany rose sharply at the beginning of the millennium especially due to the growth of solo self-employed. The expansion was even more significant than in the previous decade, when the growth of self-employment was mainly driven by the business start-ups of eastern Germany (Ortlieb and Weiss 2015). According to the 2018 microcensus (first quarter), there were 4.238 million self-employed in Germany, corresponding to about 10 per cent of the working population. Around 76 per cent of self-employed work in the tertiary sector, 17 per cent are in the secondary sector (industry) and 7 per cent are in the primary sector (agriculture, forestry and fishing). German self-employed have increased over the 2010s, despite a falling trend since 2005 (Mai and Marder-Puch 2013). The increase has been fostered by solo founders (Brenke 2013), by solo self -employed (Brehm et al. 2012), by self-employed women (Dautzenberg and Steinbrück 2013), mainly in service industries (Fritsch et al. 2012). Moreover the growth has been supported by part-time self-employment (Metzger 2014). Traditionally, studies on self-employment distinguish self-employed out of necessity from self-employed by choice, driven by market opportunities and propensity toward entrepreneurship. According to some recent studies (BMWi 2013; Amorós and Bosma 2014), despite the overall decline of the number of start-ups, the number of opportunity-driven entrepreneurs and innovative start-ups has increased, at least until 2013 (DIHK 2014).

A recent survey on solo self-employed in Germany, part of a wider study significantly entitled *Self-Employed without Personnel between Freedom and Insecurity* (Conen et al. 2016), has explored the relevant issues related to the condition of solo self-employment such as the motives in becoming self-employed, the balance between work and family life, and earnings and job satisfaction. According to the research findings the most common reasons to become self-employed are located among the pull-factors: the desire for more autonomy and the freedom from having a boss, as well as business opportunities. Nevertheless push-factors, such as the impossibility of finding a suitable wage job, the balance between work and family, the last opportunity to gain income, are significant factors for a significant minority of the respondents. Moreover the study shows how the probability of being involuntarily self-employed rises with age. Furthermore, educational level plays a relevant role indeed in 'involuntary' self-employment; evidence shows that it is more diffuse among lower educated workers.

Legal Status

Understanding the hybrid area of self-employment requires a consideration of the articulated regulatory framework. Generally speaking, German self-employment is defined mainly indirectly in opposition to dependent employment. It is considered as an economic activity characterized by independence in selecting work content, and time and place of work.

The main institutional documents regulating self-employment are the Income Tax Act[10] and the Social Security Act.[11] According to the law, the German independent professional works 'on account' and gets paid the fees in full. The worker must pay income tax and, as a rule, value-added tax. Self-employed workers are included in unemployment insurance under certain conditions and they must insure themselves against accidents at work and occupational claims for damages. The negotiation of fees and terms of contract are the normal condition, since collective agreements for self-employed persons are permitted only exceptionally. According to the existing laws there are no legal rights against dismissal or paid leave, or remuneration in case of illness. German legislation distinguishes between *Gewerbetreibende* (craftsmen, tradesmen, industrialist) and *Freiberufler* (liberal professionals regulated by public law and non-regulated professions). *Gewerbetreibende* and *Freiberufler* have different administrative and legal obligations, summarized in Table 4.2.

Basically the tax office establishes if a self-employed person is *Gewerbetreibende* or *Freiberufler* according to Paragraph 18 of the

---

[10]   Einkommensteuergesetz: https://www.gesetze-im-internet.de/estg/BJNR010050934. html.
[11]   Sozialgesetzbuch: http://www.sozialgesetzbuch-sgb.de/.

Table 4.2   Administrative and legal obligations for Gewerbetreibende *and*
Freiberufler

Gewerbetreibende	Freiberufler
Subject to income tax according to the commerce and industry tax regime	Not liable for trade tax
Must become mandatory members in the Chamber of Commerce and Industry (*IHK—Industrie und Handelskammer*)	Must register directly with the tax office (including tax registration form); registration with a professional association if the profession has a professional body
Must be registered in the German register of companies	No need to register a trade; they have to clarify whether the activity is indeed a liberal profession to tax office
Must manage a double-entry bookkeeping system	No need to manage a double-entry bookkeeping system
	Pension insurance: compulsory for regulated liberal professions
Health insurance: since 2009 compulsory (for all those living in Germany)	

Income Tax Act.[12] Section 18(1) of the Act differentiates concretely self-employment groups and thus it determines who belongs to each group according to the profession catalogue (*Katalogberufe*[13]) and the professional activities (*Tätigkeitsberufe und ähnliche Berufe*[14]). The following activities can be clearly carried out under the self-employed regime: doctors, naturopaths, physiotherapists, engineers, journalists, interpreters, translators and similar professionals or activities, as well as scientific, artistic writers, teaching or educational activities. Differently, the following activities are associated to a business: any trade (whether with art, training courses, computer hardware or software); any production (whether from books, CD-ROMs, hardware or crafts); all consultancy services that do not require higher education (such as web consultants and PR consultants); all intermediary activities (e.g. artists or literary agencies, photo agencies, content promoters, job exchanges, press agencies); all copyright holders

---

[12]   Bundesministerium der Justiz und für Verbraucherschutz: https://www.gesetze-im-internet.de/estg/__18.html.

[13]   The catalogue of professions is, so to speak, the classical liberal professions, which were listed first in the Income Tax Act.

[14]   It includes a list of additional groups of freelance new professions. The professions listed in the catalogue share numerous traits with the professions listed in the *Katalogberufe*, for example the level of professional qualifications. The list includes scientific, artistic, literary and teaching activities.

(such as galleries, publishers, event managers) as well as theatres and music organizers (Bucholz 2011).

Public Policies and Social Protection for Self-Employed Professionals

The German social protection system is mainly based on a double regime for employees and self-employed. Generally speaking a significant number of German self-employed do not have benefits or subsidies neither to cover the cost of compulsory insurances (e.g. health insurance) nor the voluntary ones (e.g. pension). However, there are exceptions for certain professional sectors and some categories of self-employed. On the one hand, there are special provisions for certain groups of self-employed (notably craftsmen), who are compulsorily insured with the statutory pension insurance and, on the other, independent social security systems for farmers (including assisting family members), self-employed artists and publicists. Moreover, there are special schemes for professions belonging to a professional body. People who have been compulsorily insured against unemployment as employees for at least twelve months during the twenty-four months preceding the self-employed activity, or persons who have received unemployment allowances before becoming self-employed, may benefit from optional continued insurance, through a request to the Federal Employment Agency (*Bundesagentur für Arbeit*) (MISSOC 2016a). Self-employed without a significant income can be insured free of charge via family insurance through the statutory health insurance of their parents or partner. If the options listed above are not practicable, the self-employed must arrange their own insurance. Self-employed artists, journalists, writers, visual artists, actors, musicians, graphic designers and similar professions are insured for pension, sickness and long-term care, through *KSK—Künstlersozialkasse*. It ensures that independent artists and publicists enjoy similar protection in statutory social security as employees. KSK is not itself a service provider, but it coordinates the transfer of contributions of its members to freely chosen health insurances as well as to statutory pension and long-term care insurance (MISSOC 2016a). Alternatively, solo self-employed in a standard condition[15] can choose between the Statutory Health Insurance (*Gesetzliche Krankenversicherung–GKV*) known as sickness funds (*Krankenkassen*), and Private Health Insurance[16] (*Private Krankenversicherung*).

---

[15]   Without specific opportunities connected with their job or family asset.
[16]   Only for public officers, self-employed people and employees with a large income (above €50,000 per year).

The traditional liberal professions,[17] have instead their own self-financed insurance schemes (managed by their professional associations) assuring compulsory coverage for old-age, invalidity and survivors on the basis of national law provisions. The professional pension schemes of the liberal professions are special systems of compulsory provision based on the law of the federal state (*Bundesländer*) according to the federal republic (Article 70 of the constitution—*Grundgesetz*). The pension schemes are applied to members of the liberal professions without distinctions related to the way they practise their profession (self-employed or employee). Each federal state decides on the appropriateness and necessity of setting up insurance bodies for professions. Benefits provided by such professional schemes are only financed through member contributions and asset returns. The state does not provide funding. According to the picture here drawn the inclusion of self-employed in the national social protection system appears extremely fragmented in relation to the profession, to the previous condition as worker, and to the overall family condition.

Collective Representation and Social Dialogue

All workers, including self-employed, are free to join a trade union, but unlike other workers, self-employed are excluded from collective bargaining along with 'civil servants, high skilled workers and managerial staff above negotiated pay levels' (Eurofound 2015). Essentially, as described above, the self-employed are considered service providers or entrepreneurs. They usually sign contracts to deliver work (*Werkverträge, Dienstverträge*), and for that reason they are not considered and treated like other workers. Despite this, since the beginning of the new millennium German trade unions, in particular Ver.di (*Vereinte Dienstleistungsgewerkschaft*–United Services Union), which is focused on the service sector where self-employment is significantly increasing, are discussing the changes underway. The unit devoted to the solo self-employed, Verd.di Selbstständige, collaborates with some associations with a significant number of freelancers such as VdÜ[18] (*Verband deutschsprachiger Übersetzer literarischer und wissenschaftlicher Werke*—Association of German-speaking literature translators), VS[19] (*Verband deutscher Schriftsteller*—Association of German Writers) and DJU[20] (*Deutsche Journalistinnen und Journalisten*

---

[17] e.g. surgeons, pharmacists, notaries, lawyers, accountants, tax agents, veterinaries, auditors and sworn auditors, dentists, psychological therapists, civil engineers.
[18] VdÜ website: http://www.literaturuebersetzer.de/.
[19] VS website: https://vs.verdi.de/.
[20] DJU website: https://dju.verdi.de/.

Union—German Union of Journalists). The debate also involves the umbrella organizations of trade unions, in particular the DGB (*Deutscher Gewerkschaftsbund*) of which Ver.di is a member. There are also other unions such as GEW (*Gewerkschaft Erziehung und Wissenschaft*—German Union of Education), itself part of DGB that counts around 2,000 self-employed members especially concentrated in the education sector (Pedersini and Coletto 2010). Moreover the largest journalist's trade union, DJV (*Deutscher Journalisten-Verband*—German Federation of Journalists) has about 40,000 members concentrated in the media sector and 15,000 of them are self-employed (Pedersini and Coletto 2010).

One of the other main German trade unions, IG-Metall, is promoting an experimental project named Fair Crowd Work, devoted to crowd workers. It aims at fostering collective identity among crowd workers through a platform where they can share useful information and publicly evaluate, anonymously, the platforms where they work. The panorama of self-employed organizations is quite fragmented. It reflects the variety of the professional sectors in which their members are involved. Some organizations deal with a single profession (e.g. BDÜ—*Bundesverband der Dolmetscher und Übersetzer*, for translators and interpreters), while other organizations are able to collect different freelancers engaged in specific sectors (e.g. VGSD—*Verband der Gründer und Selbständigen*, BFB—*Bundesverband der Freien Berufe*), and others (especially unions) are trying to connect the representation of solo self-employed with a broader framework that includes also the dependent workforce. To the extreme variety of organizations correspond an equal variety of strategies ranging from corporatism of professional associations to the inclusive approach promoted by trade unions and by some innovative subjects such as the cooperative SMart or the Platform Cooperativism Consortium in which both Ver.di, IG-Metall and SMart are involved.

Conclusion

The German case study is relevant for several reasons. Firstly, the rapid development of the advanced services sector has generated new professions and new contexts in which the self-employed are strongly present (e.g. the creative industry, IT, innovative start-ups, consultancy and services). The evolution of self-employment involves both highly skilled and low-skilled workers, who experience different working conditions including part-time work and intermittent work, as in the case of crowd workers.

Secondly, the partial and diversified inclusion of the different figures of self-employed workers in the national social protection system (see e.g. special insurance schemes for the liberal professions, journalists and artists, and the absence of special schemes for many freelancers) generates a significant fragmentation of conditions and opportunities.

Thirdly, the extreme variety of organizations involved in self-employed representation is both a strength and a weakness factor. In the first case, in fact, many organizations, both transversal to the professions and focused on specific professions, demonstrate a significant authority in exercising their function. In the second case, however, there is limited dialogue between the organizations, which are mainly focused on strengthening their presence in their areas of competence. Despite this, the German case study is interesting both for the quality of the analyses developed by the representative organizations and for the innovation that they promote.

4.4   ITALY: STEPS TOWARDS NEW SOCIAL PROTECTIONS

Anna Mori

Introduction

Self-employment has historically represented a relevant source of work in Italy (Semenza et al. 2017). Its development has followed three main phases (Ranci 2012). Since the end of the Second World War until the 1970s, the large majority of self-employed workers comprised the 'small bourgeois' in the retail and craft sectors (Sylos Labini 1974). During the 1970s and 1980s the development of industrial districts triggered the growth of self-employment in small manufacturing enterprises. A third phase started in the 1990s, and currently expanding, is characterized by the diffusion of highly specialized self-employed professionals in the tertiary sector, following the post-industrial transformation of the economy (Bologna and Fumagalli 1997; Butera et al. 2008).

Despite the numerical incidence of the self-employed and the central role they have played in economic development (Semenza 2000), such a centrality has never been fully acknowledged in the public debate and in the political sphere (Accornero and Anastasia 2006). The interplay between the deficit in political representation, the weak involvement in policymaking processes and the misleading cultural influences suffered by self-employed workers might contribute to explaining the underestimation of this important part of the productive and occupational system (Ranci 2012). Instead, a critical interpretation has traditionally accompanied the phenomenon in Italy. First, the growth of self-employment has long been associated with the widespread diffusion of small and medium enterprises which characterizes the Italian productive system. The small size of the companies was symptomatic of the inherent incapacity of industry to expand and invest in order to sustain competitiveness in a global market (Maida 2009). Second, self-employment has been interpreted as a permanent area of fiscal parasitism. The world of the liberal professions in particular is associated with the idea of political nepotism and fiscal privileges they enjoy. Third, the academic debate has been dominated by the opinion that the rise in self-employed workers has resulted from the proliferation of the bogus self-employed (Pallini 2006). Such a misconception relates to a double development in the Italian labour market since the 1990s: the diffusion of economically dependent self-employed workers (Pedersini and Coletto 2010) and the introduction of semi-subordinate contractual arrangements in the labour market as a way to raise employment. Economically dependent self-employment corresponds to an intermediate blurred area of autonomous work, where the self-employed are generally hired through a service contract featuring an exclusive contractual relationship with a unique customer. Accordingly s/he turns out to be only formally independent, but substantially characterized by economic dependency on one single employer, who also sets organizational constraints. Semi-subordinate contracts have been exploited to establish flexible working relationships and to reduce labour costs, enabling the hiring of a cheaper self-employed workforce as an alternative to subordinated workers.

Legal Status and Institutional Framework

As far as the legislative framework is concerned, self-employment is disciplined by the Civil Code where a 'genuine self-employed worker is defined as a worker who legally commits himself to perform a service or a work under payment, without being subject to any form of subordination towards the customer, working with his own assets and mainly through his own work' (Article 2222). The Civil Code also establishes a dual system of intellectual professions (regulated and non-regulated professions), a distinctive feature of the Italian configuration (Feltrin 2012). On the one hand, the law determines the regulated professions, whose practice is subordinated to a state examination and to enrolment in a professional register. The state delegates to the associations the power of control over the profession (Article 2229). This is the case for more than thirty professions, a peculiarity in Europe. On the other hand, a large and heterogeneous group of non-regulated professions has developed, not subject to the same legislative recognition. Only recently has law no. 4/2013 revised the legislative discipline for non-regulated professions, by assimilating their regulation to the regulated professions to reduce discrepancies and inequalities.

Further contractual forms of autonomous work have been introduced between the late 1990s and the early 2000s, aiming at introducing some degrees of flexibility in the labour market.[21] These new types of non-standard contractual arrangements (configuring e.g. the continuous and coordinated contract (*Contratto di collaborazione coordinata e continuativa*[22]), the project contract (*Contratto a progetto*[23]) and the occasional collaboration (*Lavoratori automoni occasionali*[24]) as non-pure forms of self-employment), were introduced with the aim of raising employment by promoting a greater contractual flexibility. What followed instead was a widespread abuse of these semi-subordinate forms of work as a contractual alternative to the traditional dependent salaried employment relationship. As explained in the previous paragraph, the specious application of these contracts triggered a proliferation of bogus self-employment. In an effort to limit the problem, the government has recently issued new measures: Law no. 92/2012 (the so-called 'Fornero reform') has tried to control in particular the improper use of the project contract[25] by imposing a new specific set of standards that configures a project contract as genuine. In this regard, the contractual relationship must be more strictly linked to a project—and not simply to a task or to a phase of work—whose final goals have to be clearly specified by the customer. The independent collaborator has to be able to autonomously manage his/her objectives and accordingly, the project contract cannot refer to merely executive tasks. Importantly, the payment has to correspond at least to the minimum salary established in the national collective agreements signed in the specific sector of reference. This reform has introduced also specific criteria enabling self-employed workers holding a VAT number and workers in a continuous and coordinated contract to be distinguished. Accordingly, self-employed work has to be treated as a coordinated and continuous relationship, hence forming an employment relationship (with the burden of proof on the

---

[21] Law no. 196/1997 (the 'Treu package') and the following Law no. 30/2003 (the 'Biagi reform') introduced increasing flexibility in the Italian labour market, by instating the Continuous and Coordinated Contractual Relationship and the Project Contract.

[22] The Continuous and Coordinated Contractual Relationship was introduced in 1997 by Law no. 196/1997 (the so-called 'Treu package').

[23] The discipline on Continuous and Coordinated Contractual Relationships has been modified by Law no. 30/2003 (the so-called 'Biagi reform') which introduced the Project Contract.

[24] Law no. 30/2003 introduced 'occasional collaborations', specifying that the contractual relationship cannot last for more than thirty days within the same year with the same employer, and the maximum annual income under this type of contract cannot exceed €5,000.

[25] The new rules apply to working relationships starting after July 2012.

customer) if at least two of the following conditions exist: (i) the relation-ship lasts more than eight months within the solar year; (ii) compensation deriving from the relationship represents more than 80 per cent of the total compensation earned by the worker within the solar year; (iii) the worker has a workspace available at the customer's offices.

A Social Security System for the Self-Employed

Overall, the social security system for self-employed workers is dominated by a deficit of protections, ranging from exclusion from pension funds to the lack of unemployment support and sickness schemes (Jessoula et al. 2017). As basic principle, in Italy there is no one homogeneous social security system applicable to all self-employed workers, but the dualism observed above in the professional models is crucial, since it mirrors important differentials also in the social protection system applied to the two groups.

Regulated professionals, in fact, belong to their own private professional social security funds which, within minimum standards defined by law, offer social security schemes to the members of the professional register according to specific rules and provisions. Conversely, the non-regulated professions have long been excluded from the protections ensured by the professional registers. Since 1995, instead, self-employed workers in professions have been regulated by Law no. 4/2013 and all the semi-subordinate workers contribute to the Separate Fund (*Fondo a Gestione Separata*) of the National Institute of Social Security (INPS—*Istituto Nazionale di Previdenza Sociale*). This fund was introduced by Law no. 335/1995 that reformed the Italian pension system (the so-called 'Dini reform'). The aim of the reform was to offer minimum levels of social assistance to these categories of workers who, until that time, had not been covered by any compulsory pension scheme; hence, all self-employed workers not covered by private professional social security funds managed by the registers were included. The two groups of workers paying social contributions to the Separate Fund differ in the extent to which they have to contribute. Self-employed workers registered for VAT are required by law to fully pay their own contributions, calculated on their total earnings declared for the relevant year. In their turn, these workers are allowed to charge their customers an additional share percentage of up to 4 per cent of gross revenue. In the case of semi-subordinate workers, the payment of their contributions is instead split between the worker (one third) and the client (two thirds).

Protection systems against unemployment for independent workers do not exist in Italy. The picture was only partly modified in 2015 when legislative decree no. 22/2015 introduced a new support scheme in case of unemployment for semi-subordinate workers. The scheme provides for a monthly subsidy called DIS-COLL to those semi-subordinate workers enrolled in the Separate Fund, but it excludes self-employed workers as beneficiaries.

The dualism between regulated and non-regulated professions persists also in the case of maternity benefits. Independent workers who are members of professional registers are covered by their own private professional social security funds, according to the specific qualifying conditions established by each fund. Generally maternity leave is fairly limited. A different regime exists for semi-subordinate workers enrolled in the Separate Fund. In such cases, maternity leave is not compulsory (as in the case of subordinate workers) but entitlement to economic benefits does not occur in case of permanence at work. Maternity benefit, paid by the INPS, amounts to 80 per cent of previous income for a maximum period of just five months.

In terms of sickness benefits, they are provided to semi-subordinate workers enrolled in the Separate Fund, only if they are not members of other compulsory social security funds. They receive sickness benefits in case of both hospitalization and illness, variable according to the total amount of contributions paid. Independent workers registered for VAT are not entitled to any sickness benefit.

The 2017 Law no. 81, 'Jobs Act for Autonomous Work' has recently introduced new important protection systems for those in self-employment. In particular the new discipline extends maternity leave to those workers who decide to not interrupt their working activity; it extends parental leave, including economic compensation and related pension contributions, to self-employed workers (both mothers and fathers) for a maximum of six months; it introduces a sickness scheme; it enlarges the application of the discipline relating to security and protection in the workplace to independent workers; and it transfers any disputes involving autonomous workers to the jurisdiction of the Labour Court.

Collective Representation and Social Dialogue

The collective representation of independent workers is particularly fragmented and often lacking (Borghi et al. 2018). Professional registers have long played a role in representing and lobbying for the interests of their members on an occupational basis. Also, first- and second-level associations have emerged, such as *Confassociazioni* (the Confederation of Professional Associations officially recognized by Law no. 4/2013) and *Confprofessioni* (a confederation which brings together the regulated professions). The latter is recognized as a social partner in collective bargaining and signs national collective agreements for employees in professional firms.

Traditional trade unions have instead shown a certain degree of organizational inertia in reorienting their actions and strategies towards the self-employed segment of the labour market (Ambra 2013). The demands emerging from a growing share of self-employed workers have been instead long neglected for twofold reasons. Firstly, trade unions have long deemed independent professional workers as a closed segment of prosperous work, in many cases protected by the professional registers; secondly, the strategic focus of unions has been devoted to the phenomenon of false self-employment, which spread markedly in the Italian labour market during the late 1990s and 2000s. Union strategies were devoted mainly to coping with the new forms of precarious, non-standard and flexible contractual arrangements.

However, it is also true that the world of professional self-employment has rarely tried to approach the unions because of cultural concerns about union activity and because of the core role played by the several professional registers in collectively representing the voices of their members. In the late 1990s, the three main union confederations started to reconsider their recruitment and representation strategies to include workers with non-standard employment relationships. To this purpose they established specific structures, but these were mainly oriented towards precarious and non-standard workers rather than the self-employed.[26] Only recently have unions' strategies specifically targeted the self-employed, as in the case of the Consultative Body for Professional Work (*Consulta delle professioni*) set up by the Italian General Confederation for Labour (CGIL) and the online community of self-employed workers vIVAce! created by the Italian Confederation of Unions (CISL).

The subject has very recently drawn attention thanks to the bottom-up pressure exercised by the growing segment of low paid self-employed workers as well as by new emerging associations (representing independent workers) and spontaneous movements. Bottom-up innovative experiences of collective representation have emerged, aiming at aggregating transversally the heterogeneous segment of self-employment: they have played a crucial role in shedding light on universal demands and new needs put forward by independent workers who have been unheard for a long time. They have been able to gain high visibility in the public and political

---

[26]   e.g. the Italian General Confederation for Labour (CGIL) has launched the union category called Nidil, devoted to all the new contractual identities and forms, while the Italian Confederation of Unions (CISL) has established the category ALAI for non-standard and contract workers).

spheres thanks to their capacity to exploit the new social media and to target their strategies towards circumscribed practical demands. This is the case, for instance, for the Association of Consultants in the Advanced Tertiary Sector (ACTA); the Chambers for Independent and Precarious Workers (CLAP) movement, a federation of independent self-managed associations that was created from the bottom up to organize and defend precarious work in general terms; and Coalition 27 February (#27F), a spontaneous movement composed of a heterogeneous group of workers (VAT registered, freelancers and professionals, and also precarious, atypical and outsourced workers and students) sharing common problems, such as a lack of social security protection, precarious working conditions and a lack of legal rights.

Conclusions

Self-employment has historically represented a relevant source of work in Italy, but despite the numerical incidence of the self-employed and the central role they have played in the economic development of the country, both political debate and academic reflection on the issues involved have long been trapped in disputes on the bogus self-employed and on the economically dependent self-employed. In Italy, self-employed professionals in fact have been traditionally viewed with suspicion, with self-employment considered an economic area of fiscal parasitism. The social protection framework is fragmented and inadequate. Nevertheless, the new Statute of Autonomous Work (Law no. 81/2017) has led to certain progress in terms of social rights, addressing a number of crucial aspects of social protection for self-employed professionals, such as economic subsidies for parental leave, specific allowances for maternity, and sickness leave. In terms of collective representation, the demands emerging from a growing share of independent workers have been instead long neglected by the trade unions, increasingly being intercepted instead by non-traditional and new collective players such as freelancer associations, cooperatives and self-organized movements. These experiences have not only filled a representation gap, but importantly have been able to encompass the specific features of this labour market segment and accordingly to channel the interests of the new self-employed generation through innovative forms.

4.5. THE NETHERLANDS: DEBATING FREEDOM, SERVICE AND PROTECTION

Bas Koene and Maylin Stanic

Introduction: Main Aspects of Self-Employed Professionals

At the end of the 1990s the Dutch social security system underwent a process of deep reform with the introduction of the 1999 Flexibility and Security Act. This heralded a period of greatly enhanced possibilities for flexible nonstandard employment relations, clear regulation for short-term flexibility and institutional appreciation of self-employment, but also a great reliance on individual responsibility for managing self-employment and limited attention for those in the grey zone of hybrid work arrangements.

In the Netherlands, autonomous workers are distinguished from temporary workers who have temporary employment contracts, either with employers directly, or with temporary work agencies. Autonomous workers are labeled *Freelance* or ZZP (*Zelfstandige Zonder Personeel*: self-employed without personnel). Their legal form is that of entrepreneur (as opposed to employee). Most self-employed professionals hold a one-man business or a private limited company (Dutch: BV). They (need to) work for multiple clients and work at their own expense and risk.

While in the past the share of autonomous workers was relatively low, since the early 2000s the growth of autonomous workers in the Netherlands has been remarkably high. In 2014 the share of autonomous workers in the working population was just above the EU average (OECD 2014). Ten years earlier, the share of self-employed without personnel was similar to that in France, Germany and Austria (about 7 per cent)—well below the EU average. While in these countries growth has been following the EU average of about one percentage point, in the Netherlands the share of self-employed without personnel has grown by three percentage points to about 10 per cent in 2014 (CBS 2014) and can be expected to grow to about 15 per cent in 2030 (CPB 2014; CPB 2015).

Especially the growth of self-employed without personnel has been high (CBS 2014). In 1999 only 5.9 per cent of the working population was self-employed. In 2008, already 8.6 per cent of the working population worked on a self-employed basis (Dekker 2010). Between 2003 and 2013 growth of the working population was almost completely due to a growing share of self-employed without personnel, whose number grew almost 50 per cent over that period.

Self-employed professionals constitute a rather heterogeneous group that shows large variations in income (CBS 2014). The stated reasons why people decide to work on a self-employed basis vary. Generally, self-report data indicate that most self-employed persons seem to be happy with their choice, reporting more positive scores (on happiness in work, possibilities for self-development, the fit of working hours with a private life and work pressure) than employees and also self-employed *with* personnel (Josten et al. 2014). However, objective data describing the situation for self-employed without personnel sketch a less positive picture. There is large income disparity within the autonomous workers sector, with one group that is relatively well-off, but another earning minimum wages. Gross income is lower than that of employees, but net income of the self-employed is often on a par, due to the availability of fiscal policies for entrepreneurs and the possibility for self-employed to make lower (or no) financial provision for unemployment, sickness, disability and/or pension schemes (IBO 2015). Self-employed are largely excluded from social insurance schemes against risks, such as sickness and disability, old age, and unemployment (Dekker 2010). Indeed, they work at their own expense and risk.

Legal Status, Institutional Framework and the Public Policy Debate: Self-Employed or Employee? From VAR to DBA to Where?

Legally regarded as entrepreneurs, self-employed without personnel are expected to make their own fiscal arrangements as they are not included in the social security system for employees (Dekker 2010) and only qualify for benefits on a minimum level. They are included (and have to pay premiums for) the basic collective old-age pension, but, as noted, they are largely excluded from other insurance schemes. Furthermore, they need to ensure that they take personal measures to increase pension benefits to an acceptable level. On the other hand, as entrepreneurs, there are a number of fiscal arrangements open to self-employed autonomous workers that are not open to employees. However, whether these fiscal instruments eventually benefit the entrepreneur or the hiring organization through lower gross rates depends on the strengths of their labour market position and negotiating power.

Due to significant differences in fiscal treatment and employment law between employees and self-employed, for both clients and self-employed the fiscal and social security related status of the business relationship is of prime importance. Is there an employer–employee relationship or not? Ever since the flexibilization of employment at the end of the 1990s this has been an issue, both for fighting bogus self-employment and to provide clarity for legitimate actors. In 2001, a so-called Declaration of Independent Contractor Status (*Verklaring Arbeidsrelatie*, VAR) was included in Dutch tax legislation (Vendrig et al. 2007). It required the self-employed to apply for a VAR declaration from the tax authority, indicating the expected nature of the working relationship. However, there were three important problems with the VAR. It had to be estimated beforehand, it made only the self-employed worker responsible for the employment relationship, and thirdly, it was administratively cumbersome, as the declarations had to be renewed annually. To deal with these issues, since 1 May 2016, the VAR has been replaced by the *Deregulation Assessment Employment Relationships Act* (*Wet deregulering beoordeling arbeidsrelaties*, DBA) that aimed to make companies and self-employed both responsible for maintaining an employment relationship that met the criteria for self-employment. However, implementation problems and fundamental unclarities about the conditions that characterize an employee status have halted the introduction of the law, leaving the status of self-employed in limbo for quite some time now.

Collective Representation and Social Dialogue

In the Netherlands, 18 per cent of employees are union members, and the proportion has been gradually falling in recent years (Fulton 2015). At the same time, many collective agreements have industry-wide coverage. There are three main union federations: the Federatie Nederlandse Vakbeweging (FNV), the Christelijk Nationaal Vakverbond (CNV) and the Vakcentrale voor Professionals (VCP). FNV is by far the largest of the three in terms of members. In 2014 CBS (2014) reported 1,131,600 members for FNV, 287,100 for CNV and 54,100 for VCP. Unease with the functioning of the traditional unions has led to increasing fragmentation of the union landscape. Currently, 'de Unie', together with smaller unions, is one of a number of organizations not affiliated to the three main confederations. Indeed, CBS figures show that the total membership of these smaller unions was 289,100 in October 2014, around 100,000 more than two years earlier (Fulton 2015).

With the fast growth of the group of self-employed without personnel and the great variation in their labour market position (Dekker 2016; IBO 2015), the questions of how to support autonomous workers and how to represent them have become a pressing issue for unions and a market opportunity for LMIs that constitute a relatively mature staffing industry in the Netherlands (Koene et al. 2014; Koene and van Driel 2011) and other, newer, organizations that see a possibility for services that would support either the self-employed, or their users, or both.

Five kinds of actors in the Dutch labour market contribute to these developments: unions, developing initiatives that extend their traditional remit and recognize the growing group of self-employed workers that is seeking support and representation; emerging platform organizations providing services to the self-employed, which after growing in size also become channels for voicing concerns; LMIs developing services for the self-employed driven by a commercial interest; initiatives of mutualization of workers where the self-employed organize to protect their own interests; and finally network organizations providing managed services to present initiatives that are not traditional service provider or advocacy organizations, but which explore and commercialize possibilities of working with and supporting independent professionals (Koene and Stanic 2018).

Conclusion: Flexible Opportunity, Responsibility and Precariousness

In all, the Dutch situation portrays a labour market where around the turn of the century the rapid development and acceptance of possibilities for flexible and temporary work stimulated the use of agency work, but also greatly enhanced the possibilities for self-employment. Self-employment grew rapidly bringing the share of self-employment in the Netherlands from a relatively low level up to the European average. Dutch self-employed are relatively highly educated, predominantly male (although the share of women is increasing), older, and relatively well paid.

Regulation in the Netherlands combines clear regulation for short-term flexibility through short-term employment solutions, partly facilitated by a mature temporary work agency industry, with a great reliance on individual responsibility for self-employed workers, with no specific recognition for workers in the grey zone of hybrid work relationships. Access to social protection is limited for the self-employed, although there are various measures of fiscal support open to these workers.

The unclear status of the self-employed is reflected in the plethora of organizations claiming to represent them and the ongoing and heated debate about how to legally distinguish self-employment from an employment status. This debate has halted the introduction of the 2016 Deregulation Assessment Employment Relationships Act (Wet DBA).

In terms of representation, self-employed without personnel are both represented by employers associations that emphasize the need for entrepreneurial choice and freedom, and by unions that highlight the precariousness of self-employed workers and their need for collective representation and support. At the same time, other actors are emerging that organize the self-employed in novel ways, ranging from membership platforms offering collective insurances, to organized cooperatives, to commercial organizations providing services for administration and project management.

Developments in the Dutch labour market thus present a wide variety of initiatives that aim to support self-employment, but with a clear reliance on individual responsibility of self-employed workers, distinguishing their position from that of dependent employees. In this context unions aim to redefine the boundaries of collective agreements, LMIs service autonomous workers as independent labour market actors, employers' associations lobby for the freedom of self-employed entrepreneurs, and self-employed workers organize themselves to protect their immediate interests.

With a relatively high proportion of skilled and well-paid self-employed workers, interest in the possibilities of self-employment is still growing. At the same time, with a rather large income disparity amongst the self-employed, issues around the increasing precariousness of a growing group of self-employed workers are noted, and there is more and more concern about short-termism, over-reliance on individual responsibility and general, but very basic, national social safety nets for the self-employed.

4.6   SLOVENIA: THE PRECARIOUS NATURE OF SELF-EMPLOYED PROFESSIONALS

Klemen Širok

National Framework

Autonomous work in Slovenia is understood as self-employment and it takes two legal forms: sole proprietors or contract work. Since the end of the twentieth century, the proportion of self-employed in Slovenia has remained close to EU average, with only minor fluctuations. The highest growth after 2009 was recorded in the arts, entertainment and recreation, and catering sectors, and other diverse business activities. One of reasons behind this growth has been an active labour market policy measure of the Employment Service of Slovenia, offering a subsidy (a grant of €4,500) if the person remains self-employed for at least two years, although this practice was abolished in 2014. Another reason for the growing number of self-employed is new employer practices. Instead of entering an employment relationship with the employee, the employer rather 'convinces' a worker to formally establish self-employed status and to enter into a contractual agreement with the employer. This is in fact the 'bogus' self-employment referred to in this volume. A third reason that could at least partly explain the growth of the self-employed in Slovenia is the (rather favourable) taxation policy of sole proprietors enacted from 1 January 2015. It is assumed that this has led to many persons acquiring self-employed status in addition to their full-time employment in order to profit from paying lower taxes instead of, for example, receiving the payment through copyright contracts when working for another employer.[27]

Over recent years Slovenia has recorded a remarkable growth of new autonomous workers. Taking Rapelli's (2012) definition of IPros, their numbers almost doubled between 2008 and 2015 to 61,000 (i.e. 6.7 per cent of the active working population), representing 67 per cent of all self-employed, which is twelve percentage points higher than in 2008. IPros' growth is even more remarkable if we take into consideration Rapelli's (2012) finding that the growth rate of IPros in Slovenia between 2008 and 2011 comes only second to Romania (78.15 per cent). Regarding the sector of economic activity, IPros in Slovenia are mostly concentrated in the professional, scientific and technical activities (38 per cent), followed by other service activities (14 per cent), information and communication (14 per cent) and arts, entertainment and recreation (14 per cent). It would be difficult to outline a typical IPro's career path, since the forms of engagement in nonstandard employments are numerous, widely different and bound to occupational context. The LFS data show that in 2015 already 23 per cent of IPros worked for only one client and 12.5 per cent worked predominately in the working space provided by the client.[28]

Legal and Institutional Framework

The legal basis for carrying out work in Slovenia is an employment contract. A standard form of employment is permanent employment. This means that employment contracts should be, as a rule, concluded for an indefinite period of time. The nonstandard forms of employment are only allowed in cases explicitly stated in the main act regulating employment relationships—the Employment Relationships Act (2013) (ERA). The nonstandard forms of employment according to ERA (2013) are: (a) fixed-term employment contracts; (b) employment contracts between the worker and the employer who carries out the activity of providing workers to another user (agency work); (c) employment contracts for the provision

---

[27]   In praxis it is also legally possible that a person who becomes self-employed in addition to being employed full-time by another employer is doing a favor for some other small business owner, who does not want his or her tax return to exceed the €50,000 annual revenue level (and thus pay higher taxes) but shifts his trade/business revenue to another small business owner.

[28]   See Labour Force Survey at https://ec.europa.eu/eurostat/web/lfs.

of public works; (d) part-time employment contracts; (e) employment contracts for home-based work; (f) employment contracts with managerial staff. It should be noted that both fixed-term contracts and part-time employment contracts provide workers with the full range of labour protection. Also relevant are other nonstandard legal forms of employment: contract work under civil law (either through work contracts or through contracts for a copyrighted work), student work and as sole proprietor. However, in cases of evident elements of the employment relationship (i.e. inclusion in employer's organized workflow, work under the direction and supervision of the employer and so on, ERA explicitly states that the work should not be carried out on the basis of civil law contracts and an employment contract must be entered into. Persons who perform work under civil law contracts and their relationship with the employer does not have the elements of employment relationship, are not entitled to the rights provided for by ERA.

As already mentioned, self-employed workers (or IPros as their subpopulation for that matter) are working either as sole proprietors or take up contract work. Self-employment is a work activity carried out independently for more clients/contract users, whereby a sole proprietor autonomously determines the price of her/his work. Self-employed persons thus perform their work under civil contracts. According to the Companies Act (2006) a sole proprietor is 'a legal person who independently carries out gainful activity on the market within a regulated company', and 'shall assume responsibility for their liabilities with all their assets'.[29] There are no type-specific/sector-specific rules on self-employment.

In the case of employees, their mandatory social protection and other contributions are divided between employee and employer, whereas in the case of the self-employed the only one paying contributions is the self-employed person.[30] In the case of illness, the self-employed are not entitled to any compensation for lost income if they are ill for less than thirty working days and are not excused from paying mandatory contributions. Regarding maternal/paternal leave, the self-employed situation is very similar to that of those in standard employment—at least in a formal sense. The government pays mandatory contributions for those self-employed on maternal/paternal leave. Self-employed are entitled to unemployment benefit if they did not choose to become unemployed or through no fault

---

[29]   See   http://www.mgrt.gov.si/fileadmin/mgrt.gov.si/pageuploads/zakonodaja/ZGD-1_PREVOD__13-12-12.pdf.

[30]   There are 1,819 self-employed workers in the culture field (whose work represents an exceptional contribution to culture) who are entitled to paid contributions for mandatory pension and health insurance from the national budget.

of their own. The benefit is calculated using the average social security contributions paid for during the self-employment period. When a self-employed worker retires, their pension is calculated again on the basis of their contributions to the pension fund. The requirements (years of service, age, etc.) apply in the same way as for the regularly employed. Self-employed, however, are not entitled to many other benefits that are tied to permanent employment: paid annual holiday (minimum twenty working days), a paid meal per working day, paid holiday days, compensation for lost income in case of illness, reimbursement of travel expenses to and from work, and so on.

Generally speaking, social protection of self-employed in comparison to workers on a permanent contract is lower. Their position is less favourable especially in the case of illness.[31] Despite mandatory inclusion in all compulsory social insurance schemes, in real life situations many self-employed don't see any point in paying higher than minimal required contributions, since the small increases in compensation (be it in the case of illness, paternal leave, unemployment, etc.) do not reflect the much higher increase in contributions. Self-employed are thus especially at risk of receiving lower-value pensions. In addition, if the self-employed person is a sole proprietor, obligations can be met with all their assets.

Public Policy to Support New Autonomous Workers

In Slovenia, the self-employed very often report lower than average wages. Since they are often in a subordinated position, they will accept worse working conditions. Generally, the self-employed report long working hours and little free time, and when they do have free time this usually means that income is negatively affected. In addition, skills development very often presumes the outlay of extra expense, and these expenses are often avoided. Other problems mentioned are uneven income flow, which makes planning and organizing even more difficult; the amount of the work is often larger (for the same salary) compared to workers on a permanent contract; they are aware that their welfare depends to a large extent upon market conditions; they usually serve as an employer's cost-reducing mechanism; competition is high, with many workers in a similar position; and they do not feel supported by the government. According to the Statistical Office of the Republic of Slovenia (2016), the at-risk-of-poverty rate for the self-employed is almost double the at-risk-of-poverty rate for

---

[31] If a self-employed person is ill for less than 45 days (or 30 working days), s/he is required to pay all their social security and other expenses; however s/he is not entitled to any compensation for the lost income for that period.

the average Slovenian resident and nearly five times that of the at-risk-of-poverty rate for the permanently employed person (22.4 per cent, 14.3 per cent, and 4.7 per cent, respectively).

In recent years the government of Slovenia has tried to address these issues. One of the objectives of the 2013 labour market reform was to reduce the segmentation between fixed-term contract and permanent contracts. With the ERA amendment, Slovenian legislation has incorporated the economically dependent worker category due to the (alarming) spread of bogus self-employed work. During the reform, the gap between employees who are engaged in a contract for a definite period of time (permanent contract), and those who work (legally or illegally) in other forms of work, additionally increased. Consequently, in 2016, the Ministry of Labour, Family, Social Affairs and Equal Opportunities prepared a programme document entitled *For Decent Work* outlining the range of measures that may provide 'a breakthrough for decent work for all citizens' (Ministrstvo za delo, družino, socialne zadeve in enake možnosti 2016). The proposed measures (should) present a comprehensive approach in tackling increasing precarization of work, while striving to respond to the challenges in relation to the future work set in the labour market. However, since 2016 no further development has taken place in this respect and autonomous workers' conditions have rather deteriorated despite an improving economic situation.

Collective Representation and Social Dialogue

The crisis that trade unions (TUs) are facing in Slovenia in the last decade is characterized by a dramatic decline in membership. The Slovenian TU movement is highly fragmented (Stanojević and Broder 2012), with ten union confederations as well as several autonomous unions. In addition, there are a large number of autonomous TUs, which have membership in specific areas. The seven confederations that are representative at national level are members of the tripartite Economic and Social Council, the highest-level body representing social partners in Slovenia, comprising representatives of the TUs, employers and government.

TUs have begun to accept self-employed, unemployed, precarious workers on different contracts, and so on in their ranks. In 2016, the Trade Union of the Precarious was established within the largest TU confederation, the Association of Free Trade Unions of Slovenia (ZSSS). Its aim is to protect the rights of precarious workers. The formation of a new TU was also supported by the TU Young Plus—the TU of students and young unemployed. The union is funded from membership fees and it intends to offer, in particular, legal security, advice and representation. There are also various (occupational) unions organizing at sectoral level protecting their labour, socio-economic, professional and other interests. These unions do not represent exclusively independent workers, but self-employed form a significant share of their membership. For example, the Union of Culture and Nature of Slovenia (GlOSA) and the Union Association of Autonomous Creators in the Fields of Culture and Information of Slovenia (SUKI) unite those employed in the fields of art, film, and natural and cultural heritage protection. The Slovenian Union of Journalists represents its members in relation to media management and owners, state institutions and other organizations.

Survey interviews identified two main problems regarding autonomous workers (i.e. the self-employed) and their collective representation. The first one is the problem of organization; namely, autonomous workers are working in a highly individualized situation, competing with each other. They are likely to perceive their position as being alone in the market as well as not represented by any official body in the social dialogue. In this context, they tend to see themselves as those who are supposed to be responsible for their own future, not counting on the help of other institutions, associations, and so on. The second problem arises when autonomous workers are actually not autonomous—when they are being forced into adopting self-employment status and can be identified as precarious workers. Three groups of these workers can be distinguished: the first comprises those in bogus self-employment; the second consists of economically dependent workers; the third are victims of the dumping forces in the market place as in the case of translators and architects.

Regarding LMIs in Slovenia (private employment placement agencies and/or temporary work agencies only) it can be stated that they often represent part of the problem contributing to higher levels of precarization rather than the solution. The exploitation of workers sent to employers by private agencies is often covered in Slovene media. Agencies are often seen as a means for employers to avoid employment legislation and reduce costs. Agencies in Slovenia do not provide any collective representation or social security protection related services to their clients.

Conclusion

As is the case in other European countries, Slovenia has been facing dramatic changes in the labour market. Although the concept of the autonomous worker has been present for a long time, Slovenia is witnessing an increase in their numbers on an unprecedented scale.

In a comparative perspective, the social protection of self-employed in Slovenia can still be considered as high since the self-employed are required to be insured under all the insurance-based schemes; however, their level of social protection is lower in comparison to the employed under employment contracts. The social position of self-employed (and IPros for that matter) is considered as problematic and often related to precariousness. While the issue of social security of autonomous workers (especially in comparison to workers employed under employment contracts) did surface in the mass media occasionally in the past, it is now seen in the media daily. However, topics related to union representation in social dialogue in relation to diverse types of autonomous work have occurred only recently. Although Slovenia falls within the group of countries with medium collective bargaining coverage, the inclusive approach of integrating atypical workers (self-employed, freelancers, etc.) in traditional unions is evolving very slowly. All in all, despite the recent economic upturn very little has been done to actively address the issue of precarious work.

To conclude, despite existing structures, current protective labour legislation and (relatively) high levels of social protection, market forces seem to have overtaken the flexibility of existing labour market structures and political will, thus predominately pushing the self-employed professional segment of the labour market into the direction of precarious work.

4.7 SPAIN: THE TREND TO PROFESSIONALS' PRECARIZATION

Antonio Martín-Artiles, Alejandro Godino and Oscar Molina

Introduction

Spain is one of the countries with the highest percentage of self-employed workers in the EU-25. Though the number of self-employed fell during the economic crisis, the recovery that started in 2013 has been accompanied by a new rise that can be partly explained by new outsourcing strategies.

Self-employment has often been seen as a way to escape long-term unemployment, particularly since the 2008 economic crisis. This partly explains the high volume of inflows and outflows from self-employment and the fact that it remains a predominantly low-skilled category that is concentrated in agriculture, construction and retailing.

The Self-Employed Workers' Statute, which came into force in 2007, was the first attempt to regulate the working conditions and access to social protection of self-employed workers in Spain. It recognized and regulated economically dependent or bogus self-employed workers. It also attempted to bridge the gap between the rights of employed and self-employed workers. The Statute was positive in many ways, but many problems remain for self-employed workers, including income uncertainty and the difficulties that it entails for paying social security contributions and achieving unemployment protection.

Legal Status and the Institutional Framework

Law 20/2007, of 11 July (*Ley del Estatuto del Trabajo Autónomo*, LETA), established the Self-Employed Workers' Statute, which aimed to provide greater protection to self-employed workers, including the right to association, maternity leave, access to unemployment protection, non-discrimination rights and health insurance. According to Riesco-Sanz (2016), the law attempted to bridge the gap between employed and self-employed workers, but Hernández Nieto (2010) criticizes the fact that the lawmakers thus opened the door to more abuses in employer strategies aimed at decentralizing and outsourcing economic activities. The Statute applies to individuals who perform an economic or professional activity for profit regularly, personally and directly, on their own, and outside the scope of the management and organization of another person. According to the expert committee that drafted the LETA, its defining trait is that it comprehensively covers very different categories of self-employees. One of its most innovative aspects was the recognition of economically dependent or bogus self-employed workers, i.e. those 'who work with a strong and almost exclusive economic dependence on the employer or client who hires them' (UPTA 2010).

Public Policies for Self-Employed Workers

Policies for promoting self-employment and entrepreneurship, implemented in Spain since the mid-1980s, are situated halfway between industrial policy and employment policy. Initially, the focus was more on developing entrepreneurship, but in recent years, and especially during the recent economic crisis, the focus has been more on employment policies aimed at unemployed people who find it difficult to find work, young people, workers with a low educational level, the long-term unemployed and unskilled women. For this reason these policies have been included in the Employment Programmes.

The promotion of self-employment has pivoted around four major mechanisms: (a) reductions in social security contributions, (b) capitalization of unemployment benefits, (c) subsidies for starting a business and (d) training accounts associated with individual workers. During the economic crisis, efforts have concentrated on the first two mechanisms.

One of the first instruments that were implemented to encourage self-employment was the capitalization of unemployment benefit as a lump-sum payment. This measure was established by Royal Decree-Law 1044/1985, but only in recent years, and particularly during the economic crisis, has there been a thorough reform in order to encourage it. The Self-Employed Workers' Statute mentioned the need to study the impact of capitalization on job creation within one year with a view to possibly increasing the capitalization rates. Indeed, in the first months of the crisis Royal Decree 1975/2008 increased the percentage of capitalization in order to provide incentives for unemployed workers to become self-employed.

As the crisis worsened, other mechanisms in addition to capitalization were developed in order to promote self-employment. The 2012 labour market reform (Law 3/2012) included the contract to support entrepreneurs, which was partly aimed at fostering growth of small businesses and allowing self-employed workers to hire other workers more easily.

The most significant changes as regards the policy of promoting self-employment came with Royal Decree-Law 4/2013 and Law 11/2013, which reduced social security contributions for self-employed workers under the age of 30 years who have not been self-employed in the previous five years. These contributions were reduced by 30 per cent during the first thirty months after the start of self-employment. Furthermore, persons under 30 years of age were entitled to capitalize 100 per cent of their unemployment benefit in order to start out as self-employed workers. Finally, receiving unemployment benefit was made compatible with starting out as a self-employed worker.

In the recent years of economic crisis, the objective of creating jobs and reducing unemployment has become more prominent. Incentives for self-employment can be interpreted more cyclically as policies giving momentum to the 'refuge effect' or 'recession/unemployment push' (Rocha Sánchez 2017), according to which times of economic crisis increase the 'forced' flow of unemployed workers (especially the less qualified) towards self-employment. In a recessionary context, the opportunity cost of starting a self-employed activity decreases due to the lack of opportunities for dependent employment, which would explain the countercyclical nature of self-employment. However, Ribó (2013) and Riesco-Sanz (2016) have pointed out that this effect would be offset by a reverse effect known as 'unemployment pull', under which unemployed workers (in principle, the most vulnerable, among other reasons because they are the lowest-skilled) are also those who are less able to set up a self-employed business, so in times of rising unemployment the growth from the push effect is offset by a low survival rate.

Hernández Nieto (2010) and Célérier et al. (2017) warn of the possible negative effects of these policies. Given the risks involved in becoming self-employed, only workers with certain skills should be expected to do so. However, if incentives for self-employment are introduced in times of economic crisis, with high unemployment rates, the flow of unemployed people into self-employment may be determined by negative selection, involving precisely the least qualified and the most affected by unemployment, or workers without the necessary skills to set up their own business. In this case of involuntary or forced self-employment, very low survival rates and a high turnover between unemployment and self-employment can be expected. In fact, for some workers self-employment will become a kind of 'hidden unemployment' that has negative consequences on their trajectory, especially in the form of acceptance of lower pay as wage earners after the period of self-employment.

The political commitment to promote self-employment has coincided with a significant increase in the number of bogus self-employed workers and new outsourcing strategies of companies. Several authors (Molina and López-Roldán 2015; Rocha Sánchez 2017; Zufiaur 2010) have criticized government incentives because, rather than promoting entrepreneurship, they help companies to use bogus self-employment. The action of the autonomous communities has been limited to offering grants and training (largely relying on the European Social Fund and other Structural Funds), because tax incentives and capitalization of benefits are regulated at the state level.

Title IV of Law 20/2007 regulates the social protection of the self-employed. Self-employees have their own social security system, the Special System for Self-Employed Workers (RETA). However, many self-employed workers are also under the general social security system. Membership is mandatory and workers are assigned a single number for their working life. The Law also provides differentiated contribution rates for economically dependent self-employed workers.

Self-employed workers have healthcare in cases of maternity and ordinary or occupational illnesses and accidents. They also have economic benefits in situations of incapacity, risk during pregnancy, maternity, paternity, permanent disability, elderly care and recovery for work.

During the economic crisis, in order to promote self-employment as an alternative to unemployment, contribution rates of self-employees have been kept low—at €50 per month during the first six months of activity. Moreover, the self-employed who hire a worker will also benefit from an additional 80 per cent reduction in their social security contributions for the first six months.

Collective Representation and Social Dialogue

The public debate on self-employment focuses on three main issues. The first is the position of self-employees in comparison with dependent employees. As pointed out by Molina and López-Roldán (2015), recent reforms have brought self-employed workers closer to wage earners in terms of rights and legal status, especially thanks to the regulation of economically dependent self-employees, who occupy a grey area of labour law because they are formally self-employed but economically dependent on a single supplier, customer or employer. According to Riesco-Sanz (2016), it is paradoxical that regulations of self-employment in Spain have tried to make it converge with dependent employment. This problem is particularly apparent in the social security contributions paid by self-employed workers, which are considered too high because they are close to the amount paid by wage earners, though some specific groups receive allowances. More importantly, these contributions consist of a fixed amount, that is, they are not linked to the income obtained by the self-employed worker in a given period. One of the priorities for the organizations representing self-employed workers is therefore to obtain a variable contribution linked to earnings.

Self-employed workers are organized, and their interests are represented, through a wide variety of associations, including employers' organizations and trade unions. This fragmentation mirrors the diversity found in types, characteristics and demands of self-employed workers. Whereas ideological reasons very often determine membership decisions of dependent workers, for self-employed workers the motivations are more related to functional criteria and to the services provided.

Since the early 2000s there has been a considerable increase in the number of organizations representing self-employed workers. This growth is a result of the quantitative increase in the number of self-employed workers in Spain in the same period and the fact that different types of self-employed workers may prefer different types of services and incentives. The most representative organizations of self-employees in 2016 were the Asociación de trabajadores autónomos (ATA) (58.48 per cent) and the Unión de Profesionales y Trabajadores Autónomos (UPTA) (22.04 per cent), followed by the Unión de Asociaciones de Trabajadores Autónomos y Emprendedores (UATAE) (13.41 per cent) and the Confederación Intersectoral de Autónomos del (CIAE) (6.07 per cent). The most representative organizations have access to certain public programmes, participate in some institutions and receive state financial support (UPTA 2014).

As in the case of wage earners, union membership figures of self-employed workers in Spain are few and fragmented. However, the government ministry does not take into account membership data provided by the represented organizations, but rather other indicators such as the number of people employed by the organization and the number of offices. For this reason, we relied on other sources to estimate the trade union membership of self-employed workers. In particular, we used the Survey on Quality of Life at Work that was conducted until 2010.[32] This survey showed that 27.5 per cent of self-employed workers belonged to a professional association or some other organization representing their interests, including employers' organizations. Trade union membership among self-employed workers showed a clear increasing trend from 2.5 per cent in the late 1990s until the outbreak of the economic crisis, when it declined rapidly. It started to recover in 2008 and reached 6.9 per cent in 2010.

The trade union membership rate of self-employed workers (6.9 per cent) was below the average for all employed workers in the economy (16.4 per cent) in 2010, the latest year for which figures are available at this level of disaggregation.

According to the survey of members made by the UPTA (the I-Wire project), the profile of emerging self-employed workers is one of journalists, photographers, publicists, graphic designers, translators, marketing consultants and labour law advisers, reflecting the increase of a new type of qualified workers, IPros, representing 41 per cent of the respondents. The majority (56 per cent) considered themselves independent workers, 70 per cent had used digital platforms to sell their professional services, and 19 per cent also had a work contract in another company.

The organizations representing self-employed workers have shown little involvement in the social dialogue. They took part in the drafting of the LETA in 2007, but their general lack of involvement in policymaking has been criticized by trade unions and the other sources (Ribó 2013).

The LETA provided for the creation of the Self-Employment Council (Consejo del Empleo Autónomo) as an advisory body that would assist the government in regulations concerning self-employed workers. Only the most representative organizations would sit on the Council, which would provide a specific voice to self-employed workers. This initiative was very much welcomed by organizations of self-employed workers, who felt excluded from the social dialogue. In particular, the only organization that participates in a high-level tripartite social dialogue with unions and the government is the Spanish Confederation of Small and Medium-Sized Enterprises (CEPYME), which also claims to represent the interests of self-employed workers.

---

[32] See https://www.eurofound.europa.eu/publications/report/2010/quality-of-life-social-policies/second-european-quality-of-life-survey-family-life-and-work.

Conclusion

Spanish legislation on self-employment has been considered one of the most advanced in Europe. It recognizes the obligation to sign a specific contract, the right to unemployment benefit, the improvement of protection against occupational hazards, the implementation of a kind of light collective bargaining on working conditions through the signing of an 'agreement of professional interest', and the recognition of the labour jurisdiction for resolving conflicts. It also includes the right to healthcare under the social security system and differentiated tax treatment. Spanish legislation has chosen an approach to the 'salaried work space' in which freelancers are considered 'workers' and may even recognize their economic dependence. This approach is similar to that of the Italian *lavoro parasubordinato* (Célérier et al. 2017).

The main challenge for the regulation of self-employment is the need to limit abusive practices related to outsourcing and leading to an increase in bogus self-employment. Furthermore, there is no legal distinction of different types of self-employed workers, with the exception of economically dependent ones. Self-employed professionals are covered by the same regulations as all other self-employed workers.

The representation of self-employed workers in Spain is very fragmented and mirrors the diversity found under this category. Though organizations representing self-employed workers provide similar services and incentives, they show some specialization according to the dominant profile of their members. In order to give a stronger voice to the self-employed, the 2007 law provided for the Self-Employment Council, an advisory body to the government on which the most representative organizations are represented.

Finally, the results of the I-Wire project survey show that the expectations of self-employed workers are to improve the associations of freelancers, professional associations, cooperative structures, mutual assistance, coalitions between professional associations and the role of trade unions.

4.8   SWEDEN: TOWARDS A SOCIAL MODEL 2.0

Maria Norbäck and Lars Walter

Introduction

Sweden is often described as a small, open and export-oriented economy which, more than many other countries, is dependent both on developments in the wider world and on being able to compete on a global market.

This has influenced the formulation of both Sweden's trade and industry policy and its labour market policy, and the institutionalized forms of collaboration between the social partners on the labour market (Thullberg and Östberg 1994), providing the foundation of what has been labelled 'the Swedish model'. The main element in this institutional model is the emphasis put on social partners to organize and regulate Sweden's labour market via collective agreements. The regulating role of the government is thus limited. Problems and conflicts arising on Sweden's labour market are dealt with in negotiation by the social partners. This means that what is perceived as a problem, in addition to which solutions can be deemed suitable and desirable, can vary between the different areas of agreement and sectors. Following this, Sweden's labour market is regulated by both legislation and collective agreements. The trade unions are responsible for each individual employer signing collective agreements—however, in practice, collective agreements are also prescriptive for workplaces not entering into them (Bergström et al. 2007). As the social partners are responsible for much of the 'rules of the game' of the Swedish labour market, the government assumes no responsibility for ensuring that collective agreements are valid. Since all economic remuneration for work is regulated via collective agreements between the partners, there is no minimum wage legislation in Sweden. This means that self-employed professionals are not covered by any kind of minimum economic remuneration for their work.

Institutional and Legal Framework

The Swedish public social insurance system is based on taxed labour income. This taxed income is then the basis for sick benefits, pension, parental leave, and so on. This means that the public social insurance system covers all workers with a taxed income, no matter in which mode (as employed or self-employed) this income was generated. There is thus a basic and—compared to many other countries, rather beneficial—social protection in place for all workers with a taxable labour income (Ståhlberg 2014). However, collective agreements often, especially for more qualified white collar workers, add further levels of protection in addition to the public basic social security (Karlsson et al. 2014). This means that many Swedish employees have better social protection compared to self-employed workers. In order to receive a similar high level of social protection, the self-employed individual must have private insurance for pension and other social securities. Also, a problem encountered by some self-employed is that the tax-deduction system where all costs related to work can be deducted means that some self-employed can maintain a fairly good standard of living on a rather low taxed income. However, if they become ill or when they retire, their low income entitles them to a rather meagre social protection.

The two central acts of Swedish employment law are the Employment Protection Act (SFS 1982) and the Employment (Co-Determination in the Workplace) Act (SFS 1976). Together, they provide the legal framework for workers in Sweden. Within this legislation, no clear legal distinction is made between being an employee and being a self-employed worker. Instead judgements are dependent on praxis developed by labour courts, in which the relation between the worker and the employer is evaluated against a set of prerequisites in order to determine whether a particular contractual arrangement is to be defined as an employment relation or not. In the Swedish legal system there is thus no 'third' or 'middle' category between employee ('worktaker'/*arbetstagare*) and contractor ('assignment-taker'/*uppdragstagare*). In the Swedish laws regulating unemployment insurance, social insurance, and tax, each have different definitions of what constitutes an employee and contractor/self-employed, respectively. In the tax law, there is a clear difference between rules for employees versus contractors, concerning the responsibility for payment of taxes and VAT. In the social insurance law, amongst other things, there are different rules for how to calculate the income that sick pay is based upon (*sjukpenning-grundande inkomst*), which can cause problems especially for combinators who combine short employments with self-employed work. This means that a self-employed professional could, at least in theory, be regarded as an employee in regard to one law and a contractor as defined by another law, since the laws were written for specific purposes and the definitions reflect this. However, it is especially in relation to the unemployment insurance law that self-employed workers find themselves in an insecure situation.

A report from the Swedish Inspection for the unemployment insurance (Inspektionen för arbetslöshetsförsäkringen 2016) surveying all Swedish unemployment funds states that they all report problems with deciding whether workers working on assignments ('assignmenttakers'/contractors) should be entitled to unemployment benefits or not. According to Swedish unemployment insurance law, whether the worker should be considered employee (*arbetstagare*) or firm-owner (*företagare*) is the basis on which they should be entitled to benefits or not. The most important criterion for defining a worker as one or the other is her/his *independence* in relation to the client. If the worker is seen as *dependent* upon the client, then she *is* entitled benefits; if she is regarded as *independent* she is *not* entitled to unemployment benefits. When deciding whether a person is a dependent or independent contractor, the unemployment funds must make an individual judgement for each case. Factors that are taken into account are (among other things): if the worker does her own marketing, if she pays her own taxes and social fees, if she gets paid per hour or per commission, if the person uses her own equipment, and if the work takes place at the site of the client. For the workers, this creates uncertainty as to whether they will be covered by unemployment benefits, since this is decided from case to case, and not until the worker has applied for it.

Swedish Public Policies for Self-Employed Professionals

In many Swedish trade unions there is an ongoing debate about whether the unions should extend their services and membership to organize not only traditionally employed workers but also firm-tax permit holders (the permit needed by tax law in order to work as self-employed in Sweden). These firm-tax permit holders have traditionally been regarded as firm owners. Hence they have, at least historically, been seen as the very opposite of the kind of employed workers that unions were formed to protect. However, following the transformation of the labour market where the amount of workers working as self-employed firm-owners are increasing in all sectors (albeit with a different speed) (Arbetskraftsbarometern 2016) most unions are now beginning to realize that this group of workers is important to reach and 'get onboard', for the sake of all workers within the trade. For example, during recent years the Swedish trade union Unionen (organizing white-collar workers) which by membership is the biggest union in Sweden, has worked intensely to organize firm-tax permit holders and lobby for reformation of the Swedish social security systems so that they cover also firm-owners and so called 'combinators'.

Collective Representation of Self-Employed Workers

The trade unions are also painfully aware that when the amount of self-employed and freelancers in a buyers' labour market (where there is an excess supply in relation to demand) increases, there is an unavoidable downward pressure on freelance rates, which eventually will also affect the pay levels of employed workers in the same professions (Thörnquist 2013). Since self-employed are not covered by the Swedish collective bargaining agreements where minimum wages are stipulated, the collective agreements will therefore run the risk of becoming hollowed out. This is a problem that the Swedish journalists' union is currently dealing with. This union discusses how to investigate the so-far untried but often implicitly assumed presumption that 'collective bargaining' on the part of freelance professionals would be formation of a cartel, which is illegal under Swedish competition law. The reasoning put forward by the union is that competition law is designed in order to protect the (most often) weaker part in the market, namely consumers, against the stronger part of big corporations. In the case of freelance journalists, even though they are indeed suppliers, the stronger market actors are in this case the buyers of content. Also, according to the Employment (Co-Determination in the Workplace) Act contractors that are 'equal' or dependent on the commissioning client have the right to engage in collective bargaining, which is in fact a way to sidestep the competition law in terms of allowing cartels for those selling their labour. According to the law, 'equal or dependent' contractors are those that do work for another part and are not employed but have a standing which is 'to all intents and purposes that of an employee'. Thus, one way forward for the Swedish unions could be to collectively encourage their self-employed members to solidarize by refusing to do work for a fee that is below a certain agreed-upon level.

Conclusion

According to the overview of the institutional framework for self-employed work in nine EU-countries (Chapter 5), the Swedish setting would be characterized as a system of 'universal coverage'. Based on this overview, one can assume that universal coverage (old age and survivor's pension, parental leave, healthcare, sickness benefits, unemployment insurance, family benefits, invalidity and accident insurance) means that self-employed and employees in Sweden are equally well covered by its public social security system. However, as we have discussed in this section, it is more complex in practice as many collective agreements provide additional coverage to employees. Also, since the public social security system is based on the principle of taxed income of work, economic levels of coverage depend on the levels of taxed income. As self-employed work is inherently volatile, with often 'bulimic' work patterns and periods of work shortage (Barley and Kunda 2004; O'Mahony and Bechky 2006), the volatility of self-employed work makes the situation more insecure for self-employed workers than for employees. For employed workers there is most often a continuous and steady stream of work and a consistent salary (on which social security is based) which creates a factual as well as a psychologically perceived sense of economic security and social protection.

Hence, even though Sweden, compared to many other EU countries, could be described as 'best in class' for social protection of self-employed professionals, it is still from many aspects more secure to be employed than to be self-employed. This is mainly due to the inherent work volatility of self-employed work. As some self-employed are what should be described as 'underemployed' (that is, they work less than 40 hours per week or at least are paid for less than a 40-hour working week) their taxed income is lower than for the employee in the same profession who is covered by a collective agreement. Also, even though self-employed professionals in theory have the same possibilities to use the beneficial Swedish parental leave insurance, there is still the problem that all self-employed professionals face: clients will turn elsewhere if you are on leave during an extended period of time, and when you come back to work you find yourself without clients (Barley and Kunda 2004). For employed workers, these problems are shouldered by the employer rather than the individual worker. Additionally, other problems may arise for self-employed professionals. The ability to get loans for housing or a contract to rent housing is often dependent on having employment, as employment contracts are seen by banks and landlords as a way to secure against risk (Leighton and Brown 2013).

For the future of self-employed professional work in Sweden, the issue of economic remuneration will probably become even more crucial, as collective bargaining traditionally has been the principle for setting the lowest allowed levels of wages in the country. The legal status of self-employed professionals will probably be under future scrutiny, as independent contractors are not permitted to engage in 'rate-cartels' under Swedish competition law. However, one way forward for the Swedish unions is to sign collective agreements on a case by case basis with each single contracting organization, in which levels of economic compensation could be settled.

4.9   UNITED KINGDOM: THE INSTITUTIONAL IMPULSE TO SELF-EMPLOYMENT

Anna Mori

Introduction

Self-employment has played a central role in the development of the British economy. The volume of VAT-registered workers in fact continued to display an upward trend even during the financial crisis following 2008. Only in 2016, the number of VAT registrations grew by about 4.3 per cent, rising from 2.45 million businesses to 2.55 million (Office for National Statistics 2016). The increase in the number of self-employed professionals in the advanced tertiary sector is particularly relevant: increasing from 1.22 million in 2008 to 1.86 million in 2016, they now account for half of total self-employment. The picture shows an overall transformation of the British business landscape. Not simply symbolically, the Department of Trade and Industry has been substituted by the new Department for Business, Innovation and Skills (Dellot 2014). The political class has also spotlighted the relevance of self-employment for the British economy, with former prime minister David Cameron depicting self-employed work in 2014 as 'the lifeblood of the UK economy'.[33] Similarly, Iain Duncan Smith described the rise in self-employment as an indicator that 'the entrepreneurial spirit is alive and well in the UK'.[34] Such support for entrepreneurship is, however, bipartisan in the political sphere, with former Labour leader Ed Miliband promising in 2013 to go 'into the next election as the party of small business and enterprise'.[35] In a nutshell, self-employment and entrepreneurships seem to embody the new zeitgeist, the new spirit of the age, in the UK (Dellot 2014).

The political orientation of successive governments since the 1980s towards an 'enterprise culture' has helped in laying a favourable and accommodating ground for self-employment (Schulze Buschoff and Schmidt 2009). 'By creating a climate whereby starting up is relatively easy, with the minimum of costs and bureaucracy' (European Commission 2010, p. 13), self-employment has been largely encouraged. Public policies have played a major role in creating opportunities for self-employment and small business, and in influencing public attitudes to taking up such opportunities (Bennett 2014). The privatization and outsourcing programmes launched since the 1980s have triggered the spread of small production and service companies, many of them single-person self-employed workers supplying services as subcontractors (Kitching 2015). A second important driver for self-employment is the active labour market policies promoted by government since the 1980s to help unemployed people return to work. In 1981, Margaret Thatcher's Conservative government issued the Enterprise Allowance Scheme (EAS) (renewed in 2013 under the name New Enterprise Allowance), a policy initiative designed to guarantee mentoring support and financial assistance to unemployed people setting up their own businesses. A further explanation of the boom in self-employment relates to the lack of employment opportunities in the UK labour market, and in particular the lack of good job opportunities ensuring affordable and decent living standards and working conditions. In a sense, unemployed workers and the working

---

[33]   See https://www.bbc.co.uk/news/av/business-25909235/cameron-small-businesses-are-lifeblood-of-uk-economy.

[34]   See https://www.telegraph.co.uk/news/politics/conservative/10783556/Benefit-cuts-creating-new-generation-of-entrepreneurs-Bank-of-England-suggests.html.

[35]   See https://www.theguardian.com/politics/2013/dec/06/ed-miliband-labour-small-business-champion.

poor have been somehow 'pushed' or 'forced' into self-employment by the total lack of and/or unattractive employment alternatives (Dellot 2014).

Legal Status and Institutional Framework

In the British regulatory framework, the definition of self-employment is a questioned subject open to debate, partly because no legal definition exists (Dellot 2014). Regulation of self-employment is minimal, limited to governmental guidelines oriented towards supporting workers, inter alia pointing out that their employment status determines their related rights and the responsibilities of the entity making use of their services. Her Majesty's Revenue and Customs (HMRC) has explicated a set of working behaviours and conditions that help to distinguish when a person is an employee, a self-employed or a worker. The latter category represents an intermediate status between subordinate employment and self-employment, displaying intermediate characteristics in terms of contractual relations and employment rights. The website of the British government provides a guide to employment status that allows workers to point out their employment status and determines their related rights and their employer's responsibilities.[36] In particular, they specify that self-employed workers do not enjoy the employment rights and protections accorded to employees, and partly to workers. Accordingly, 'a person is self-employed if they run their business for themselves and take responsibility for its success or failure. Self-employed workers are not paid through PAYE [Pay As You Earn system[37]], and they don't have the employment rights and responsibilities of employees.'[38] According to the guide, a worker can be identified as self-employed if most of the following criteria hold true: (a) he is in business for himself, is responsible for the success or failure of his business and can make a loss or a profit; (b) he can decide what work he does and when, where or how to do it; (c) he can hire someone else to do the work; (d) he is responsible for fixing any unsatisfactory work in his own time; (e) his employer agrees a fixed price for his work—it doesn't depend on how long the job takes to finish; (f) he uses his own money to buy business assets, cover running costs, and provide tools and equipment for the work; (g) he can work for more than one client.

In general, the legal status of self-employed workers without employees can configure in different ways. Sole trader/sole proprietorship, partner-

---

[36]   See https://www.gov.uk/.
[37]   In which income tax and national insurance contributions are deducted from employer wage/salary payments.
[38]   See https://www.gov.uk/employment-status/selfemployed-contractor.

ship and limited company are the most adopted forms, differing according to the number of workers involved. In the case of the sole trader, the self-employed works on his own account; in a partnership two or more workers are involved in the business; while in the case of limited companies, the company has to be registered and have at least one shareholder. These legal forms differ also in terms of tax and national insurance regimes and implications. Freelancers may also operate under a PAYE umbrella company: in this case, they become employees, but not directors, of the umbrella company, where the umbrella organization is responsible for invoicing clients on behalf of freelancers and for paying the freelancer's salary net of tax and national insurance deductions (Kitching and Smallbone 2008).

Consistent with an economic culture oriented towards free market competition, overall the country displays the lowest restrictions to professional practice in Europe (OECD 1999). Professional associations are autonomous in the regulation of the respective practice, as are professional ethics, self-regulated through codes of conduct. The principle of free competition imposed by the Monopolies Commission prohibits the setting of minimum or maximum standards regarding payment rates for professional practice (Feltrin 2012). Generally speaking, professions are divided between those with regulated access (i.e. legal, medical and accounting professions) and all other non-regulated ones.

Social Security System

Concerning the social security system, the institutional configuration is characterized by weak protections and limited benefits which are increasingly being made conditional on activation requirements in the labour market for both subordinated and self-employed workers (ESPN 2017).

Self-employed workers are eligible for many of the protections enjoyed by wage-earners, including housing benefits, council tax reductions and working tax credit. There are, however, some policy areas where coverage for self-employed is still very limited. Overall the main differences relate to sickness and maternity allowances, where self-employed cannot benefit from paid leave (statutory maternity pay and statutory sick pay), and old-age pensions (MISSOC 2016b). Moreover, self-employed workers forgo statutory paid paternity leave, as well as the industrial injuries disablement benefit (Dellot and Reed 2015). However, a maternity allowance is payable to women who have been self-employed for at least 26 weeks out of the 66 weeks, ending with the week before the baby is due, and have average weekly earnings of at least £30 (€36).

Self-employed persons could qualify for the contributory (state) basic retirement pension on the same basis as employees, but they are generally not entitled to benefit from a state earnings-related pension, the additional state pension (including state second pension, state earnings-related pension, and state graduated pension). However, the newly launched reform of the pension system, enacted from 2016–17, replaced the basic state pension and state second pension with a new single-tier pension for everyone below the state pension age. The new system should be essentially universal, thus it should ensure considerably more extensive crediting of unpaid activities than before (Crawford et al. 2013).

The overall picture is characterized by an average lower rate of contributions levied by self-employed workers compared to their counterpart in wage-work: 'This disparity, to a certain extent, reflects a lower entitlement to contributory benefits for the self-employed, and this is particularly true in the domain of pensions (prior to the introduction of the Single Tier Pension). However, the disparity in contribution levels between the two groups seems large in relation to the difference in benefit entitlement' (Social Security Advisory Committee 2014, p. 29). In March 2017 the government attempted to raise Class 4 National Insurance contributions for the self-employed, equalling the personal rate applied to employees (12 per cent instead of 9 per cent). The proposal of such a tax rise has met fierce opposition from business groups, trade unions, a number of MPs and the press.

An overall evaluation of the system of social protections ensured to the population of self-employed workers shows a lack of welfare protections (Social Security Advisory Committee 2014). A major problem concerns the lack of measures to support self-employed workers on low incomes (Dellot and Reed 2015).

Incentives and Public Policy to Sustain and Promote Self-Employment

Public policy in the UK has played an important role in promoting opportunities for self-employment (Bennett 2014). There have been specific labour market measures providing direct encouragement to self-employment. As part of wider programmes aiming to help people get back into the labour market, these activation policies have promoted self-employment as an exit route to unemployment. The New Deal and Flexible New Deal provide help in becoming self-employed through advice and guidance and some financial assistance, mainly in the form of the government self-employment credit available to claimants of the Jobseeker's Allowance.

Another policy initiative promoting self-employment is the EAS. Introduced in 1981 by Margaret Thatcher's Conservative government, it provided a guaranteed income of £40 per week to unemployed people who set up their own business. This type of scheme was recently renewed in 2013 when the New Enterprise Allowance was launched. This scheme is designed to support claimants in starting their own business by moving into self-employment. It provides mentoring support and financial assistance in the form of the New Enterprise weekly allowance (administered by Jobcentres Plus) to specific groups of unemployed people already claiming some form of income support or benefits, such as Jobseekers Allowance, Employment and Support Allowance, Income Support for lone parents, or Universal Credit.[39]

Collective Representation and Social Dialogue

The collective representation of the interests of self-employed professionals is segmented across professional categories, with both professional associations and trade unions responsible for the organizing (Borghi et al. 2018). Beyond lobbying and self-regulating, the professional bodies can engage in representation and negotiation tasks for their members. This is particularly the case with the education and medical professions, such as, for nurses (the Royal College of Nurses). As far as the trade unions are concerned, the Trades Union Congress has traditionally not sponsored the idea of establishing general unions for the self-employed. In the absence of a specific TUC guideline, individual trade unions have taken the initiative to develop services and branches for the self-employed in specific sectors. Trade union representation of self-employed workers is concentrated in productive sectors with a high incidence of such workers beyond a subordinate workforce with whom they share interests and working conditions (Pedersini and Coletto 2010). The artistic and creative sector is rich in experience. On an occupational basis, occupation-related unions have been established, organizing for both salaried and self-employed workers, despite the latter being prevalent. This is the case, for example, with the Broadcasting Entertainment Cinematography and Theatre Union in the media and entertainment sector; Equity (British Actors' Equity Association) which includes actors and performers, but also directors, choreographers and dancers; and the Musicians' Union in the music industry. Recognized as social partners, these unions sign collective agreements mainly with individual employers to set working conditions and pay levels for self-employed workers.

Alongside these sectoral experiences, cross-industry organizations have emerged, trying to give voice to self-employment in general terms, mainly through lobbying activities. The Professional Contracting Group was

---

[39]   See https://www.gov.uk/browse/benefits.

formed in May 1999 to provide independent contractors and consultants with a representative voice in opposition to the original IR35 tax system reform proposals introduced in 2000, which placed additional burdens on the self-employed. It has since evolved from being a single-issue campaign group to a fully fledged, not-for-profit professional body, and into the largest association of independent professionals in the EU. In 2014 it was renamed the Association of Independent Professionals and the Self-Employed (IPSE). It currently represents 22,000 freelancers, contractors and consultants from every sector of the economy, with an ambition to become the voice for 4.8 million self-employed people across the UK. IPSE acts as a lobbying group in order to give public visibility to the phenomenon by extensively financing research into freelancing, and organizing roundtables and discussions of key policy issues.

Conclusion

Self-employment has played a central role in the development of the British economy. In fact, in the UK the political-institutional context appears strongly favourable towards self-employed professional work, simultaneously encouraged by flexible regulation and active labour market policies. The political orientation of successive governments since the 1980s towards an 'enterprise culture' has helped lay a favorable and accommodating ground for self-employment. Concerning the social security system, the institutional configuration is characterized by weak protections and limited benefits which are increasingly being made conditional on activation requirements in the labour market for both subordinated and self-employed workers. The collective representation of the interests of self-employed professionals is segmented across professional categories, with both professional associations and trade unions responsible for the organizing. Beyond lobbying and self-regulating, professional bodies can engage in representation and negotiation tasks for their members. This is particularly the case with the education and medical professions. Trade union representation of self-employed workers is concentrated in productive sectors with a high incidence of such workers beyond a subordinate workforce with whom they share interests and working conditions, such as in the artistic and the creative sectors.

REFERENCES

Accornero, A. and B. Anastasia (2006), 'Realtà e prospettive del lavoro autonomo: un p.di attenzione, please', *Giornale Di Diritto Del Lavoro e Di Relazioni Industriali*, **28** (4), 743–55.

Acoss (2016), *Les Auto-Entrepreneurs Fin 2015*, Acoss Stat n° 235, accessed at https://www.acoss.fr/home/observatoire-economique/publications/acoss-stat/20 16/acoss-stat-n235.html.

Ambra, M. C. (2013), 'Modelli di rappresentanza sindacale nella società post-industriale. Come i sindacati si stanno ri-organizzando', *Quaderni Rassegna Sindacale*, **4**, 75–94.

Amorós, J. E. and N. Bosma (2014), *Global Entrepreneurship Monitor 2013 Global Report: Fifteen Years of Assessing Entrepreneurship across the Globe*, accessed at http://www.gemconsortium.org.

Antonmattei, P.-H. and J.-C. Sciberras (2008), *Le travail économiquement dépendant: quelle protection?*, Rapport à M. le Ministre du Travail, des Relations sociales, de la Famille et de la Solidarité, 7 November.

Arbetskraftsbarometern (2016), *The Swedish Annual Labour Resource Report*, SCB, accessed at http://www.scb.se/Statistik/_Publikationer/UF0505_2016A01_BR_AM78BR1604.pdf.

Barley, S. R. and G. Kunda (2004), *Gurus, Hired Guns, and Warm Bodies: Itinerant Experts in a Knowledge Economy*, Princeton, NJ: Princeton University Press.

Bennett, R. J. (2014), *Entrepreneurship, Small Business and Public Policy: Evolution and Revolution*, London: Routledge.

Bergström, O., K. Håkansson, T. Isidorsson and L. Walter (2007), *Den nya arbets-markaden: bemanningsbranschens etablering i Sverige [The New Labour Market: The Establishment of Staffing Agencies in Sweden]*, Lund: Academica Adacta.

BMWi (2013), *Gründerland Deutschland 2013: Zahlen und Fakten. Unterneh-mensgründungen und Gründergeist in Deutschland*, Berlin: BMWi.

Bologna, S. and A. Fumagalli (1997), *Il lavoro autonomo di seconda generazione: Scenari del postfordismo in Italia*, Milan: Feltrinelli.

Borghi, P., A. Mori and R. Semenza (2018), 'Self-Employed Professionals in the European Labour Market. A Comparison between Italy, Germany and the UK', *Transfer: European Review of Labour and Research*, first published online 26 February 2018, https://doi.org/10.1177/1024258918761564.

Brehm, T., K. Eggert and W. Oberlander (2012), *Die Lage der Freien Berufe*, Nürnberg: BMWi.

Brenke, V. K. (2013), *Allein tätige Selbständige: starkes Beschäftigungswachstum, oft nur geringe Einkommen*, DIW Wochenbericht, July, Berlin: DIW.

Bucholz, G. (2011), *Der Ratgeber Selbstständige*, Berlin: Ver.di-Mediafon.

Butera, F., S. Bagnara, R. Cesaria and S. Di Guardo (2008), *Knowledge Working. Lavoro, lavoratori, società della conoscenza*, Milan: Mondadori Università.

CBS (2014), *Achtergrondkenmerken En Ontwikkelingen van Zzp'ers in Nederland*, Heerlen: Centraal Bureau voor de Statistiek.

Célerier, S., A. Riesco-Sanz and P. Rolle (2017), 'Trabajadores autónomos y transformación del salariado: las reformas española y francesa', *Cuadernos de Relaciones Laborales*, **35** (2), 303–14.

CESE (2017), *Les nouvelles formes du travail indépendant: mandature 2015–2020—*

avis présenté par Mme Sophie Thiéry, Paris: Conseil économique, social et environnemental (CESE).

Companies Act (2006), *ZGD-1*, accessed at https://www.google.si/url?sa=t&rct=j &q=&esrc=s&source=web&cd=1&cad=rja&uact=8&ved=0ahUKEwj6veqIhY jbAhWFhiwKHUncB10QFggoMAA&url=http%3A%2F%2Fwww.mgrt.gov. si%2Ffileadmin%2Fmgrt.gov.si%2Fpageuploads%2Fzakonodaja%2FZGD-1_ PREVOD__13-12-12.pdf&usg=AOvVaw0oZcsV_MG5fCw1mEVc8lAr.

Conen, W., J. Schippers and K. Schulze Buschoff (2016), *Self-Employed without Personnel between Freedom and Insecurity*, Study n° 5, August, Berlin: WSI— Institute of Economic and Social Research.

CPB (2014), *The Dutch Labour Market during the Great Recession*, CPB Background Document, June, Den Haag: Centraal Planbureau.

CPB (2015), *Position Paper t.b.v. 'IBO Zelfstandigen Zonder Personeel'*, CPB Notitie, Den Haag: Centraal Planbureau.

Crawford, R., S. Keynes and G. Tetlow (2013), *A Single-Tier Pension: What Does It Really Mean?*, IFS Report R82, London: Institute for Fiscal Studies, accessed at https://www.ifs.org.uk/comms/r82.pdf.

D'Amours, M. (2010), 'Les logiques d'action collective d'associations regroupant des travailleurs indépendants', *Relations industrielles/Industrial Relations*, **65** (2), 257–80.

Dautzenberg, K. and A. Steinbrück (2013), *Gründerinnen Und Unternehmerinnen in Deutschland I—Quantitative Daten Und Fakten*, N° 33, Stuttgart: bundesweite gründerinnenagentur (Bga).

Dekker, F. (2010), 'Self-Employed without Employees: Managing Risks in Modern Capitalism', *Politics & Policy*, **38** (4), 765–88.

Dekker, F. (2016), 'Flexibilisering: geen tijd te verliezen', *Socialisme & Democratie*, **73** (4), 20–24.

Dellot, B. (2014), *Salvation in a Start-up? The Origins and Nature of the Self-Employment Boom*, RSA report, London, May, accessed at https://www.thersa. org/globalassets/reports/226768356-salvation-in-a-start-up-the-origins-and-nat ure-of-the-self-employment-boom1.pdf.

Dellot, B. and H. Reed (2015), *Boosting the Living Standards of the Self-Employed*, RSA Report, accessed at https://www.thersa.org/globalassets/pdfs/reports/ boosting-the-living-standards-of-the-self-employed-.pdf.

DIHK (2014), *Pioniergründer bringen frische Brise. Zahlen und Einschätzungen der IHK-Organisation zum Gründungsgeschehen in Deutschland*, DIHK-Gründerreport, Berlin: Deutscher Industrie- und Handelskammertag (DIHK).

Employment Relationships Act (2013), *ZDR-1*, accessed at http://www.mddsz. gov.si/fileadmin/mddsz.gov.si/pageuploads/dokumenti__pdf/word/zakonodaja/ zdr1_en.doc.

ESPN (2017), *Synthesis Report on 'Access to Social Protection for People Working on Non-Standard Contracts and as Self-Employed in Europe'*. A study of national policies, accessed at http://ec.europa.eu/social/main.jsp?langId=en&catId=1135 &newsId=2798&furtherNews=yes.

Eurofound (2015), *Germany: Working Life Country Profile*, Eurofound, 25 November, accessed at http://www.eurofound.europa.eu/sites/default/files/ ef_national_contribution/field_ef_documents/germany.pdf.

European Commission (2010), *Self-Employment in Europe*, European Employment Observatory Review, Luxembourg: Publication Office of the European Union.

Faniel, J. and K. Vandaele (2012), *Implantation syndicale et taux de syndicalisation (2000–2010)*, N° 2146–2147, Courrier hebdomadaire du CRISP.

Feltrin, P. (ed.) (2012), *Trasformazioni delle professioni e regolazione in Europa: Una comparazione dei mutamenti nei sistemi professionali in Francia, Germania, Italia e Regno Unito*, I Quaderni di Confprofessioni.

France stratégie (2016), *L'avenir du travail: Quelles redéfinitions de l'emploi, des statuts et des protections?*, Document de travail N° 2016-04, March, Paris.

France stratégie (2017), *Salarié ou indépendant: Une question de métiers?*, Note d'analyse N° 60, September, Paris.

Fritsch, M., A. Kritikos and A. Rusakova (2012), *Who Starts a Business and Who is Self-Employed in Germany?*, Discussion Papers of DIW Berlin N° 1184, Berlin: DIW Berlin, German Institute for Economic Research.

Fulton, L. (2015), *Worker Representation in Europe*, Labour Research Department and ETUI, accessed 4 October 2016 at http://www.worker-participation.eu/ National-Industrial-Relations/Countries/Netherlands/Trade-Unions.

Hernández Nieto, J. A. (2010), 'La desnaturalización del trabajador autónomo: el autónomo dependiente', *Revista universitaria de ciencias del trabajo*, **11**, 177–94.

IBO (2015), *IBO Zelfstandigen Zonder Personeel*, Ministerie van Financiën, Inspectie der Rijksfinanciën/Bureau Strategische Analyse.

InSEE (2015), *Emploi et Revenus Des Indépendants*, Paris: Insee.

Inserm (ed.) (2011), *Stress au travail et santé: Situation chez les indépendants*, Rapport, Paris: Les éditions Inserm.

Inspektionen för arbetslöshetsförsäkringen (2016), *Uppdragstagare i Arbetslöshetsförsäkringen: Kartläggning Initierad Av IAF [Assignment Taker in the Unemployment Insurance: Overview Initiated by IAF]*, accessed at https://www.iaf.se/globalassets/dokument/rapporter/2015-2016/2016-3-uppdragstagare-i-arbetsloshetsforsakringen.pdf.

Jessoula, M., E. Pavolini and F. Strati (2017), *ESPN Thematic Report on Access to Social Protection of People Working as Self-Employed or on Non-Standard Contracts. Italy*, European Union, accessed at http://ec.europa.eu/social/key Documents.jsp?pager.offset=10&&langId=en&mode=advancedSubmit&year= 0&country=0&type=0&advSearchKey=ESPNsensw.

Josten, E., J. D. Vlasblom and C. Vrooman (2014), *Bevrijd of Beklemd? Werk, Inhuur, Inkomen En Welbevinden van Zzp'ers*, November, The Hague: Sociaal en Cultureel Planbureau.

Karlsson, N., Malm Lindberg, H., Larsson, AS., Stern, L., Lundqvist, T. (2014), *Lönebildning iverkligheten: kollektivavtalens effekter på företagens lönesättning och utvecklingskraft / Salaries in reality: the effects of collective agreements on companies' salary setting and development*, Studentlitteratur: Lund.

Kenney, M. and J. Zysman (2016), 'The Rise of the Platform Economy', *Issues in Science and Technology*, **32** (3), 61–69.

Kitching, J. (2015), 'Tracking UK Freelance Workforce Trends 1992–2014', *International Review of Entrepreneurship*, **13** (1), 21–34.

Kitching, J. and D. Smallbone (2008), *Defining and Estimating the Size of the UK Freelance Workforce*, A Report for the Professional Contractors Group, October, Kingston Hill: Kingston University, accessed at http://eprints.kingston.ac.uk/3880/1/Kitching-J-3880.pdf.

Koene, B. and H. van Driel (2011), 'The Rhetoric of Restraint: The Struggle for Legitimacy of the Dutch Temporary Work Agency Industry, 1961–1996', *Enterprise & Society*, **12** (3), 562–600.

Koene, B., N. Galais and C. Garsten (2014), 'Management and Organization of Temporary Work', in B. Koene, N. Galais, and C. Garsten (eds), *Management and Organization of Temporary Agency Work*, London: Routledge, pp. 1–20.

Koene, B. and M. Stanic (2018), *Country Case Study: Netherlands*, I-WIRE Project.

Leighton, P. and D. Brown (2013), *Future Working: The Rise of Europe's Independent Professionals (IPROs)*, European Forum of Independent Professionals.

Léonard, E. and F. Pichault (2016), 'Belgique: l'adaptation d'un "modèle" de concertation sociale', in *Syndicats et dialogue social: Les modèles Occidentaux à l'épreuve*, Brussels: Peter Lang, pp. 55–75.

Lorquet, N., J.-F. Orianne and F. Pichault (2017), 'Who Takes Care of Non-Standard Career Paths? The Role of Labour Market Intermediaries', *European Journal of Industrial Relations*, available at https://doi.org/10.1177/0959680 117740425.

Mai, C.-M. and K. Marder-Puch (2013), 'Selbstständigkeit in Deutschland', *Statistisches Bundesamt*, 482–97, available at https://www.destatis.de/DE/Publikationen/WirtschaftStatistik/Arbeitsmarkt/SelbststaendigkeitDeutschlan d_72013.pdf?__blob=publicationFile.

Maida, B. L. (2009), *Proletari della borghesia. I piccoli commercianti dall'Unità a oggi*, Rome: Carocci.

Metzger, G. (2014), *KfW-Gründungsmonitor 2014: Gründungstätigkeit Wiederbelebt— Impuls Aus Dem Nebenerwerb*, KFW Economic Research, Frankfurt am Main: KFW.

Ministrstvo za delo, družino, socialne zadeve in enake možnosti (2016), *Za Dostojno Delo*, Ljubljana: Ministrstvo za delo, družino, socialne zadeve in enake možnosti, accessed at http://www.mddsz.gov.si/fileadmin/mddsz.gov.si/pageuploads/dokumenti__pdf/dpd/21_03_2016_Dostojno_delo_final.pdf.

MISSOC (2016a), *Mutual Information System on Social Protection*, accessed at https://www.missoc.org/missoc-database/comparative-tables.

MISSOC (2016b), *Social Protection of the Self-Employed*, accessed 16 January 2017 at www.missoc.org.

Molina, O. and P. López-Roldán (2015), 'Occupational Growth and Non-Standard Employment in the Spanish Service Sector: From Upgrading to Polarisation', in W. Eichorst and P. Marx (eds), *Non-Standard Employment in Post-Industrial Labour Markets: An Occupational Perspective*, Cheltenham: Edward Elgar Publishing, pp. 110–49.

OECD (1999), *Competition in Professional Services*, policy roundtables, accessed at http://www.oecd.org/regreform/sectors/1920231.pdf.

OECD (2014), *Employment Outlook 2014*, OECD Publishing.

Office for National Statistics (2016), *UK Business; Activity, Size and Location: 2016*, statistical bulletin, accessed at https://www.ons.gov.uk/businessindustry-andtrade/business/activitysizeandlocation/bulletins/ukbusinessactivitysizean dlocation/2016.

O'Mahony, S. and B. A. Bechky (2006), 'Stretchwork: Managing the Career Progression Paradox in External Labor Markets', *Academy of Management Journal*, **49** (5), 918–41.

Ortlieb, R. and S. Weiss (2015), *Business Start-Ups and Youth Self-Employment in Germany: A Policy Literature Review*, STYLE Working Papers, WP7.1/DE. CROME, Brighton: University of Brighton.

Pallini, M. (2006), *Il lavoro a progetto in Italia e in Europa*, Bologna: Il Mulino.

Pedersini, R. and D. Coletto (2010), *Self-Employed Workers: Industrial Relations and Working Conditions*, Dublin: Eurofound.

Ranci, C. (ed.) (2012), *Partite iva. Il lavoro autonomo nella crisi Italiana*, Bologna: Il Mulino.

Rapelli, S. (2012), *European I-Pros: A Study*, London: Professional Contractors Group Ltd.

Ribó, J. (2013), *Perspectiva sindical del trabajo autónomo en España*, Madrid: CCOO.

Riesco-Sanz, A. (2016), 'Trabajo, independencia y subordinación. La regulación del trabajo autónomo en España', *Revista Internacional de Sociología*, **74** (1), e026.

Rocha Sánchez, F. (2017), 'El trabajo autónomo económicamente dependiente en España. Diagnóstico y propuestas de actuación', *Revista de Derecho de la Seguridad Social, Laborum*, **10**, 301–26.

Schmidt, F. A. (2017), *Digital Labour Markets in the Platform Economy: Mapping the Political Challenges of Crowd Work and Gig Work*, Bonn: Friedrich-Ebert-Stiftung.

Schulze Buschoff, K. and C. Schmidt (2009), 'Adapting Labour Law and Social Security to the Needs of the "New Self-Employed"—Comparing the UK, Germany and the Netherlands', *Journal of European Social Policy*, **19** (2), 147–59.

Semenza, R. (2000), 'Le nuove forme del lavoro indipendente', *Stato e Mercato*, **1**, 143–68.

Semenza, R., A. Mori and P. Borghi (2017), 'Alla ricerca di cittadinanza: il lavoro autonomo professionale in Italia, Germania e Regno Unito', *Quaderni di rassegna Sindacale*, **18** (1), 41–59.

SFS (1976), *Employment (Co-Determination in the Workplace) Act [Lag Om Medbestämmande i Arbetslivet] (SFS 1976:580)*, available at https://www.government.se/government-policy/labour-law-and-work-environment/1976580-employment-co-determination-in-the-workplace-act-lag-om-medbestammande-i-arbetslivet/.

SFS (1982), *Employment Protection Act [Lag Om Anställningsskydd] (SFS 1982:80)*, available at https://www.government.se/government-policy/labour-law-and-work-environment/198280-employment-protection-act-lag-om-anstall ningsskydd/.

Social Security Advisory Committee (2014), *Social Security Protection and the Self-Employed*, Occasional Paper No. 13, September, London: SSAC.

Ståhlberg, A.-C. (2014), *Socialförsäkringarna i Sverige [Social Insurance in Sweden]*, Lund: Studentlitteratur.

Stanojević, M. and Ž. Broder (2012), 'Trade Unions in Slovenia: Historical Development and the Current Situation', *SEER: Journal for Labour and Social Affairs in Eastern Europe*, **15** (3), 303–13.

Statistical Office of the Republic of Slovenia (2016), *Kazalniki Dohodka in Revščine, Slovenija, 2015*, accessed 14 June 2016 at http://www.stat.si/statweb/prikazi-novico?id=6070&idp=10&headerbar=8.

Supiot, A. (1999), *Au-delà de l'emploi: Transformations du travail et devenir du droit du travail en Europe*, Paris: Flammarion.

Sylos Labini, P. (1974), *Saggio Sulle Classi Sociali*, Rome: Laterza.

Thörnquist, A. (2013), *Falskt Egenföretagande—Ett Fenomen i Arbetsmarknadens Gråzon [Bogus Self-Employment—a Phenomenon in the Grey Zone of the Labour Market]*, **3–4**, 37–42.

Thullberg, P. and K. Östberg (eds) (1994), *Den svenska modellen [The Swedish Model]*, Lund: Studentlitteratur.

UPTA (2010), *El trabajo autónomo en el modelo social Europeo y en el reordenamiento jurídico de la UE en la estrategia de Lisboa después de 2010*, Madrid: UPTA.

UPTA (2014), *Eurostat: Análisis de los trabajadores autónomos de la UE*, Madrid: UPTA.

Vendrig, J. P., P. J. M. Vroonhof, M. Folkeringa and M. J. Overweel (2007), *Evaluatie Wet Uitbreiding Rechtsgevolgen Verklaring ArbeidsRelatie*, Zoetermeer: EIM.

Volkmann, C. K., K. O. Tokarski and M. Grünhagen (2010), *Entrepreneurship in a European Perspective: Concepts for the Creation and Growth of New Ventures*, Wiesbaden: Gabler Verlag.

Zufiaur, J. M. (2010), *Dictamen tendencias en materia de trabajo autónomo*, SOC/244, 8 March, Brussels.

5. Comparing the national contexts

Laura Beuker, François Pichault and Frédéric Naedenoen

1. INTRODUCTION

Following Rapelli's (2012) definition, IPros are self-employed without employees; engaged in an activity that does not belong to the farming, craft or retail sectors; and practise activities of an intellectual nature and/ or which come under the heading of the services sector.

For the purposes of our transversal analysis of the institutional framework, we will therefore focus on self-employed professionals or solo self-employed workers (i.e. self-employed workers without employees) that can be considered as the closest category to IPros. We must keep in mind, however, that many new independent professionals can be engaged simultaneously in different jobs (multi-activity), mixing different statuses—not only as self-employed—and probably different social regimes, as shown by the results of the survey presented in Chapter 3.

We will compare the situation of solo self-employed workers in nine countries—Belgium, France, Germany, Italy, the Netherlands, Slovenia, Spain, Sweden, and the UK—by examining four main institutional dimensions likely to characterize the diversity of industrial relations systems at a macro level.[1] The first dimension refers to the potential recognition, in the regulatory framework of each country, of specific working situations located in a 'grey zone' between classical employment and self-employment. The second dimension concerns union density and the coverage rate of collective bargaining in each country. It also explores the strategies developed by traditional unions vis-à-vis self-employed workers: to what extent are they ready to include them among their members? The third dimension refers to the fiscal support offered to the self-employed in each country. Finally, the fourth dimension characterizes the social

---

[1] Unlike the considerations in Chapter 3, here we do not consider individual factors located at micro level, such as level of education, family composition, age, professional activity, etc.

protection offered to self-employed workers: how big are the differences, if any, between provisions for the self-employed and regular employees? Answering these questions will allow us identify the main institutional factors likely to provide better social protection for self-employed workers and, by extension, for new independent professionals. Our comparative analysis not only includes structural factors (regulatory and fiscal frameworks, union density and coverage rate of collective bargaining) but also agency factors (unions' strategies vis-à-vis self-employed workers) in order to explain the level of social protection offered. We must admit, however, that this analysis remains a very difficult exercise: rough indicators must be used in order to make the comparison feasible, which unavoidably simplifies descriptions of the institutional complexity of each country.

2.   REGULATORY FRAMEWORKS

The comparative analysis of national regulatory frameworks reveals that one country does not provide any legal distinction between work statuses; three countries legally oppose employee and self-employed statuses and five countries consider an intermediate working situation, located 'in between' employee and self-employed statuses (Table 5.1).

2.1   The Binary Approach

Sweden is the only country in which there is no clear legal distinction between employee and self-employed statuses. Judgements of labour courts examine the relation between workers and employers according to a set of prerequisites. However, even though no legal definition is offered, the ability to make such a distinction is imperative to the Swedish regulatory system because different laws are applicable according to the work status (e.g. fiscal law, unemployment law, social security law). Despite the lack of opposite work statuses defined by the law, we can thus consider that a binary approach is adopted in Sweden.

Four countries (Belgium, France, Sweden and the Netherlands) offer a clearer distinction between the two work statuses. In Belgium, the prevailing regulatory framework remains organized around standard employment relationships—while self-employment is defined by default—and does not really take into account nonstandard work arrangements, even though some exceptions do exist for certain categories of workers. For example, the legislation on intermittency, also called the 'Lumberjack rule' (that also applies to artists) facilitates access to unemployment benefits for certain categories of workers. There is an ongoing debate around the potential

Table 5.1   Legal/regulatory categories used in each European country

Countries	Employee	Hybrid work status	Self-employed
Sweden	No legal definition: work statuses are defined in tax-law and their differences are mainly shaped by praxis		
Belgium	Employee		Self-employed
Netherlands	Employee		Entrepreneurs
France	Employee		Defined in opposition to employment
Spain	Employee	Economically dependent self-employed (TRADE)[1]	Self-employed
Slovenia	Employee	Economically dependent worker (ERA 2013)[2]	Self-employed
Germany	Employee	Employee-like person	Indirectly defined in opposition to employment
Italy	Employee	Semi-subordinated contracts[3]	Self-employed
UK	Employee	Workers[4]	No legal definition

Notes:
1   LETA (2007): 'Ley del Estatuto del Trabajo Autónomo'.
2   Article 213.
3   Law N° 196/1997 ('Treu package') and Law N° 30/2003.
4   See https://www.gov.uk/employment-status/worker.

creation of a third status but no political agreement has been reached so far on this question.

In France also, there is no legal positive definition of self-employment: the latter is defined in opposition to employment (characterized by subordination links). Besides the classical status of employee, France has developed the status of 'micro-entrepreneur'[2] (Law of 4 August 2008). However, it is mainly a fiscal status that does not provide any specific social rights to individual workers. The micro-entrepreneur status is very often denounced as disguised employment or can be misused as a (long) trial period. In France, there is a legal presumption of independent work for physical persons listed in the commercial register, the craft/profession

---

[2] 'Micro-social regime for independent workers pursuing small-scale activities which means the right for them to benefit from simplified tax-returns and social security contributions subject to a maximum turnover' (ESPN FR 2017, p.4).

list or other companies' registers.[3] There is no specific status for economically dependent workers, even though the law organizes the collective bargaining for some categories of independent workers who perform their activities under economic dependency. Certain vulnerable groups, such as moviemakers and journalists, are automatically classified as employees (presumption of salaried status) (Schmid-Drüner 2013, p. 28). Many French judges have been tempted to classify situations of economic dependency as employment contracts, by referring to a supposed relationship of subordination. The 'Arrêt Labbane' states that the existence of working relationship depends on the effective conditions in which the work is actually done (and not on the willingness of the parties or the designation of the work's convention). The Labour Court thus plays an important role in reassigning labour statuses (Spasova et al. 2017, p. 58).

Over recent years, the growth of autonomous workers in the Netherlands has been remarkably high (OECD 2014). Workers are legally classified either as employees or as self-employed workers. In 1999, the Dutch Flexibility and Security Act has broadened the status of employment by reclassifying some self-employed workers as working under employment contracts. This Act has introduced a presumption that an employment contract exists when work has been carried out for another person in return for pay on a weekly basis or during a period of at least twenty hours per month over three consecutive months (Schulze Buschoff and Schmidt 2009). Consequently, all applicable labour rights, protection, and social insurance obligations of employees apply to the person concerned. In the Netherlands, the concept of dependence is founded on the authority relationships with the employer (i.e. the right to direct work). In 2001 the 'Declaration of Independent Contractor Status' (*Verklaring Arbeidsrelatie* (VAR)) was introduced to fight against bogus self-employment and to provide clarity (regarding fiscal and social security systems). Self-employed workers can apply for a declaration of self-employed status to clarify the expected nature of the working relationship for their clients and how the Tax and Custom Administration would assess the nature of the business relationship beforehand. On 1 May 2016, the Deregulation Assessment Employment Relationships Act replaced the VAR. Self-employed workers and hiring companies can now choose the work status according to a standard model agreement specifying that it is not an employment relationship. Therefore, the hiring party is exempted from withholding any payroll taxes and contributions to collective insurances. However, some implementation problems have been reported: for example, slow adoption

---

[3] L8221-6 article of the Labour Code (modified by Law N° 2011-1906 of 21 December 2011).

of the new model due to its lack of clarity, and the vague definition of concepts.

2.2 The Hybrid Approach

A second group of countries comprises Slovenia, Spain, Germany, Italy and the UK. All of them offer a specific recognition of hybrid working situations (between employees and self-employed workers). This regulatory recognition can take various forms: legal recognition of economic dependence in order to grant workers more social and labour rights, assimilation to the wage-earning, and so on.

In Slovenia, the topic of 'new autonomous work' is currently included in the debate on precarious work.[4] Self-employment, part-time and fixed-term employment are all deemed as flexible employment schemes: there is no tangible difference regarding social insurance or even the social security system. In 2013, the Labour Market Regulation Act introduced the category of economically dependent worker (i.e. workers 'that obtain at least 80% of his/her annual income from the same contracting authority'[5]), with specific labour protection.

While self-employment is remarkably high on the Spanish labour market,[6] the legal status of self-employed workers was approved in July 2007. The new legislation has also officially recognized the specific situation of economically dependent self-employed workers (*trabajador (a) autónomo (a) dependiente económicamente* (TRADE)). These workers are defined as 'formally self-employed, but economically dependent on a single supplier or customer or employer' (Reyna Fernández 2010).

In Germany, the labour law 'provides for another conception of dependency than only that of legal subordination' (Schulze Buschoff and Schmidt 2009, p. 152), that is, dependency on place, time, work content, integration within the organizational chart and the use of employer's equipment.[7] The 'employee-like person' (Collective Agreements Act 1969) is economically dependent. S/he is 'defined as a person who works under either a business contract or a free contract for services, performing the service or work personally and without employees, and working mainly for one principal' (Schulze Buschoff and Schmidt 2009, p. 153). Thanks to this status,

---

[4] See 'Trade Union of the Precarious' created in October 2016 in order to gather autonomous workers in Slovenia.

[5] Article 213 of ERA (2013)

[6] See https://www.eurofound.europa.eu/observatories/eurwork/comparative-information/national-contributions/spain/spain-self-employed-workers.

[7] See https://www.eurofound.europa.eu/observatories/eurwork/comparative-information/travailleurs-economiquement-dependants-droit-du-travail-et-relations-industrielles.

self-employed workers have gained more labour protection rights in some sectors.

In Italy, a series of reforms in the late 1990s have defined specific forms of self-employment that can be located at the border between dependent and independent employment: the semi-subordinated contracts (forms of independent work). Two of them are of interest. From a legal point of view, both are forms of self-employment: the short contract called 'continuous and coordinated contractual relationship' (*Contratto di collaborazione coordinata e continuative* (co.co.co)[8]) and the occasional collaborator (*Lavoratori autonomi occasionali*[9]). The reference point for co.co.co is Article 409 (N° 3) of the Civil Procedure Code where coordinated and continuous collaborations are defined as 'the performance of continuous and coordinated work, mainly personally, even if outside of the scope of an employment relationship'. There is no formal subordination to the employer but the latter is entitled to coordinate the worker's activities according to the company's demands. The second semi-subordinated contract is a specific form of independent work: the occasional collaborator. It is defined in Law N° 30/2003 as 'an autonomous worker engaged in a contractual relationship with a customer to provide a service but with neither forms of subordination, nor coordination power from the customer'.

There is one essential condition to fill in: the contractual relationship has to be occasional and discontinuous. Over the years, these two types of contracts have been widely used and often misused by employers. Abuses have mainly consisted in contracting workers at lower costs than employees, even though the work carried out presents all the characteristics of subordinate work. Two important legislative changes were recently introduced in Italy, which directly affected both employees and self-employed: Legislative Decree 81/2015[10] (reform of employment contracts) and Legislative Decree 81/2017,[11] also called the Self-Employment Statute. Both decrees are part of a broader labour reform called Jobs Act. One of the main goals of Decree 81/2015 was to reorganize and rationalize the various 'atypical' contracts and to introduce relevant changes in

---

[8]   The Continuous and Coordinated Contractual relationship was introduced in 1997 by Law No. 196/1997 (the so-called 'Treu package').

[9]   Law No. 30/2003 introduced occasional collaborations, specifying that the contractual relationship cannot last for more than thirty days within the same year with the same employer, and the maximum annual income under this type of contract cannot exceed €5,000.

[10]   D. Lgs. 15 giugno 2015, n. 81. Disciplina organica dei contratti di lavoro e revisione della normativa in tema di mansioni, a norma dell'articolo 1, comma 7, della legge 10 dicembre 2014, n. 183.

[11]   L. 22 maggio 2017, n. 81. Misure per la tutela del lavoro autonomo non imprenditoriale e misure volte a favorire l'articolazione flessibile nei tempi e nei luoghi del lavoro subordinato.

employment contracts.[12] Some of the changes affected coordinated and continuous collaborations' (co.co.co.) and contracts based on specific projects (co.co.pro[13]) (Caponetti 2015). From 1 January 2016, as stated in the Legislative Decree, 'employment rules will also apply to collaborative relationships consisting in the performance of work which is exclusively personal, continuous and whose performance is organized, also in terms of place and working hours, by the employer'. At the same time project contracts are to be suppressed (starting 25 June 2015), while the previous rules and regulations continue to govern existing contracts until their expiration. After 25 June 2015, co.co.co contracts remain valid and fully effective when collaborations consist in the performance of work, which is 'mainly' (not 'exclusively') personal and the collaborator, in coordination with the employer, decides the details of the activity.[14] With the Legislative Decree 81/2017, some crucial aspects of self-employed workers have been tackled in a systematic way, although some issues, especially related to social protection, were already granted in the past (Perulli 2017).

The UK has experienced the third largest percentage rise in total self-employment in Europe since 2009, amounting to 18 per cent,[15] even though we must be aware that there is no legal definition of self-employment. Lawyers still 'refer to the concept of "master and servant" when distinguishing a contract of employment from other contractual relationships'.[16] There is just a set of working behaviours and conditions set by HRMC[17] that help indicate whether a worker is self-employed or not. English law (common law) distinguishes three types of working situations: self-employed, employee and workers (between employees and self-employed). The UK has thus opted for a 'partial extension of employment law to the broader legal concept of the worker, also including

---

[12] It has introduced progressive protection in case of dismissal of an employee. This change significantly decreases the economic risks for employers related to dismissals, therefore making employment contracts more attractive.

[13] Contracts based on specific projects. In this type of contract, each contractual relationship has to be linked to a specific project or service specified by the customer (Law No. 30/2003, abolished by the Job Acts in 2015).

[14] There are some exceptions to these changes. Co.co.co remain valid in any case when they are specifically provided for and regulated by national collective agreements in order to meet peculiar production and organizational needs of the relevant business sector. Similarly remaining valid are the collaborations provided for and by registered professionals (i.e. accountants and lawyers), the activities of the members of corporate bodies (i.e. directors and auditors) and collaborations for associations and amateur sports associations affiliated to the national sports federations and their affiliated sports promotion bodies.

[15] Percentage change in self-employment (2009–14): Office for National Statistics, based on Eurostat, https://ec.europa.eu/eurostat/web/main.

[16] See http://www.employmentlaws.co.uk/guide/worker_or_self-employed.html.

[17] See Her Majesty's Revenue and Customs Department (HMRC), https://www.gov.uk/government/organisations/hm-revenue-customs.

a part of dependent self-employed automatically'.[18] A worker is 'defined to include employees and others who personally undertake to do work for another under a contract, whether written, oral, implied, or express but not where the work is part of a professional business undertaking carried on by the worker'.[19] The distinction between workers, employees and self-employed workers is made on the basis of a matrix of indicators on the following four dimensions: control over how the work is done; integration (or not) into the employer's organization; the extent to which the employer is required to offer work; the extent to which the worker concerned must bear the economic risks (Schulze Buschoff and Schmidt 2009, p. 152). In practice, the distinction between self-employed and workers, or between workers and employees can be difficult (Heyes and Hastings 2017, p. 18). In the UK, as in Sweden, there is no statutory definition of dependent self-employment. Case law is thus the most important source of assessment.[20] Dependent self-employment has been the subject of media and political debate in the UK; it is, for example, a big issue in the construction sector (Schmid-Drüner 2013, p. 83). Figure 5.1 presents the two main regulatory approaches among EU countries regarding working situations.

The binary approach	The hybrid approach
Belgium France Sweden Netherlands	Slovenia Spain Germany Italy UK

Figure 5.1   Main regulatory approaches to working situations

3.   INDUSTRIAL RELATIONS

Another important institutional variable to consider is the way in which the industrial relations system is organized in each country. We will

---

[18]   See   http://www.europarl.europa.eu/RegData/etudes/etudes/join/2013/507449/IPOL-EMPL_ET%282013%29507449_EN.pdf, p. 32. It is also defined as 'any individual person who works under a contract, whether or not it is a contract of employment, to provide a "personal service"' (Social protection rights of economically dependent self-employed workers, p. 43).

[19]   See http://www.employmentlaws.co.uk/guide/worker_or_self-employed.html.

[20]   See   http://www.europarl.europa.eu/RegData/etudes/etudes/join/2013/507449/IPOL-E MPL_ET%282013%29507449_EN.pdf.

successively examine unionization rates, coverage rates of collective bargaining and union strategies regarding self-employed workers.

3.1   Trade Union Density

According to the OECD (2017) Employment Outlook report, the employees'
unionization rate varies considerably across countries: from 7.7 per cent in
France to 67.3 per cent in Sweden. Conversely, although the report underlines a global steady decline of unionization rates, three countries (Belgium,
Spain and Italy) have experienced a slight increase of membership, while the
membership rates in other countries have declined slightly (except in Slovenia
where a fall of 37 per cent can be observed) during the period covered by the
report. According to the OECD, Slovenia is following a more general trend
of Central and Eastern European countries 'after the fall of central planning'
(OECD 2017, p. 133). For Spain, an interesting explanatory factor of the
evolution of union membership is certainly the increase of unionization
among the self-employed, from 2.5 per cent in 1999 to 6.9 per cent in 2010,
with a peak of 8.7 per cent in 2006.[21] Overall, the affiliation rate in the differ-

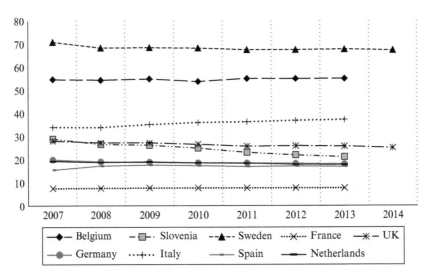

Source: OECD 2017.

Figure 5.2   Employees' unionization rate

---

[21]   See   https://www.eurofound.europa.eu/publications/report/2010/quality-of-life-social-
policies/second-european-quality-of-life-survey-family-life-and-work.

ent countries covered in this volume remains stable, with an average of 30.9 per cent in 2009 and 29.7 per cent in 2013 (Figure 5.2).

There are three clusters of countries. The first group with high unionization rates (higher than 50 per cent) comprises Sweden and Belgium, two countries that have adopted the Ghent system in which unions (partially) take charge of the administration of employment benefits. In Sweden, eligibility for unemployment benefit requires that a fee is paid to an unemployment fund in the appropriate work sector. These funds are governed and organized by the unions. To receive unemployment allowances in Belgium, workers may choose between the services offered by unions and those provided by the government, but the latter is considered as less accessible and less efficient than union schemes. The second group comprises four countries with low unionization rates of less than 20 per cent: Spain, France, Germany and the Netherlands. The third group comprises three countries that display a medium unionization rate: Slovenia, Italy and the UK (Table 5.2).

Table 5.2 Categories of unionization rates

Countries	Unionization rate
Sweden	High
Belgium	High
Slovenia	Medium
Italy	Medium
UK	Medium
Spain	Low
France	Low
Germany	Low
Netherlands	Low

3.2 Coverage of Collective Bargaining in Each Country

Collective bargaining coverage, 'usually computed as the number of employees covered by the collective agreement, divided by the total number of wage and salary-earners' (OECD 2017, p.167), is a useful indicator to measure the impact of social dialogue on the working conditions of all salaried workers. While in some countries collective bargaining only applies to workers and employers who are signatories to agreements, several national regulations have historically adopted *erga omnes* clauses extending agreements to all workers, whether affiliated to unions or not. Two thirds of OECD countries have legally adopted the 'extension' principle through which the legislation imposes collective bargaining agreements on all established employers in the country, not only on members of signing parties (OECD 2017, p. 141). The collective bargaining coverage rate could be influential when considering the working conditions of self-employed workers. Figure 5.3 highlights the evolution of collective bargaining coverage in the nine countries considered in this book.

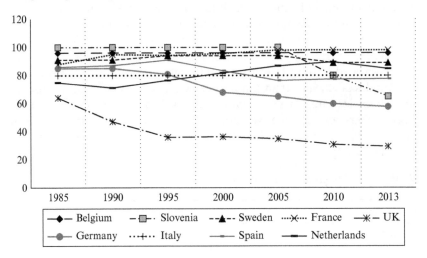

Source: OECD 2017.

*Figure 5.3   Evolution of collective bargaining coverage in the nine
                countries*

Coverage rates are clustered in three categories. Most countries experience a high level of collective bargaining coverage. According to the OECD:

> [A]ll in all, collective bargaining coverage is high and stable only in countries where multi-employer agreements (mainly sectoral or national) are negotiated (even in several of the Southern European countries where trade union density is quite low). A second key element which matters for bargaining coverage is the relative strength, and willingness to negotiate, of employer organizations since they negotiate and sign collective agreements which in most countries then apply to all workers of their affiliated firms. (OECD 2017, p. 137)

The highest rates (80 per cent and over) are found in the countries belonging to the Ghent system (Belgium and Sweden). High rates can, however, be observed in Southern European countries (i.e. Spain, Italy and France). For Northern and Central European countries, a distinction must be made between the Netherlands, where the coverage rate remains high, and

Germany where a fall can be observed since the 1990s (around 60 per cent). Slovenia also faces an important drop in its collective bargaining coverage rate, due to 'the collapse of the old regime [which] led to abrupt changes in the role of trade unions and collective bargaining' (OECD 2017, p. 137). Finally, the UK, where deep reforms took place in the 1980s, experiences the lowest rate in our sample (under 40 per cent) (Table 5.3).

Table 5.3   Collective bargaining coverage

Countries	Collective bargaining coverage
Sweden	High
Spain	High
France	High
Italy	High
Belgium	High
Netherlands	High
Slovenia	Medium
Germany	Medium
UK	Low

3.3   Unions Strategies vis-à-vis Self-Employed Workers

This section characterizes the degree of inclusion of non-standard workers (self-employed, freelancers, etc.) in traditional unions. This issue remains controversial in the literature. Eurofound (2009) stated that 'in recent years trade unions in a number of countries have tried to extend their representation to new groups of workers which are formally self-employed but have a less clear-cut professional identity'. However, Gumbrell-McCormick (2011) asserted that, even if unions have integrated some requests of non-standard workers in collective bargaining, their efforts have remained mainly focused on part-time and temporary workers. Self-employed workers seem to be less concerned by these initiatives and remain 'outside the scope of most trade union activity' (Gumbrell-McCormick 2011, p. 306).

Seven countries can be identified in which more inclusive approaches are taken (i.e. in which union membership is open to self-employed workers). This variable is here considered as an agency factor, reflecting the strategic intent of unions vis-à-vis self-employed workers.

In Italy, at the end of the 1990s, the trade union confederations started to rethink their organizations in order to extend collective representation to a broader category of non-standard workers (Ambra 2013), including self-employed workers. Eurofound explains that these efforts are centred on self-employed workers regarded as 'economically dependent' (Eurofound 2009, p. 43).

In Slovenia, self-employed workers are organized in both associations and unions. Some of these latter (like the Union of Culture and Nature of Slovenia, the Slovenian Union of Journalists and the Union of Emitters of Slovenia) include self-employed issues in negotiations.[22] Moreover, a new union was established in 2016—the Trade Union of the Precarious—within the largest trade union confederation ZSSS. This union voices the concerns of autonomous workers who fall into the category of 'precarious' work, which is mainly composed of self-employed workers.

In the UK, individual trade unions have taken the initiative to develop services and branches for the self-employed in industries where they are highly concentrated, such as journalism, construction, media and entertainment sectors, and creative sectors.[23]

In Spain, a multiplicity of organizations representing self-employed workers can be observed since the early 2000s and the two main trade unions (the Workers' Commissions and the General Union of Workers), along with the Union of Professionals and Self-Employed Workers of Spain, have undertaken the representation of the self-employed under different forms.[24]

In the Netherlands, some units of the trade union movement have been established to offer a specific representation of self-employed workers: FNV Zelfstandigen and CNV Zelfstandigen: 'They provide services to members, especially consultancy on contractual and legal matters, and act as pressure groups' (Eurofound 2009, p. 47).

In Germany, 'besides the many trade associations that protect the interests of self-employed workers mainly on a professional basis, a number of trade unions organize self-employed workers as well as employees' (Eurofound 2009, p. 40), meaning that all workers are free to join a trade union. We must add that interesting initiatives have been developed by unions in order to defend dependent self-employed against lay-offs (Holst 2008).

In Sweden, most unions have realized that self-employed workers are important to reach and 'get onboard'. During the 1990s, increasing numbers of Swedish trade unions developed a more welcoming attitude towards accepting self-employed people as union members. This fact may

---

[22] See https://www.eurofound.europa.eu/publications/report/2009/slovenia-self-employ ed-workers.

[23] See https://www.eurofound.europa.eu/es/publications/report/2009/uk-self-employed-workers.

[24] See https://www.eurofound.europa.eu/publications/report/2009/spain-self-employed-workers.

be seen as a response to changes in the labour market.[25] Furthermore, the Swedish trade union Unionen (organizing white-collar workers) which by membership is now the biggest union in Sweden, offers various services to the self-employed.[26] It has worked intensely to organize firm-tax permit holders and lobby for reformation of Swedish social security systems.

When unions open their membership to non-standard workers, two categories of strategies may be considered.[27] Most unions have adopted the *servicing model*, that is, offering specific legal, fiscal and social support to new categories of members. For instance, the Swedish journalists union has developed a 'service company' catering to freelancers by providing legal and professional advice, support with taxes and administration, customized insurance for freelance journalists and professional development courses. Servicing activities are also significant in Spain since the motivation of self-employed to choose a union has to do more with the nature of services provided.

Nevertheless, many unions also offer larger support to non-standard workers by organizing collective mobilization through methods and actions transferred from the most organized segments (*organizing model*). Charhon and Murphy's (2016) study of the media, arts and entertainment sectors highlights various original initiatives such as advanced training packages (Netherlands Union of Journalists), use of social media and digital tools in order to raise awareness and share information (Swedish Confederation of Professional Employees), 'fair play guides' for both venue promoters and artists in order to support decent places to work for fair compensation (UK Musicians' Union), and so on. In Slovenia, we have already mentioned that the Union of the Precarious aims at protecting the rights of precarious workers. Another recent union has addressed students and young unemployed—Young Plus—and intends to 'offer particularly legal security, advice and representation'.[28] In Germany, most union initiatives go beyond the simple servicing model. Verband der Gründer und Selbständigen e.V., for instance, promotes campaigns against tax dodging, in support of professional careers, for the inclusion of freelancers in the welfare system. Bundesverband der Dolmetscher und Übersetzer e.V., the largest association of technical translators in Germany, has developed a strong lobbying activity towards national institutions in order

---

[25] See https://www.eurofound.europa.eu/publications/article/1999/trade-unions-open-their-doors-to-the-self-employed.

[26] See https://www.unionen.se/in-english/membership-self-employed.

[27] Unions may also offer specific activities to self-employed workers in some economic sectors, but they are not taken into account here in order to keep the transnational comparison as simple as possible.

[28] RTV Slovenija (2016).

to achieve, for example, higher minimum prices. In Italy, most initiatives seem to develop organizing actions, such as the Association of Atypical and Temporary Workers (*Associazione Lavoratori Atipici e Interinali*), that gather nonstandard workers whose aim is to enlarge collective representation to the new forms of work. In Spain, organizations representing the interests of self-employed workers undertake specific lobbying actions in order, for example, to modify the calculation of social security contributions. Such voicing actions have been facilitated by the creation of the Self-Employment Council a consultative body whose role is to assist the government in the regulations concerning the self-employed.

By contrast, in Belgium and France, unions persist in excluding self-employed workers from their membership. In France, the global trend is exclusion even if some local initiatives have been undertaken for self-employed in specific situations,[29] as noted by Eurofound: 'In France, some trade unions organize self-employed workers or "independent professionals" who are assimilated by the Labour Code as employees: this is the case, for instance, for freelance journalists (so-called "pigistes"), but also artists and fashion models' (Eurofound 2009, p. 42). In Belgium, beyond the willingness of the National Federation of White-Collar Workers to create a new specific union for freelancers, the opportunity to affiliate these new types of workers is still under discussion. Currently, self-employed workers cannot be affiliated to a trade union and are supposed to be represented on the employer side in (inter-)sectorial social dialogue (Table 5.4).

Table 5.4   Union strategies vis-à-vis self-employed workers

Countries	Unions' strategies
Sweden	Inclusive
Slovenia	Inclusive
Spain	Inclusive
Netherlands	Inclusive
UK	Inclusive
Italy	Inclusive
Germany	Inclusive
Belgium	Exclusive
France	Exclusive

[29]   In France, discussions are under way with CGT and CFDT. See https://syndicollectif.fr/la-cfdt-veut-organiser-les-travailleurs-independants/ and https://www.lesechos.fr/13/12/2016/LesEchos/22338-012-ECH_independants--vtc---les-syndicats-commencent-a-voir-au-dela-du-salariat.htm.

4. FISCAL SUPPORT TO SELF-EMPLOYMENT

Numerous fiscal policy measures aim to enhance business opportunities for self-employed workers. For example, in Belgium, since 1 March 2017, a reduced taxation system has been in place to support the rise of the digital economy. If an individual worker provides a service via a collaborative platform, the user must pay directly the platform, which will deduct fees and taxes. Such a favourable taxation system (10 per cent instead of 33 per cent) is limited to additional revenues below €5,000 per year generated via platforms certified by the public fiscal authorities.[30] Beyond this amount, workers are considered as being professionals and are subject to the classical tax regimes for self-employed. It is clearly a way to promote small-scale entrepreneurial activities in the digital economy. Furthermore, the administrative burdens are minimal for such workers: for example, they do not have to meet the Crossroad Bank for Enterprises registration requirements.

Public authorities often present fiscal measures as a way to support new work arrangements in the digital economy. However, these measures can encourage workers to develop their business activities without imposing any specific work status. Therefore, many of them may choose an informal status, being neither an employee nor self-employed, which paves the way to an increasing black market.

In order to avoid a detailed presentation of fiscal measures in each national context, we will consider three main categories: financial incentives to the development of business activities as a self-employed worker; tax or social contribution exemptions; and access to loans at preferential rates. The following procedures were used to cluster the different countries: if the three categories of measures are implemented, a score of 3 ('high') is given. If two measures only are implemented, the proposed score is 2 ('medium'). With only one measure, the score is 1 ('low') (Table 5.5). This exercise must be regarded with caution because the three fiscal measures under consideration combine elements of different nature and scope. However, the method provides an interesting global overview of the fiscal protection offered to self-employed workers across Europe.

5. THE SCOPE OF SOCIAL PROTECTION

The level of social protection independent professionals can access in each country largely depends on the work category in which they are classified.

---

[30] This amount was increased to €6,000 in 2018.

Table 5.5　Fiscal support to self-employment

Countries	Financial incentives	Tax or social contribution exemption	Access to loan at preferential rate	N =
France	ESPN/NR	ESPN/NR	ESPN/NR	3
Belgium	ESPN/NR	NR	NONE	2
Netherlands	ESPN/NR	ESPN/NR	ESPN/NR	3
Germany	ESPN/NR	NR	ESPN	3
Italy	NR	ESPN/NR	ESPN	3
UK	ESPN/NR	NONE	NONE	1
Slovenia	ESPN	ESPN/NR	NONE	2
Sweden	ESPN	ESPN/NR	ESPN	3
Spain	ESPN/NR	ESPN/NR	ESPN	3

We must admit that social protection not always supports the changing nature of work, which may create important gaps in terms of social rights. In many countries, self-employed workers do not enjoy the same statutory social security schemes as employees. Accessibility (eligibility conditions which are often hard to meet) and the level of social protection (amount of grant, duration, level of coverage) may vary significantly. Self-employed workers may receive lower benefits than standard workers because they pay lower social contributions and/or the income basis on which benefits are calculated is more volatile.[31]

In addition, it must be remembered that the population of independent professionals is heterogeneous: due to their multiple activities, many of them juggle different legal statuses, which usually results in more complexity and fragmentation of rights. If the social protection system distinguishes different regimes with accessibility determined by income thresholds, it can be even more difficult for individual workers to access benefits whatever their social/legal status.

We will first consider the social protection offered to self-employed in general and then focus on the situation of workers provided with specific institutional recognition where it does exist.

5.1　Social Protection for Self-Employed Workers

The comparative Table 5.6 was constructed by referring to the following primary source material: the national reports produced within the I-Wire project; the Mutual Information System on Social Protection (MISSOC)

---

[31]　European Commission (2017, p. 24).

Table 5.6 Social security schemes for self-employed workers

Country	Old age and survivor's pension	Maternity, paternity cash benefits and benefits in kind	Healthcare	Sickness Benefits	Unemployment Insurance	Family benefits	Invalidity, Occupational accident/disease insurance
Sweden	**Universal** (access to an income-related pension and a guaranteed pension)	**Compulsory** insured.	**Universal** and almost free of charge	**Compulsory** Self-employed can apply for sickness benefits (less favourable benefits for freelancers)	**Universal** and compulsory but workers must stop all their activities + one voluntary system (small fee to pay)	**Universal** Applies to **all** families	**Universal**[1]
Germany[2]	**Choice between** statutory or private insurance, in principle,[3] no statutory social pension insurance for self-employed	**Choice between** voluntary insurance in the public scheme or private health insurance	**Compulsory** health insurance for any worker Self-employed member of the private system can **voluntarily enter** the statutory health insurance system	**Compulsory** affiliation to private or public health insurance	**Cannot claim unemployment benefits**	**Compulsory** The general system applies	**Voluntary members, compulsory for certain** groups of self-employed
Spain	Universal **(compulsory)**	**Compulsory** Similar to standard employees	**Mandatorily insured**	**Compulsory** for the RETA scheme + TRADE	Can join **voluntarily:** cessation of business	**Compulsory** Same conditions except for	**Voluntary** for the self-employed, **compulsory** for TRADE

Table 5.6 (continued)

Country	Old age and survivor's pension	Maternity, paternity cash benefits and benefits in kind	Healthcare	Sickness Benefits	Unemployment Insurance	Family benefits	Invalidity, Occupational accident/ disease insurance
					activity benefit[4] (special tax for unemployment)	the first two years of parental leave	
Netherlands	Almost identical. The third pillar (voluntary individual pension savings arrangements) is used more often by self-employed	**Compulsory** Self-employed do have the right to maternity benefits, but only to the minimum wage (16 weeks of maternity leave, 3 days of paternity leave)	**Compulsorily insured**	Can insure themselves either through public or private insurance[5]	**No unemployment insurance system**	**Universal** (identical)	**None**, can opt for voluntary insurance (work incapacity)
Slovenia	**Compulsory insured** + arising from the invalidity insurance	For all persons covered by pension and disability insurance, e.g. persons on employment contract +	**Compulsory** Contribution rates are more or less the same (for standard and non-standard contracts);	**Compulsory insured** Self-employed are entitled only after 30 days of illness (80% of compensation)	**Compulsory insured** Eligible if not unemployed by their own will or fault	**Universal** Entitlements are based on permanent residence and actual residence in Slovenia	Covered by **compulsory** health and pensions and invalidity insurance

158

	Pension	Maternity	Health care	Sickness	Unemployment	Work accidents	Invalidity / other
France	**Compulsory** (except for liberal professions) — compulsory self-employed + temporary agency workers; the amount of contributions paid depends on the definition of contribution bases	**Compulsory** Maternity benefits: Less favourable	**Universal protection** (2016): identical contribution rates	**Compulsory** In line with the general system (waiting period of 3 days in case of hospitalization or 7 days in other cases)	**No unemployment insurance system** but self-employed can claim the RSA[6]	**Compulsory** The general system applies	**Not compulsory, voluntary** members (Invalidity: compulsory)
Italy	Own insurance system for the regulated professions + co.co.co **compulsorily insured**	Maternity insurance: fewer weeks off. Maternity leave not compulsory (for the non-regulated professions). Self-employed have lower likelihood of accessing public services than other types of households	National Health System (available to all residents): **universal**	Right to sickness benefits (for members of *gestione separata*)[7]: self-employed must pay contributions during 3 months in the 12 last months before illness	**Does not exist in Italy** (except for semi-subordinate workers: DIS-COLL)[8]	**Compulsory** Partial benefits, no benefits for licensed professions	According to the qualifying conditions provided within their special scheme (Invalidity: compulsory)

Table 5.6 (continued)

Country	Old age and survivor's pension	Maternity, paternity cash benefits and benefits in kind	Healthcare	Sickness Benefits	Unemployment Insurance	Family benefits	Invalidity, Occupational accident/ disease insurance
UK	**Compulsorily covered** (Statutory pension scheme), excluded from the additional state pension system New single tiers pension: National Insurance Contributions on a equal basis (between self-employed and employed)	No access to the maternity or paternity pay, can qualify for insurance-based benefits, can claim the maternity allowances No maternity leave for the workers	**Universal** Provided free at the point of need by the National Health Service	No access to the statutory sick pay for the self-employed, who are eligible to the contributory Employment and Support Allowances (means-tested, tax-financed benefit)	Does not exist for self-employed, who can claim the income-based jobseeker's allowance (means-tested benefits)	**Universal** The general system applies	**Not compulsory**: no special protection afforded
Belgium	**Compulsory insured**, if the self-employed can demonstrate a career equal to 2/3 of a full	**Compulsory** for maternity benefits Exemption of paying the social security	**Compulsorily insured** (Same entitlement and reimbursement in healthcare	**Compulsorily insured** (1 month waiting period, lump-sum payment)	**No protection system** but there is a special social insurance in case of bankruptcy (Gateway law)	**Compulsorily** insured	**Invalidity: compulsory insured** No protection system for the accident at work and

160

				occupational disease
Belgium	career, they can claim minimum pension	contributions (during the maternity leave) 4 weeks of maternity leave (3 are compulsory and 12 weeks are possible): no obligation to use up all weeks	as regular employees)	

Notes:

1. Freelancer must pay for their liability insurance.
2. In Craft and Commerce sectors.
3. There is a multitude of derogations: teachers, lecturers, child minders, etc. (ESPN DE 2017, p.12).
4. See the 'cessation of business activity benefit' (Spasova et al. 2017, p.38).
5. 'The level of benefits depends on the daily wage level for which they have chosen to insure themselves, which in turn determines their monthly insurance premium' (ESPN NL, 2017, p.12).
6. In French: revenu de solidarité active.
7. Self-employed in commerce and craftsmen do not have any type of statutory/compulsory sickness insurance (ESPN IT 2017, p.9).
8. They enjoy rights concerning insurance against sickness, maternity, accident at work and family benefits that are similar to those of employees (although benefits are usually less generous). European Parliament, IP/A/MPL/ST/2012-02, 2012, p.49.

161

database;[32] and recent documents of the European Commission (Access to social protection for people working on non-standard contracts and as self-employed in Europe, 2017;[33] Second phase consultation of social partners under Article 154 TFEU on a possible action addressing the challenges of access to social protection for people in all forms of employment in the framework of the European Pillar of Social Rights, 2017[34]).

In Sweden, the system of social protection does not discriminate between employees and self-employed workers. This system is thus fundamentally founded on the principle of national insurance,[35] meaning that any self-employed person can enjoy the social protection of the general system. Access to social benefits is based either on residence or work in Sweden. All types of social benefits result from the individual income of labour. For individuals with no income, there is minimum social security coverage. Parental leave has three different compensation levels, depending on income (and not on work status). Pension insurance or even occupational accident/disease insurance applies to self-employed workers as well as to employees. Access to unemployment benefits requires that a self-employed worker can show that all activity related to their business has stopped and a guarantee that unemployment benefits will not become a supplementary income. If the self-employed activity is reactivated, the worker is excluded from unemployment benefits for a period of five years in order to reduce the risk of social fraud. This rule can thus discourage workers from applying for unemployment benefits (Commission Staff Working Document: European Commission 2017, p. 39).[36] During sickness, the compensation usually amounts to 80 per cent of income (for everybody); there are, however, some differences between groups (regarding the number of qualifying days, a maximum amount of sickness and maternity pay of around €1,500 per month for independent contractors, or the level of compensation which is higher for employees, thanks to collective bargaining agreements).

In Slovenia, there is one integral social insurance and social security system covering employees, self-employed workers, public servants and other groups of the population. During the last twenty years, social security legislation has gone through numerous changes, and forms a very complex system. Self-employed workers in the field of culture can ask the

---

[32]   See https://www.missoc.org/missoc-database/.
[33]   See https://publications.europa.eu/en/publication-detail/-/publication/fb235634-e3a7-11e7-9749-01aa75ed71a1/language-en.
[34]   See https://ec.europa.eu/social/BlobServlet?docId=18309&langId=en.
[35]   See http://www.missoc.org/MISSOC//INFORMATIONBASE/COUNTRYSPECIFICDESCS/SELFEMPLOYED/2017_01/SE-Self-01-17-EN.pdf.
[36]   See https://ec.europa.eu/social/BlobServlet?docId=18596&langId=en.

government to pay their contributions.[37] If self-employed workers are sick for more than thirty days, they are entitled to 80 per cent compensation, calculated from the mandatory contributions paid during the previous calendar year. As far as maternal/parental leave is concerned, the self-employed are entitled to parental benefits (if they have social security insurance the day before the start of the leave or have been insured for at least twelve months in the previous three years). It is important to note that in practice, the position of self-employed workers is not the same as regular employees. Their wages are often very low. When they are ill, they receive minimum wage compensation. A high proportion of self-employed workers pay social contributions by reference to the minimum base. Consequently, they are entitled to the minimum old-age pension (ESPN SI 2017).

In Spain, there is a special scheme for self-employed workers (RETA) in craft, commerce and other areas, and another for self-employed agricultural workers. There is also a special scheme for maritime workers. Approved by the Spanish government in 2007, the main aim of the schemes is to bring social security entitlements of self-employed workers closer to those offered to employees.[38] Self-employed workers have to pay their social protection fees (an overall 29.80 per cent) in an integral and non-progressive way (for healthcare benefits in the event of sickness and maternity, invalidity insurance, old-age provision and death benefits for survivors).[39] This subsystem (RETA) includes some innovative elements such as benefits for the stoppage of activities, social protection for temporary sickness and an early retirement option (that covers self-employed workers involved in toxic, dangerous or painful economic activities). The 2007 legislation has also introduced measures in the field of maternity and parental leave, thereby creating more equality between workers. Self-employed can voluntarily join the social security scheme regarding accidents at work and occupational injuries benefits, as well as unemployment benefits.

In Germany, most of the social security system (offering individuals a comparatively high degree of protection against social risks) is available via voluntary participation, so that self-employed workers can enjoy a somewhat comparable level of protection (Schmid-Drüner 2013, p.48). They are, however, excluded from unemployment benefits. There are four

---

[37] See https://www.eurofound.europa.eu/publications/report/2009/slovenia-self-employ ed-workers.

[38] See https://www.eurofound.europa.eu/observatories/eurwork/comparative-informati on/self-employed-workers-industrial-relations-and-working-conditions#seccion0000.

[39] See http://www.missoc.org/MISSOC//INFORMATIONBASE/COUNTRYSPECIFI CDESCS/SELFEMPLOYED/2017_01/ES-Self-01-17-EN.pdf.

different social security schemes: for farmers, for self-employed artists and publicists, for employees and for traditional liberal professions with professional chambers. Admitted self-employed artists have to pay half of the contributions due: *Künstlersozialkasse* (KSK) contributes the remaining amount from a federal subsidy (20 per cent) and social contributions from companies that use services of artists and journalists (30 per cent).[40] Traditional liberal professions have their own self-financed schemes (managed by professional associations) assuring compulsory coverage for old age, invalidity and survivors on the basis of national law provisions.

In the UK, the overall picture is characterized by an average lower rate of contributions levied by self-employed workers compared to their counterpart in wage work. Self-employed workers have no access to maternity or paternity pay although maternity allowances are payable to women 'who [have] been self-employed in at least 26 weeks out of the 66 weeks, ending with the week before the baby is due'.[41] There is no protection system regarding unemployment or even occupational disease or accident at work for self-employed workers. They can qualify for the contributory state basic retirement pensions (on the same basis as employees) but they are excluded from the additional state pension, even if important progress has been realized with the reform of the UK's state pension system, starting in 2016/17 with the new single-tier state pension. This system treats the national insurance contributions from self-employed and employees on an equal basis.

In the Netherlands, 'the general protection system applies as a rule to all residents of the Netherlands'.[42] There are a few special regulations excluding self-employed workers from social insurance schemes against risks (sickness, disability, old age and unemployment). They only qualify for the basic collective old-age pension. In case of maternity or family allowances, they are entitled to the same benefits as anybody else (Schulze Buschoff and Schmidt 2009, p. 156). In 2004, social security for self-employed workers was reduced (due to the abolition of their own income-based insurance). The Netherlands is one of the rare countries in which self-employed workers can decide to opt into private or public insurance schemes regarding invalidity (Spasova et al. 2017, p. 40).

In Belgium, there are three social security schemes: one for salaried, one for self-employed and one for civil servants. Self-employed workers are covered by a special system against all traditional risks (except for

---

[40]   See http://www.kuenstlersozialkasse.de/die-ksk/die-kuenstlersozialkasse.html.
[41]   See https://www.gov.uk/maternity-allowance/eligibility.
[42]   See http://www.missoc.org/MISSOC//INFORMATIONBASE/COUNTRYSPECIFI CDESCS/SELFEMPLOYED/2017_01/NL-Self-01-17-EN.pdf.

accident at work, occupational disease and unemployment).[43] Compared to the regular employees' scheme, social rights of the self-employed are lower. Furthermore, there is no protection system against unemployment, despite special insurance in case of bankruptcy, forced discontinuation or economic difficulties. However, insurance for sickness and maternity is compulsory for self-employed persons, helpers and assisting spouses (as well as invalidity insurance, a retirement pension system and family benefits).

In France, the social protection system distinguishes employees and self-employed. Furthermore, 'supplementary schemes for the self-employed workers are subject to different heterogeneous rules within the same professional category' (Spasova et al. 2017, p. 37). Four different regimes are provided: the general scheme, the agricultural scheme (MSA), the scheme for self-employed workers[44] (known as *Régime Social des Indépendants* (RSI)) and a separate scheme for liberal professions (CNAVPL) (even if they also come under the RSI insofar as sickness insurance is concerned).[45] Despite the standardization of many schemes in order to improve accessibility to non-standard workers and self-employed, significant differences remain concerning the distribution rates and protection afforded. There is no compulsory system, for example, that covers the risk of accident in the workplace or unemployment, even if there is a specific unemployment insurance system for workers in the entertainment and audio-visual industry: under certain conditions linked to their intermittent status, artists and entertainment workers receive unemployment benefits every day off (Bureau and Corsani 2016). However, new important reforms are planned by the current president of the French Republic. One of them concerns the right for self-employed workers to benefit from unemployment allowances. Until now, self-employed workers have not enjoyed any protection against the risk of job loss. It is indeed difficult to determine the risks against which self-employed workers must be protected, since they constitute a heterogeneous category of workers (Charpin et al. 2017), and that is why the problem remains under discussion. Moreover, the RSI has been finally removed, leading to a general system of social protection for both employees and self-employed, and the financing of unemployment insurance benefits via taxation.

In Italy, there is no homogeneous social security system applicable to all

---

[43] See http://www.missoc.org/MISSOC//INFORMATIONBASE/COUNTRYSPECIFI CDESCS/SELFEMPLOYED/2017_01/BE-Self-01-17-EN.pdf.

[44] i.e. craftsmen, retailers and manufacturers.

[45] See http://www.missoc.org/MISSOC//INFORMATIONBASE/COUNTRYSPECIFI CDESCS/SELFEMPLOYED/2017_01/FR-Self-01-17-EN.pdf.

self-employed workers but there are differences that trace back to a dualism in the regulatory framework between the regulated and the non-regulated professions. The social security system for self-employed workers is dominated by a lack of protections: they are excluded from pension funds, unemployment insurance and sickness schemes. The dual system of liberal professions (regulated versus non-regulated professions) is crucial in the perspective of social protection. Professional registers effectively control access to regulated professions, and provide the self-employed with specific private social protection schemes. By contrast, non-regulated professions lack the majority of these social protections. Self-employed workers in associative professions and semi-subordinate workers (co.co.co and co.co. pro) are thus requested to contribute to the Separate Management Fund of the National Institute of Social Security (their enrolment is compulsory).

It is evident that specific social protection schemes for self-employed workers are present in Belgium, Spain, Germany, the Netherlands, France and Italy. Furthermore, specific social protection schemes have been developed for some categories of workers (e.g. artists) within the general social status of salaried or self-employed workers (Table 5.7).

Table 5.7   Social protection schemes

Countries	Specific schemes	Non-specific schemes
Sweden		Universal system
Slovenia		One integral social insurance
Spain	Employees, RETA, REA	
Germany	Farmers, artists and publicist (*KSK)* employees, liberal professions	
UK		Lower rates of contributions
Netherlands	Not included in the social security system for employees	
Belgium	Employees, self-employed and civil servants	
France	4 different regimes (MSA, RSI, General, CNAVPL)	
Italy	General system + INPS (*gestione separata*)	

Globally, the self-employed are required to be insured for sickness protection (Belgium, Germany, Spain, France, Sweden, Slovenia and the UK) but they are subject to different eligibility conditions or have less favourable benefits compared to those of employees (Belgium, France, Slovenia and the UK). In Italy and in the Netherlands, self-employed workers are not compulsorily covered by sickness insurance.

As far as maternity/paternity schemes are concerned, self-employed are mandatorily insured (Belgium, Spain, France and Italy). They can qualify for insurance-based benefits in the UK, but are excluded from employer-provided maternity/paternity benefits (Spasova et al. 2017, p. 35). There is no independent statutory protection system for craftsmen and retailers in Germany regarding maternity benefits.[46] In Slovenia, self-employed are insured for parental protection and have the right to parental leave and parental benefits. In Sweden, parental insurance is universal (based either on residence or on work).

The self-employed are mandatorily covered by statutory pension schemes in Belgium, Sweden, Spain, Slovenia, France, Italy and the UK. In Germany, self-employed can choose between the statutory system and private insurance. In the Netherlands, self-employed only qualify for the basic collective old-age pension (they have to make specific arrangements on a personal level in order to increase their pension to an acceptable level).

According to the ESPN report (Spasova et al. 2017, p. 27), 'unemployment benefits are among the social benefit schemes which are the most difficult to access for some non-standard workers and the self-employed in general'. In some countries, the self-employed do not have any access to unemployment benefits (Belgium, Germany, France, Italy, Netherlands and the UK). However, in Belgium, there is the 'Gateway Law' (social insurance in case of bankruptcy) and in Italy, semi-subordinate workers are eligible for unemployment allowances. In Spain, the self-employed can *voluntarily* join a specific unemployment protection scheme while in Sweden and Slovenia, they are compulsorily insured against unemployment.

Employers are usually responsible for insuring workers against the risks of accident at work and occupational disease. This is why most self-employed workers do not access this protection, except in Italy, Sweden and Slovenia. In France, the UK and Belgium, the self-employed are not compulsorily insured against such risks. In Germany, France and Spain, self-employed can voluntarily join either the public scheme or a private insurance, which can be very expensive, especially for those with low incomes. Dutch self-employed workers are the only ones who can decide to opt into either public or private insurance schemes regarding permanent invalidity.

Family benefits do not depend on employment status. It is thus a universal payment in most countries (Spasova et al. 2017, p. 41). The self-

---

[46]   See http://www.missoc.org/MISSOC//INFORMATIONBASE/COUNTRYSPECIFI CDESCS/SELFEMPLOYED/2017_01/DE-Self-01-17-EN.pdf.

employed receive only partial family benefits in Italy. Furthermore, there is no family benefit for liberal professions. In other countries, the general system applies.

5.2 Degrees of Social Protection

5.2.1 Social protection under the binary approach
Belgium, France, Sweden and the Netherlands do not provide any specific institutional recognition of working situations located between classical self-employment and employment: as mentioned earlier, these countries have adopted a binary approach to working situations. But what does that mean in terms of social protection?

In Belgium, the Netherlands and France, self-employed workers are excluded from unemployment insurance. In Belgium, there is no protection system offered to self-employed workers for an accident at work and occupational disease; in the Netherlands, self-employed workers can opt voluntarily for protection against these risks. In the Netherlands, however, own-account self-employed who regularly work for one principal have all the rights of employees and are compulsorily subject to statutory insurance. Generally speaking, we can consider the social protection of self-employed in these three countries as limited.

By contrast, in Sweden, all types of social benefits are based on individual labour incomes. The Swedish welfare state is universal, with a national system of social insurance that includes all groups whatever their status. Therefore, the social protection of self-employed must be considered as full.

5.2.2 Social protection under the hybrid approach
Italy, Germany, the UK, Slovenia and Spain provide a specific institutional recognition of working situations located between classical employment and self-employment. As mentioned earlier, they have adopted a hybrid approach. We will see that here again, the social protection offered to self-employed workers varies strongly.

In Italy, semi-subordinated contracts lead to some social security rights which are not open to other classical self-employed, such as unemployment benefits and sickness benefits if self-employed workers do not contribute to other compulsory social security funds. Semi-subordinate workers are thus 'slightly better off in terms of social security provisions than other categories of self-employed' (European Parliament 2013, p. 49). Such self-employed are compulsorily insured through a special regime managed by the National Institute for Social Security (INPS). The payment of social security contributions is split between the worker (one third) and the client (two thirds). Even though self-employed workers on semi-subordinated contracts are entitled to some social rights not open to classical self-employed workers, the social protection offered to them is subject to several restrictions. It must be added that these specific forms of contracts are not often used. Globally speaking, Italian self-employed workers have thus limited access to social protection whatever their form of contract.

In Germany, classical self-employed are excluded from unemployment insurance. 'Employee-like' workers (*arbeitnehmerähnliche personen*) are 'neither "ordinary" self-employed workers nor employees' (Waas and Heerma van Voss 2017). The term is mentioned in several acts (e.g. the 1969 Collective Agreements Act). They 'are considered to be in need of social protection because of their economic dependency on their principal' (Schulze Buschoff and Schmidt 2009, p. 152). Employee-like persons, while remaining self-employed, enjoy some rights of employees because they are recognized as weaker than classical self-employed workers. Their social protection needs are therefore presumed to be somewhat higher. Nevertheless, many of them do not claim their rights because they are not informed about them or they are not aware of their economic dependency. The global social protection of self-employed workers in Germany thus remains limited.

In the UK, classical self-employed are excluded from occupational accidents/disease insurance. Some legal protections (working time regulations, minimum wage conditions, no discrimination) apply to the hybrid category of workers, but the right to be protected against unfair dismissal and to receive redundancy allowances only relates to employees. 'In terms of employment law, a worker has fewer rights than an employee' (ESPN UK 2017, p. 5). Once again, even though the situation of workers may be considered as slightly better, social protection rights remain limited when not categorized as an employee.

In Slovenia, with the recent amendment of the Employment Relationship Act (ERA), the legislation has defined the category of economically dependent workers. Such workers 'are entitled to limited legal job protection related to the prohibition of discrimination, provision of minimum notice period, prohibition of cancellation of a contract in cases of unfounded reasons for cancellation, enforcement of liability for damage and assurance of payment for contractually agreed work' (Article 214 of ERA-1). However, they enjoy full access to social security, like any self-employed worker (ESPN SI 2017). Therefore the social protection of self-employed workers must be considered as full, even though the general level of protection in Slovenia remains low compared to richer EU countries like Sweden.

In Spain, classical self-employed workers are not compulsorily covered by one or more insurance based-schemes (unemployment insurance and occupational accident/illness insurance) but they can opt in. Economically dependent self-employed workers (TRADE) have access to some legal protection regarding annual leave, collective bargaining and unjustified dismissal (Heyes and Hastings 2017, p. 13). They are included in the RETA scheme and have similar access to social protection as any regular employee under the general scheme. The only significant difference is that the insurance for accidents at work and occupational illness is voluntary for classical self-employed workers and compulsory for TRADE (ESPN SP 2017, p. 40). Their social security protection is thus a little bit higher compared to classical self-employed workers. Furthermore, TRADE are entitled to holidays, rest between workdays, limited duration of work assignments, notice in the event of unilateral termination of the contract with the possibility of compensation when sufficient causes are identified for the temporary suspension of the employment relationship, all provided for under 2007 government legislation. In a nutshell, the social protection of Spanish self-employed workers and TRADE may be considered midway between full and limited access, due to the opt-in system for some insurance-based schemes.

To summarize, three degrees in the social protection of self-employed workers can be distinguished (Table 5.8):

- limited (self-employed are excluded from one or more schemes and cannot opt in)
- medium (self-employed are insured under all schemes, sometimes via opt-in solutions)
- full (self-employed are insured either universally or compulsorily under all schemes).

Table 5.8   *Degrees of social protection for self-employed workers per country*

Degree of coverage	Full	Medium	Limited
Countries	Slovenia, Sweden	Spain	Belgium, France, Italy, UK, Netherlands, Germany

5.3   Towards a Better Social Protection for Self-Employed Workers?

We are now in position to explore the main interrelations between the aforementioned institutional factors and the level of social protection offered to self-employed workers. This analysis might directly feed the current debate on the appropriate social regulation for new independent professionals and other categories of autonomous workers (Stewart and Stanford 2017). We will survey each factor separately and discuss its potential impact on the level of social protection.

5.3.1   Creation of a third status

The creation of a third status between classical employment and self-employment is often presented as a relevant institutional answer to respond to the specific working situations of new independent professionals. If the Slovenian context seems to support this position, our transversal analysis provides a much more nuanced view.

In the UK, Italy and Germany, where the hybrid approach has been adopted, social security protection offered to self-employed workers remains limited. The institutional recognition of specific working situations between classical employment and self-employment may be attractive for users only, who can pay lower social security contributions compared to regular employees and benefit from more flexible contracts. In such conditions, the hybrid approach appears as a low-cost alternative to fixed-term and permanent contracts, and does not necessarily lead to better social security rights for self-employed workers. This is probably why in some countries (Spain and Germany), such hybrid statuses are not very successful: their complexity and lack of attractiveness for both workers and users has hindered any massive development so far.

By contrast, the Swedish binary approach—with a distinction between salaried and self-employed workers—leads to a much higher level of social protection. It must be remembered that the Swedish social security system is based on the principle of national insurance, which means that any worker—whatever his/her status—can enjoy the (high) level of social protection offered in this country.

Therefore, the creation of a third status may not be considered as a sustainable solution per se.

5.3.2   Fiscal support

Different fiscal measures can be introduced to support business opportunities for self-employed workers: financial incentives, tax or social contributions exemptions and access to loans at preferential rates.

In Belgium, for example, a specific taxation system has been introduced for autonomous workers in the gig economy (10 per cent instead of 33 per cent), limited to additional revenues below €5,000 per year. Beyond this amount, workers are subject to the usual tax regimes of the self-employed. This kind of financial measure does not provide any legal protection in terms of minimum wage, liability of users in cases of accidents at work, and so on. The problem becomes crucial when platform managers can determine the work of contributors through maximal prices or sanctions in case they do not want to work or do not work to a high enough standard (Lambrecht 2016, p. 22).

In France, the micro-entrepreneur regime is open to self-employed workers pursuing small-scale activities: 31 per cent of self-employed (excluding agricultural activities) are economically active micro-entrepreneurs. But a significant amount of self-employed workers are affected by poverty: they represent 27 per cent of the 461,000 working poor and a majority of them work as micro-entrepreneurs (ESPN FR 2017, p. 6).

To conclude, specific fiscal measures, if they can contribute to the growth of business activities developed by self-employed workers, do not offer them any progress in terms of social protection.

5.3.3 Inclusiveness of union strategies

In recent years, trade unions have tried to extend their representation by opening their membership to new groups of workers. Inclusive strategies vis-à-vis self-employed workers have been detected in seven countries out of the nine. In Germany for example, unions succeeded in defending dependent self-employed against lay-offs (Holst 2008). Inclusive strategies do not, however, guarantee a high level of social protection for self-employed workers. In Italy, the UK, the Netherlands and Germany—where unions have adopted inclusive strategies—their social security rights remain limited, exactly like in France and Belgium, where exclusive union strategies are observed.

Therefore the presence of inclusive union strategies vis-à-vis self-employed workers cannot help us to predict the level of social protection offered to them in a particular national context.

5.3.4 Collective bargaining coverage

Collective bargaining coverage is a useful indicator to measure the impact of social dialogue on the working conditions of salaried workers. In some countries, collective bargaining only applies to the signing parties, while in others agreements are extended to all workers (whether affiliated to trade unions or not). Collective bargaining coverage could be influential when considering the working conditions of self-employed workers. A high coverage rate can indeed represent an isomorphic pressure (DiMaggio and

Powell 1983), likely to become a common target for all categories of workers. Spain seems to confirm this tendency: with a high rate of collective bargaining coverage, medium social protection is offered to self-employed workers. Conversely, the UK, with a low collective bargaining coverage rate, does not provide a high level of social protection. However, Belgium and France, countries with the highest rates of collective bargaining coverage in the EU, offer limited social protection to self-employed workers. By contrast, Slovenia faces an important drop in its collective bargaining coverage but self-employed workers still benefit from high social protection.

We must once again conclude that collective bargaining coverage cannot guarantee, per se, sustainable social protection for self-employed workers.

6.   CONCLUSION

If we consider separately each of the institutional factors studied throughout this transnational chapter, we are not able to predict the quality and the level of social protection likely to be offered to new independent professionals. Such factors must probably be combined to explain the diverse situations observed in each country. A contextual approach is thus needed. However, traditional explanations in terms of varieties of capitalism (Hall and Soskice 2001) or again in terms of welfare states (Esping-Andersen 1990) cannot directly help in interpretation of the differences of social protection displayed in Table 5.8. The time periods and the countries concerned in our analysis are indeed different. Moreover, the structure of risks is changing, generating new challenges to be faced. However, the key variables taken into account by Esping-Andersen (1990) are still relevant for studying contemporary labour markets. Whatever the period considered, the sole existence of social insurance is not enough to ensure decommodification:[47] real alternatives to market dependence must be offered.

Access to social protection must therefore be questioned in each country, beyond fiscal measures adopted by local governments and often presented as a way to support new work arrangements in the digital economy. Although fiscal measures can indeed help self-employed workers develop their businesses, they do not provide any kind of social protection. Therefore, we will not take them into account in our final considerations.

Generally speaking, self-employed workers may benefit from formal

---

[47]   Decommodification is 'the degree to which individuals or families can uphold a socially acceptable standard of living independently of market participation' (Esping-Andersen 1990, p. 37).

coverage regarding all security schemes, except unemployment benefits and occupational accident/illness insurance. The latter are, however, compulsory in Slovenia and universal in Sweden. Self-employed can voluntarily enter these schemes in Spain and Germany. It must be remembered that compulsory insurance does not mean 'effective' coverage, that is, 'offered under comparable conditions, irrespective of the type of employment' (Commission Staff Working Document: European Commission 2017, p. 32). The coverage can be partial, due to tighter eligibility conditions compared to standard workers. The periods during which the benefits are received can be shorter for self-employed workers. Furthermore, the waiting period before receiving benefits can be longer, as in Slovenia for sickness benefits.

Is the voluntary coverage via opt-in clauses a better solution? If it gives individuals the opportunity to adhere to a scheme of social protection, we must keep in mind that self-employed workers have to pay to be covered. There is an evident risk of a 'vicious circle' in which low professional incomes generate low payment capacity in terms of social protection and thus no insurance or lower benefits. In addition, when voluntary coverage is proposed, the take-up rates may be very low.[48] Such considerations on effective coverage are thus essential, given the complexity and the heterogeneity of social protection levels offered in each country. Moreover, the transferability of rights and entitlements (when workers switch from one status to another) is often neglected, despite current evolutions of the labour market.

Multiple other factors have to be taken into account. They must include the socio-demographic characteristics of each country. In general, expenditure related to the 'old age and survivors' and the 'sickness/ healthcare' functions prevail. But expenditure concerning other branches of social security beyond the 'common core' may vary strongly from one country to another, reflecting significant differences in terms of economic development.

Further analysis must also integrate legal, political and cultural dimensions. The high variations observed in the numbers of IPros across EU countries should support this multidimensional view. Therefore a combination of structural factors (regulatory framework, industrial relations system, economic development, cultural openness vis-à-vis new work arrangements, socio-demographic characteristics, etc.) and agency factors (institutional entrepreneurship and strategies emanating from unions, quasi unions and labour market intermediaries, political reforms, etc.) is

---

[48]   European Commission, COM (2018) 132 final, proposal for a council recommendation on access to social protection for workers and self-employed, p. 4.

probably the best way to better understand the specific dynamics occurring in each country. In France, for example, the current government seems to support an evolution towards homogeneous social protection for all workers whatever their status. Would this mean an evolution towards the Swedish system? Nothing could be less certain: key institutional factors (in terms of economic development, socio-demographic characteristics and cultural openness) radically differ between the two countries.

In summary, our transversal analysis pleads for a multidimensional approach to the social protection of new independent professionals in each country rather than considering a one-size-fits-all solution likely to be replicated from one country to another (the creation of a third work status or the provision of opt-in schemes). Moreover, effective coverage must be guaranteed to new independent professionals whatever their work status. It is probably by exploring more complex options—like enforcement of existing laws, clarifying or expanding definitions of 'employment' and reconsidering the concept of an 'employer' (Stewart and Stanford 2017)—and by taking into account the various interrelations with other institutional variables in each national context, that sustainable solutions could be developed for new independent professionals in terms of social protection, rather than the formal application of a series of principles likely to support the European Pillar of Social Rights.

REFERENCES

Ambra, M. C. (2013), 'Modelli di rappresentanza sindacale nella società post-industriale. Come i sindacati si stanno ri-organizzando', *Quaderni Rassegna Sindacale*, **4**, 75–94.

Bureau, M.-C. and A. Corsani (2016), 'New Forms of Employment in a Globalised World: Three Figures of Knowledge Workers', *Work Organisation, Labour & Globalisation*, **10** (2), 101–12.

Caponetti, B. (2015), *Italy: Economically Dependent Self-Employed Work in the Jobs Act*, European Observatory of Working Life, accessed at https://www.eurofound.europa.eu/it/publications/article/2015/italy-economically-dependent-self-employed-work-in-the-jobs-act.

Charhon, P. and D. Murphy (2016), *The Future of Work in the Media, Arts & Entertainment Sector: Meeting the Challenge of Atypical Working*, accessed at https://www.fim-musicians.org/wp-content/uploads/atypical-work-handbook-en.pdf.

Charpin, J.-M., P.-M. Carraud, C. Durrieu, C. Freppel, L. Caussat, E. Robert, C. Cadoret and S. Baubry (2017), *Ouverture de l'assurance Chômage Aux Travailleurs Indépendants*, Rapport de l'Inspection générale des finances et de l'Inspection générale des affaires sociales, October, accessed at http://www.igas.gouv.fr/IMG/pdf/Rapport-Assurance_chomage_independants.pdf.

DiMaggio, P. J. and W. W. Powell (1983), 'The Iron Cage Revisited: Institutional

Isomorphism and Collective Rationality in Organizational Fields', *American Sociological Review*, **48** (2), 147–60.

ERA (2013), *Employment Relationship Act: National Assembly of the Republic of Slovenia*, accessed at http://www.mddsz.gov.si/fileadmin/mddsz.gov.si/pageuploa ds/dokumenti__pdf/word/zakonodaja/zdr1_en.doc.

Esping-Andersen, G. (1990), *The Three Worlds of Welfare Capitalism*, Princeton, NJ: Princeton University Press.

ESPN DE (2017), *ESPN Thematic Report on Access to Social Protection of People Working as Self-Employed or on Non-Standard Contracts – Germany*, accessed at http://ec.europa.eu/social/keyDocuments.jsp?pager.offset=0&langId=en&mo de=advancedSubmit&year=0&country=0&type=0&advSearchKey=ESPNse nsw.

ESPN FR (2017), *ESPN Thematic Report on Access to Social Protection of People Working as Self-Employed or on Non-Standard Contracts – France*, accessed at http://ec.europa.eu/social/keyDocuments.jsp?pager.offset=0&langId=en&mo de=advancedSubmit&year=0&country=0&type=0&advSearchKey=ESPNse nsw.

ESPN IT (2017), *ESPN Thematic Report on Access to Social Protection of People Working as Self-Employed or on Non-Standard Contracts – Italy*, accessed at http://ec.europa.eu/social/keyDocuments.jsp?pager.offset=0&langId=en&mode =advancedSubmit&year=0&country=0&type=0&advSearchKey=ESPNsensw.

ESPN NL (2017), *ESPN Thematic Report on Access to Social Protection of People Working as Self-Employed or on Non-Standard Contracts – the Netherlands*, accessed at http://ec.europa.eu/social/keyDocuments.jsp?pager.offset=0&langI d=en&mode=advancedSubmit&year=0&country=0&type=0&advSearchKey= ESPNsensw.

ESPN SI (2017), *ESPN Thematic Report on Access to Social Protection of People Working as Self-Employed or on Non-Standard Contracts – Slovenia*, accessed at http://ec.europa.eu/social/keyDocuments.jsp?pager.offset=0&langId=en&mode =advancedSubmit&year=0&country=0&type=0&advSearchKey=ESPNsensw.

ESPN SP (2017), *ESPN Thematic Report on Access to Social Protection of People Working as Self-Employed or on Non-Standard Contracts – Spain*, accessed at http://ec.europa.eu/social/keyDocuments.jsp?pager.offset=0&langId=en&mode =advancedSubmit&year=0&country=0&type=0&advSearchKey=ESPNsensw.

ESPN UK (2017), *ESPN Thematic Report on Access to Social Protection of People Working as Self-Employed or on Non-Standard Contracts – United Kingdom*, accessed at http://ec.europa.eu/social/keyDocuments.jsp?pager.offset=0&langI d=en&mode=advancedSubmit&year=0&country=0&type=0&advSearchKey= ESPNsensw.

Eurofound (2009), *Self-Employed Workers: Industrial Relations and Working Conditions*, Luxembourg: Publications Office of the European Union.

European Commission (2017), *Commission Staff Working Document*, (SWD (2017) 381 final), 20 November, European Commission.

European Commission COM (2018) 132, *Access to Social Protection for Workers and the Self-Employed – EU Monitor* (n.d.), accessed 13 September 2018 at https://www.eumonitor.eu/9353000/1/j9vvik7m1c3gyxp/vkmnk364z9xq.

European Parliament (2013), *Social Protections Rights of Economically Dependent Self-Employed Workers*, Study IP/A/EMPL/ST/2012-02, Directorate General for Internal Policies, April, accessed at http://www.europarl.europa.eu/RegData/ etudes/etudes/join/2013/507449/IPOL-EMPL_ET%282013%29507449_EN.pdf.

Gumbrell-McCormick, R. (2011), 'European Trade Unions and "Atypical" Workers', *Industrial Relations Journal*, **42** (3), 293–310.

Hall, P. A. and D. W. Soskice (eds) (2001), *Varieties of Capitalism: The Institutional Foundations of Comparative Advantage*, Oxford and New York: Oxford University Press.

Heyes, J. and T. Hastings (2017), *The Practices of Enforcement Bodies in Detecting and Preventing Bogus Self-Employment*, European Platform of Undeclared Work, available at http://ec.europa.eu/social/BlobServlet?docId=17971&langId =en.

Holst, H. (2008), 'The Political Economy of Trade Union Strategies in Austria and Germany: The Case of Call Centres', *European Journal of Industrial Relations*, **14** (1), 25–45.

Lambrecht, M. (2016), 'L'économie des plateformes collaboratives', *Courrier hebdomadaire du CRISP*, **2311–12**, 5–80.

OECD (2014), *OECD Employment Outlook 2014*, accessed at https://www.oecd-ili brary.org/employment/oecd-employment-outlook-2014_empl_outlook-2014-en.

OECD (2017), *OECD Employment Outlook 2017*, Paris: OECD Publishing.

Perulli, A. (2017), 'Il Jobs Act degli autonomi: nuove (e vecchie) tutele per il lavoro autonomo non imprenditoriale', *Rivista Italiana di Diritto del Lavoro*, **2**, 173–203.

Rapelli, S. (2012), *European I-Pros: A Study*, London: Professional Contractors Group.

Reyna Fernández, S. (2010), 'El trabajo autónomo en el modelo social europeo y en el reordenamiento jurídico de la UE en la Estrategia de Lisboa después de 2010', *Revista Del Ministerio de Trabajo y Asuntos Sociales*, **10**, 109–20.

RTV Slovenija (2016), *Prekarci Se Bodo Za Pravice Bojevali S Svojim Sindikatom: Prvi Interaktivni Multimedijski Portal*, RTV Slovenija, accessed 16 November 2016 at http://www.rtvslo.si/gospodarstvo/prekarci-se-bodo-za-pra vice-bojevali-s-svojim-sindikatom/404559.

Schmid-Drüner, M. (2013), *Social Protection Rights of Economically Dependent Self-Employed Workers*, European Parliament's Committee on Employment and Social Affairs, accessed at http://www.europarl.europa.eu/studies.

Schulze Buschoff, K. and C. Schmidt (2009), 'Adapting Labour Law and Social Security to the Needs of the "New Self-Employed"—Comparing the UK, Germany and the Netherlands', *Journal of European Social Policy*, **19** (2), 147–59.

Spasova, S., D. Bouget, D. Ghailani and B. Vanhercke (2017), *Access to Social Protection for People Working on Non-Standard Contracts and as Self-Employed in Europe: A Study of National Policies 2017*, European Social Policy Network (ESPN), Brussels: European Commission, Directorate-General for Employment, Social Affairs and Inclusion.

Stewart, A. and J. Stanford (2017), 'Regulating Work in the Gig Economy: What Are the Options?', *Economic and Labour Relations Review*, **28** (3), 420–37.

Waas, B. and G. Heerma van Voss (eds) (2017), *Restatement of Labour Law in Europe. Vol. 1 The Concept of Employee*, Oxford and Portland, OR: Hart Publishing.

6. Continuity and discontinuity in collective representation

Anna Mori and Bas Koene

Since 2000, the socio-economic landscape has undergone rapid change, and is still in flux. A comparative analysis of initiatives oriented to the collective representation and support of self-employed workers in Europe is helpful in fostering an understanding of the novel possibilities for organization and representation under conditions where the traditional industrial relations model, hinged on an open-ended subordinated employment relationship, is in decline.

This chapter reports the outcomes of an investigation into how traditional and novel actors in the labour market organize their support for self-employed workers and what strategies they employ to represent them. We find differences in the ways in which they structure their activities and the strategies they deploy to support their members. This chapter thus enriches our understanding of the possibilities for organizing representation and support for self-employed workers, the bases for establishing a collective identity around shared interests, and how relevant collective capabilities can be developed, sustained and promoted, building new forms of solidarity from below.

1. EROSION OF THE BASIS FOR TRADITIONAL COLLECTIVE ACTION

Over recent decades the labour movement in Europe has displayed a growing erosion (Martin and Ross 1999; Waddington and Hoffmann 2000). Across European member states, the role of the trade union as primary actor of the collective representation of workers has begun to decline (Regini 1992). Despite differences, all union movements have increasingly experienced various forms of 'crisis': decline in membership, either in aggregate terms or among specific segments of the labour market (e.g. among young workers or precarious workers); erosion of collective bargaining coverage; declining mobilization capacity (also following members' reluctance to take part in union activities); increasing membership heterogeneity and related difficulties in the definition and aggregation of interests; more constrained opportunity structures; and erosion of the structures of interest representation, such as workplace representation bodies (Gumbrell-McCormick and Hyman 2013).

On a general level, the causes of such 'hard times' for trade unionism (Gumbrell-McCormick and Hyman 2013) can be tracked down in, among other areas, industrial, economic, political and social transformations which have challenged the traditional role played by these collective organizations: 'European economic integration; intensified internationalization of financial and product markets; decentralization of neo-corporatist and industry-level collective bargaining; and changing structures of employment (individualization, feminization and tertiarization)' (Frege and Kelly 2003, p. 8). The intense globalization of the labour market, prompted by a boost in the movement of workers, has not only promoted new employment opportunities but also undermined unions' capacity to advocate and ensure fair and protected working conditions across borders (Bieler and Lindberg 2011). The opening up of national labour market boundaries has, in fact, allowed employers leeway in cutting labour costs by circumventing national employment protection measures and looking for more advantageous labour regulations in different institutional frameworks. Phenomena like posting workers and subcontracting of work along international value chains, which paved the way to a race to the bottom in the definition of terms and conditions of employments, represent well-known cases where the capacity of trade unions to organize workers is seriously weakened (Drahokoupil 2015). At the same time, the proliferation of non-standard contracts, ranging from temporary contracts, part-time jobs and self-employment, to collaborations, project-based contracts, on-call jobs and zero-hour contracts, has paved the way for the gradual dismantling of the traditional contractual arrangement based on the standard full-time open-ended subordinate contract, which has historically represented the rank-and-file of labour movements (Gumbrell-McCormick 2011).

Accordingly, the new fragmented geography of work, but importantly also the diversified and segmented new structure of contractual arrangements, have triggered a growing individualization of terms and conditions of employment. This process has made traditional industrial relations models based on collective bargaining between social partners hardly applicable. They are becoming less and less effective for a growing part of traditional jobs, due to weaker coverage, decreasing coordination in collective bargaining, and a marked decentralization and their application is far more complex for all non-standard forms of employment. Given that collective bargaining has become increasingly weak even at company level, individual bargaining has gained a foothold (Crouch 2012). But the application of the word 'bargaining' to such a circumstance can be misleading: in fact companies often offer a pre-defined job position and the worker can only accept or refuse the terms and conditions of employment proposed. Indeed, a real negotiation process at workplace level generally occurs when the worker displays strong bargaining power in the labour market, in other words when the worker has highly developed specific skills, their professional ability is in great demand in the marketplace, and they are not easily replaceable. Conversely, the spread of individual bargaining is often strictly connected to a process of weakening of labour and of erosion in labour standards which has taken place in every industrialized country. Indeed, despite the fact that individual bargaining power should allow more freedom and self-determination in accommodating the terms and conditions of employment to the specific needs of each worker, the worker is actually forced to face all the risks of their working activity on an individual basis (Banfi and Bologna 2011). Hence the process is ambiguous as it bears both risks (many) and opportunities (few).

Such individualization of work has eroded unions' role in collective representation at workplace level, but also at national level where workers enjoy different degrees of labour protection and safeguards against social risks. Overall, trade unions have become increasingly less effective in attracting new workers in the traditionally organized sectors where, conversely, they are witnessing a significant loss of collective identity. A major challenge is represented by the new emerging industries—the gig economy represents a prime example—and new segments of the labour market displaying peculiar features, like the platform workers, where a collective identity still has to be built (Wood et al. 2018).

1.1 Recruitment and Organization of Self-Employed Workers

Against this changing socio-economic landscape, the recruitment and organizing of self-employed workers has turned out to be notably troublesome, condensing the different challenges and ambiguities mentioned above. First, it is highly problematic to reach this labour market segment since it is geographically scattered and fragmented across many different and dispersed workplaces. Second, self-employment is an inherently individualistic working condition: accordingly, promotion of the paradigm of collective action in the labour market is a preliminary to recruitment, rather than the individual action self-employed workers generally pursue. Third, the demand for collective representation of self-employed workers is a relatively recent phenomenon following the rapid growth of these workers during the 2010s: it follows that trade unions have to quickly adapt their structures to these continuous transformations of the labour market. Fourth, the difficulty in organizing this category of workers is further exacerbated by the fact that traditional industrial relations models have increasingly little relevance.

The recent growth of self-employment in Europe (for a more detailed account see Chapter 2) in such a socio-economic landscape highlights the need to revise our understanding of organizing actions in the labour market. Furthermore, the emergence of traditional and novel organizations with this specific purpose begs us to explore two main interrelated issues: the significance of organizing in the light of the evolving characteristics of the labour market and the ambitions of the organizations to collectively represent this segment of workers.

While in the traditional paradigm, trade unions had come to a clear understanding of who shared common interests and demands, what these shared interests were, and how and at what level these shared interests had to be sustained and developed, given the wider institutional frameworks, over recent years these issues have needed to be reconsidered in the context of globalization, marketization, individualization and changing regulation of the labour market. More specifically, two developments are particularly prominent when analysing the position of self-employed workers in the labour market in comparison to regular employees.

Firstly, the question of organizational structure addresses the relevant context for establishing a collective identity. It addresses the core question of what needs to be organized for. A collective actor should address clear collective interests, collective capabilities to be built, maintained and protected. As shared interests by employers or industry seem to have become less relevant, where do we find relevant collective interests for the future between those of an individual in the workplace and the broad societal interests covered by labour market regulation?

Secondly, the nature of required strategies and ambitions for collective representation are not self-evident, given the changing nature of the socio-economic context characterized, on the one hand, by the fragmentation and individualization of the workforce and, on the other hand, by the possibilities provided by the rich institutional environment in most EU countries, which can facilitate ways to overcome individual vulnerability and address the collective challenges of workers more than previously was the case. Rather than deductively establishing what is needed, our contribution provides a transversal analysis that investigates initiatives in various EU countries, focusing especially on the support of highly skilled self-employed workers.

2. TRADITIONAL AND INNOVATIVE FORMS OF COLLECTIVE REPRESENTATION IN THE LABOUR MARKET

Considering research to date, several approaches have been recognized to counteract the individualization trajectory in the labour market described above and to address these emerging challenges. Over the last decade European trade unions have tried to build membership among under-represented segments, including self-employed workers. In some countries, they have implemented new organizational strategies in order to adjust their logics of action to the protection needs of these specific workers. Extending representation to new labour market segments means taking greater account of their distinctive demands and specific needs (Bernaciak et al. 2014). Different strategies have been put in place. In some cases trade unions have offered services, such as legal, fiscal and social security assistance. They have adopted the servicing model not only for self-employed workers, but more generally for all non-standard workers. Other trade unions have adopted innovative strategies by enacting new organizational patterns to promote direct participation of workers and their collective mobilization. This last model represents a more active approach, given that the trade unions do not try to attract workers in a traditional way but actively look for new members by recruiting them one by one.

The search for innovative responses by trade unions in many European countries has encouraged the establishment of new alliances and a coalition-building approach. This strategy seems to be an attractive and effective one for various reasons:

> It can increase access to new constituencies: this is particularly important for efforts to recruit previously unorganized (or weakly organized) groups of workers. Coalitions may also be a source of added legitimacy for union campaigns: working with community or religious organizations may help unions recruit ethnic minority members, and a common campaign with relevant NGOs (non-governmental organizations) may strengthen union claims to represent a broad public interest. Finally, alliances can strengthen unions' mobilization capacity, particularly when working with NGOs that possess a vibrant activist base. (Bernaciak et al. 2014, p. 21)

In parallel to union revitalization attempts, new innovative organizational forms have emerged, responding to otherwise unaddressed demands of representation in modern economies: this is the case of quasi-unions (Heckscher and Carré 2006) and labour market intermediaries (LMIs) (Autor 2008). Quasi-unions are defined as 'the broad range of organizations that have emerged to represent the interests of otherwise unrepresented people in their work lives and in their relationships with their employer, seeking to address matters of worker rights and to improve working conditions' (Heckscher and Carré 2006, p. 606). These organizations embody a heterogeneous field through a multitude of diverse organizational forms. What they have in common, however, is the fact that, in spite of representing their members and affiliates in the workplace, these organizations are not formal unions. They are generally member associations, but they often lack formal membership mechanisms and related systems to collect dues. Overall, they do not seek to become formal unions in the short term: in fact quasi-unions are self-organized entities, with limited financial resources that do not follow the traditional collective bargaining approach. They are mainly based on voluntary work, with a strong core staff whose commitment is permanent, complemented by a very loose and shifting membership. Their notion of members' affiliation is loose and varied: members can be 'supporters' who take part in specific collective actions, 'registered members' who sign up for websites/social media, or 'paying members' who pay a yearly subscription fee to support the activities of the association. In terms of primary functions and levers for actions, the quasi-unions follow a logic of action between service and advocacy.

LMIs represent a second innovative organizational form that growingly supports and organizes self-employed workers. Embodying an organization for career management located between the hierarchy and the market, these novel initiatives developed by third-party actors appear in the labour market in order to support workers throughout non-standard job transitions. These organizations play an intermediary role between individual workers on nonstandard paths and the end-users of their services (the latter can no longer be considered as their employers). Moreover, in a context of growing task hyper-specialization, it becomes more and more difficult for companies to find appropriate workers without the support of such third parties, very often through IT solutions (Malone et al. 2011; Koene et al. 2014). LMIs' logic of action focuses particularly on the matchmaking process. Moreover, they may also act as a service supplier during job transitions: in fact LMIs deliver various services including networking activities—with potential employers and colleagues—and providing information on vacant positions. They can arrange training for workers and offer them access to facilities for individual and/or collective activities, which reinforces their feeling of belonging to a community.

To recap, the transition from a labour market primarily grounded in a salaried dependent workforce towards a society where the demand and supply of labour are growingly dominated by self-employed workers highlights the inefficacy and the incongruity of the traditional model of collective representation. Such a shift triggers a profound redefinition of employment relations, which in turn calls for a revitalization in the organizational forms and strategies needed to collectively represent workers' interests. Some scholars agree on the concern of integrating the increasingly heterogeneous constituencies of self-employed workers into the union movement (e.g. Dølvik and Waddington 2002; Gottschall and Kroos 2003). However, the difficulty in building a class consciousness within the population of self-employment workers is recognized, since they have limited personal contacts with other workers in similar conditions of employment (Pernicka 2006).

The following sections of this chapter map out how a broad range of actors organize new and non-traditional segments of self-employed workers in the light of the evolving characteristics of the labour market and what strategies they choose to support and collectively represent them. With this approach we investigate the traditional and new emerging forms of collective representation of self-employed workers in the European labour market, by focusing in particular on two analytical dimensions: the structure of these organizations and the strategies they opt for to support and give collective voice to these workers. Empirical evidence is based on a transversal comparative analysis of experiences of collective organization and representation of self-employed workers in Europe (the analysis has been carried out specifically in the following nine countries: Belgium, France, Germany, Italy, the Netherlands, Slovenia, Spain, Sweden and the United Kingdom) (for a detailed list of the organizations investigated, refer to Table 6.1a in the Appendix to this chapter).

3. ORGANIZATIONAL STRUCTURE: TRAJECTORIES OF CREATION AND ORGANIZATIONAL EMBEDDING

Considering the various structural configurations through which collective representation for self-employed workers is established, three elements stand out: the timeframe or moment of establishment of the initiatives to support self-employed workers, the trajectories of creation (i.e. whether the initiatives followed a top-down or bottom-up trajectory), and the type of membership that the organizations are aiming for.

3.1 Timeframe: A Recent Development

The establishment of organizational experiences aimed at the collective representation of self-employed workers represents a recent phenomenon. Across Europe we have witnessed a proliferation of organizational structures mainly during the last two decades, allegedly in conjunction with the growth of this segment in the tertiary sector. New innovative experiences have been launched in recent years, such as the German cooperative for artists SmartDE in 2013; the German experience of the platform cooperativism movement called Supermarkt in 2012 for artists; and the Chambers for Independent and Precarious Workers (CLAP), a federation of independent and self-managed associations created in Rome in 2013 to offer services and information to self-employed workers in occupied warehouses managed by networks of volunteers.

Interestingly, the origins of the innovative experiences of quasi-unionism and labour market intermediation, although recent, predate the wave of unions' revitalization to encompass the self-employed workforce in their structures. The cooperative Société Mutuelle pour ARTistes (Smart) was created in 1998 in Belgium for artists (SmartBE); the Italian quasi-union Association of Consultants in the Advanced Tertiary Sector (ACTA) was established in 2004; the British quasi-union Association of Independent Professionals and the Self-Employed (IPSE) was set up in 1999; and the Dutch labour market intermediary Yacht was launched in 1999 by the Randstad group for highly skilled independent professionals. Only very recently have traditional trade unions either, in a few cases, revitalized their structure to also encompass the self-employed (e.g. the Christian Trade Union (CSC) in Belgium in 2015) or, in most cases, created new ad hoc internal structures to build membership among the group of self-employed. Just to mention some relevant examples across Europe, this option was pursued among others by: the vIVAce! online community launched in Italy in 2015 by the union confederation CISL; the Platform Union set up in 2016 by the Federation of Communication (Conseil); Culture F3C of the French trade union CFDT; the Ver.di Selbstständige, the specific unit devoted to self-employment of the trade union Ver.di created in Germany in 2001; the Trade Union of Precarious Workers established in Slovenia in 2016; and the Confederation of Autonomous Workers of Catalonia (CTAC) set up in the Spanish region in 2001.

Longstanding experiences of collective representation are instead limited, concentrated in economic sectors and traditional professions historically dominated by a self-employed workforce: this is the case of the Association of Professional Journalists (AJP) created in Belgium that traced back to 1886; the German Federal Association of Interpreters and Translators (BDÜ) established in 1955; the Dutch trade union for artists created in 1977; the Journalist Union (JU) established in Sweden during the 1960s; the

British Musicians' Union (MU) set up in 1921, and the union for professional performers and actors Equity created during the 1930s.

3.2 Twofold Trajectory of Creation: Bottom-Up and Top-Down

As far as the process of creation of these organizational experiences is concerned, we can observe in Europe a twofold trajectory that interestingly recalls the division between traditional and innovative organizational forms. On the one hand, in fact, we witness a top-down development: this is mainly the case of creation of novel ad hoc internal structures that the trade unions built to target the interests of self-employed workers. This top-down pattern can be tracked in the establishment of the CSC, vIVAce!, Conseil, Culture F3C, Ver.di Selbstständige, CTAC, and Yacht. On the other hand, the most innovative experiences followed the opposite trajectory, evolving from bottom-up initiatives undertaken by activists and the same self-employed professionals who decided to set up their own associations. This is the case of the cooperative SmartBE, launched by a manager of musical bands and an engineer whose wife works in the artistic industry, who jointly aspired to assemble artists to defend their professional interests and to provide services. As in Belgium, the German cooperative SmartDE followed a similar process of bottom-up establishment. This was also the case for the Alliance Française des Designers (French Alliance of Designers (AFD)), created by a group of designers with the aim of federating all the designers regardless of their area of specialization. The origins of quasi-union ACTA in the advanced tertiary sector in Italy traces back to the initiative of a small group of twenty professionals from different occupations that opted for self-organization to fill a gap they identified in the collective representation of self-employed workers. By definition, the advent of movements in defence of the rights of self-employed workers follows a bottom-up pattern. The Movement for Decent Work in Slovenia and CLAP in Italy were launched and animated by groups of activists and volunteers deeply committed to their cause.

3.3 Mixed and Heterogeneous Membership

The type of membership is often mixed and heterogeneous: the organizations investigated in fact targeted several diverse economic sectors and occupations. Their main strategic focus is to recruit and give collective voice and visibility to professional self-employment in general, as a working condition per se, rather than to specific professions. This is the case of the initiatives launched by the trade unions for self-employed workers. Having long refused to represent autonomous workers, the CSC decided to 'initiate a debate over the enlargement of our union to self-employed work-ers without employees' during its 2015 congress,[1] hence agreeing to tackle the needs of self-employed in general. The Platform Union in France offers services to all independent workers, apart from the regulated professions. Ver.di Selbstständige organizes across several economic sectors including the media and communication, education, culture, ICT, and the creative industry. Likewise vIVAce! addresses its services to all independent work-ers who are not assisted by other associations, such as the professional registers. CTAC was created in response to the lack of legislative initiatives in defence of self-employed workers. Similarly, when innovative experi-ences of quasi-unionism and cooperativism were launched, the strategic and organizational focus was oriented towards the specific condition of self-employment, rather than on single occupations. Hence the coopera-tives SmartBE and SmartDE, despite being launched initially in the artistic industry, quickly enlarged their focus, firstly to the creative industries more generally and then to the wider world of freelancing. The quasi-unions Platform for Independent Entrepreneurs (PZO-ZZP) in the Netherlands, ACTA in Italy and IPSE in the UK were launched to represent professional independent workers in the advanced tertiary sectors of the economy in their respective countries and more widely at European level, since they are all affiliated to the European Federation of Independent Professionals (EFIP). PZO-ZZP presents itself as 'an association of self-employed, for self-employed, by self-employed'.

Less numerous, some organizations circumscribe their constituency to a specific occupation or profession. In this case the organizations con-solidate their action in a selected sector of the economy, grouping together both self-employed and employees working in the targeted industry. Generally these economic sectors are dominated by self-employment. This is the case of the AJP in Belgium where freelance journalists represent 75 per cent of the members; the MU in the UK, where 90 per cent of member-ship comprises self-employed musicians; and Equity in the UK, with a large majority of independent actors and performers. Likewise the AFD in France specifically focuses on the design industry (including spaces, products and communication design). The Dutch union Kunstenbond (Art Union) serves professionals in the art and creative sectors. The BDÜ organizes 7,500 members, corresponding to 80 per cent of professional translators and interpreters enrolled in the German professional register.

To recap, the enquiry about the organizational structure addresses the relevant context for establishing a collective identity within a changing

---

[1] Congrès annuel de 2015, ligne de force n°29, https://cne.csc-en-ligne.be/csc-en-ligne/La-CSC/congres-2015/themes-du-congres/elargir/elargir.html, accessed 18 May 2017.

labour market composition, in particular by elucidating what patterns emerge in terms of types and characteristics of structures adopted to respond to such challenges. First, although pioneer innovative experiences initially focused on professionals in specific sectors or occupations, they then often enlarged their organizational structures to collectively represent self-employed workers more in general. Initiatives were mostly created bottom-up by the autonomous initiative of groups of workers looking for collective visibility and voice, or by organizations recognizing possibilities in the support of self-employed, hence filling a gap in collective representation left by traditional unions. Conversely, trade unions were less responsive to these new developments, retaining focus on their historical constituencies comprising subordinated employees.

Second, although most of these pioneer innovative organizations built their membership on belonging to a specific economic occupation sector, addressing the specific challenges of their members, over time they have often broadened their reach to the wider category of self-employed in general.

Third, when comparing top-down versus bottom-up initiatives, organizations that were founded bottom-up more clearly have the interests of workers at the core of their mission objectives (mutualization by employees). Commercial LMIs established top-down in order to grasp a market opportunity and follow corporate interests. Trade unions adjusted their structures to build membership among self-employed workers. The dominant pattern, however, was the creation of ad hoc structures, separate from the core union structure, to organize the whole segment of self-employment. In many instances, unions for self-employed also strived for more independence as they found it difficult to serve their members within the confines of the regular union structure.

4. ORGANIZATIONAL STRATEGIES FOR ENGAGING IN SUPPORT AND REPRESENTATION

The collective representation of self-employed workers in Europe displays a threefold pattern in terms of dominant or primary organizational strategies adopted. As collective bargaining is hardly a feasible option for the self-employed, the three dominant strategic models are the servicing model, the lobbying model, and the coalition-building model. The three models are not mutually exclusive. For the most part, organizations either follow a core strategy of servicing or lobbying, depending on their historical development, over time often accompanied by secondary initiatives in lobbying and servicing respectively, and in most cases accompanied by some form of coalition-building strategy to increase their reach and legitimacy. These strategies document the main way in which organizations aim to connect to their members. Most organizations also employ novel ways of communicating and networking, using social networks and membership platforms with registered users, which are indicative of the shifting relationships catered for between organizations and their members.

4.1 Servicing Model

A number of organizations focus their logic of action on the provision of services for self-employed workers. A variety of ad hoc services are supplied to respond to the specific needs of those professionals who work autonomously. These include in particular: fiscal and accounting services, legal advice and support in case of judiciary proceedings, administrative support for business contracting, training, personalized and individual general assistance, and customized insurance packages at discounted rates. The servicing model has proven to be strategically valuable in attracting new members or clients both in the case of trade unions and innovative emerging organizations. The former include, for instance, the Platform Union of the French CFDT (for further detail on this refer to Box 6.1); the vIVAce! community of the Italian CISL and the Trade Union of Precarious Workers in Slovenia. Innovative emerging organizations encompass both LMIs with a market focus (attracting clients) and cooperatives that develop mutualized solutions (attracting members). The Dutch LMI Yacht provides a range of legal, fiscal and administrative services, besides its core function of matching and placement activities in the labour market for professional independent workers. Moreover, it organizes events and sets up online networks to facilitate meetings between clients and professionals. Particularly interesting in the latter group are the cooperatives SmartBE and SmartDE. They represent experiences of new mutualism for their members: they provide mutual guarantee funds, customized insurance packages, leasing for professional equipment, microcredit for the development of professional activities, and subsidies.

4.2 Lobbying Model

Other organizations have, instead, opted for focusing their main organizational strategy on lobbying. Advocacy and lobby actions are carried out towards governments, parliaments, public administration bodies, local policymakers, and institutionalized consultative bodies. This is the case for some quasi-unions, auto-entrepreneurs' associations and professional

---

BOX 6.1   F3 CFDT'S UNION PLATFORM SERVICE PRACTICE (FRANCE)

CFDT is a union confederation created in 1964 that recently became the first confederation of trade unions in France. The F3C CFDT was created in October 2005 by the merger of the former CFDT Federation of Post and Telecoms (FUPT-CFDT), Federation of Communication and Culture (FTILAC-CFDT), and the business services part of the federation of CFDT Services (IT services, service providers, advertising and accounting activities). This organization has more than 50,000 members and it represents those independent workers who are not in regulated professions and some specific activities not covered by professional insurance.

The creation of this new federation responded to the challenges and the impacts of digital technology on working conditions. To this purpose, in 2015 the CFDT's Federation of Communication, Conseil, and Culture (F3C) organized a meeting and a Bar-Camp with digital workers in a co-working space in Paris (the NUMA), in order to understand the specific needs of these workers. Following this event, taking into account the social and employment protection requests raised by the workers, the CFDT (F3C) decided to experiment with a new platform launched at the end of 2016 (http://www.f3c-cfdt.fr/union) to support independent workers (non-salaried workers, auto-entrepreneurs, freelancers) by providing ad hoc tools and services, financed through 1 per cent of the turnover and used by freelancers, especially in high-skilled intellectual occupations.

In particular, the platform provides:

- tools for purchase management
- support in customer relationships management
- a free bank account
- professional insurance (Axa)
- a digital safe (La Poste)
- legal advice (also in case of problems of accessing welfare services)
- coaching and accounting support (optional).

In the future, the platform intends to extend its services to customer rating, integrative health insurance and loss of earnings insurance.

---

associations for self-employed workers which concentrate their strategic actions in pursuing the approval of ad hoc measures and regulatory interventions that improve the condition of self-employed workers. The German BDÜ is strongly oriented towards structured lobby activities, carried out also though specifically hired personnel. The lobbying actions are developed through vis-à-vis contacts with policymakers, courts and official bodies, organizations, and clients, oriented to ensure long-term improvement of general working conditions for interpreters and translators. Moreover the BDÜ is consulted when legislative interventions affecting its professional groups are under discussion in parliament: it has played a core role in the definition of the German Judicial Remuneration and Compensation Act (JVEG68), which provides the basis for remuneration of linguists and other professionals for services provided to courts, public prosecutors' offices and other governmental agencies.

The quasi-union ACTA was launched in Italy to lobby for the rights of independent professionals who work outside the protection of the professional registers. ACTA's lobbying actions are centred on three core spheres: welfare issues (high social security contributions combined with exclusion from protection systems and very low pensions); fiscal issues (higher taxes compared to other workers); and rights (in the Italian legislative framework, labour law applies only to subordinated workers). In the Netherlands, PZO-ZZP is a lobbying organization set up to give collective voice to the world of professional self-employment, without focusing on specific professions. Thanks to a seat on the Dutch Social Economic Council, PZO-ZZP has a privileged position from which to carry out lobbying and advocacy actions. Similarly the Spanish professional association Autònoms Pequeña y Mediana empresa de Cataluña (PIMEC) (Autonomous Small and Medium Enterprises) focuses on lobbying actions to influence members of the government or the opposition to defend the interests of the self-employed. In that sense, the organization has pressured at political level over the issue of the adoption of laws to fight against defaulting. In Belgium, the AJP has developed two categories of vis-à-vis actions with political actors (for further details refer to Box 6.2): reactive actions in lobbying to maintain the specific status of (self-employed) journalists and proactive actions concerning issues that the association wants to raise in the political debate. A telling example is the question of whistle-blowers for which the association wants to create legal protection, similar to the protection of information sources. This lobbying activity was particularly intense when the specific status of journalists was at stake, for example during the reform of their pension schemes and copyright taxes.

The French Federation of Auto-Entrepreneurs (FEDAE) has implemented important advocacy actions, being politically very active: for instance, it has recently published a practical guide geared towards candidates for the presidential election 'for a renewal of the independent work'. Moreover it launches petitions, white papers and press releases, and participates in meetings with ministers. FEDAE has also contributed in the Commission Grandguillaume about the simplification of legal, social and fiscal regimes for individual contractors, while in 2014, it supported the Agence pour la creation d'entreprises (APCE) (Agency for the Creation of Enterprises) whose future was threatened. In 2015, FEDAE launched the operation *je suis un caillou* ('I am a little stone') and sent an open letter to Nicolas Sarkozy who described auto-entrepreneurs as 'stones in his shoe'.

BOX 6.2   LOBBYING INITIATIVES: 'FREELANCER NOT
EASILY FOOLED (*PIGISTE PAS PIGEON*)' AND
JOURNALISTEFREELANCE.BE NETWORK
LAUNCHED BY THE ASSOCIATION OF
PROFESSIONAL JOURNALISTS (BELGIUM)

The lobbying initiatives 'Freelancer not easily fooled (*pigiste pas pigeon*)' and the Journalistefreelance.be network were carried out by the Association of Professional Journalists (AJP), a Belgian quasi-union. This organization cannot be considered as an official worker union given that its membership is below the legal threshold of 50,000 members and it does not have inter-professional coverage as required by law. Accordingly, the AJP is not allowed to take part in collective bargaining systems. Hence the AJP often engages in advocacy and lobbying activities involving journalists, unions, employer organizations and public authorities, in particular when the specific status of journalists is at stake, for instance with reference to pension schemes or copyright taxation.

Importantly, two specific initiatives have been successively undertaken for self-employed journalists:

The '**Freelancer not easily fooled (*pigiste pas pigeon*)**' campaign was launched in 2006 to denounce the poor working and financial conditions of such workers. This initiative followed up on three successive surveys (2005, 2011, 2015) on working conditions and the income levels of self-employed journalists. The results of the surveys were collected in a sort of 'black book' that outlines the specific problems of these workers, such as their feeling of isolation, the difficulty of individual bargaining with clients and the strong competition they face in this sector, a continuous worsening of working conditions and a decrease in income level.

journalistefreelance.be network was launched in 2015 to involve and mobilize freelance journalists. This web network, besides representing a virtual space where journalists can engage in dialogue, provides useful information relating to:

- the list of its members, to favour the partnerships and the networking activities
- legal resources
- the minimum threshold for the articles of self-employed journalists in accordance with a civil agreement signed with the General Association of the Belgian Press
- the pay rate scales which, despite not being compulsory, represent useful indications to help freelancers negotiate with their client
- an income calculator which helps freelancers to negotiate a fair income
- job opportunities and intranet.

These different advocacy and lobbying actions have increased public authority awareness of the working conditions of freelance journalists thanks also to extensive coverage by the Belgian media.

It also founded the 'Observatory of the Uberization', in order to improve the social protection of workers in digital platforms, and contributed to the Barbaroux Report, which aims to simplify the auto-entrepreneur regime. Likewise, the British IPSE combines a wide range of services with lobbying actions in order to gain public visibility and awareness of professional self-employment. IPSE has established a stable liaison with parliament, and it engages extensively with politicians and civil servants. IPSE participates in government consultations, with feedback from the members and research. It works with other organizations such as the Confederation of British Industry (CBI) and the Recruitment and Employment Confederation (REC) to proactively campaign on issues that matter to businesses. A dedicated team of policy and public affairs professionals regularly meets with MPs, ministers and shadow ministers to brief them on issues affecting independent professionals and the self-employed. IPSE also lobbies parliament on series of issues including maternity, better regulation for the self-employed, agency workers' regulation, pensions, freelancer limited companies and work hubs.

4.3 Coalition-Building Model

A third dominant organizational strategy is to take part in more or less structured and formal partnerships with other organizations. This third model represents a strategy for broadening the reach and strengthening the legitimacy of organizations already engaged in servicing or lobbying. The search for new alliances and coalition-building has been widely explored by the organizations, since partnership represents a positive-sum game for all the actors involved. Coalitions can facilitate access to new constituencies of workers: this aspect is particularly important when recruitment in the labour market examines new unorganized segments, such as in the case of self-employed workers. Moreover, the creation of coalitions can increase the legitimacy of campaigns and lobbying actions carried out together, on behalf of a wider rank and file membership. Partnerships enable the strengthening of an individual organization's capacity to mobilize, in particular when movements and innovative bottom-up associations are involved, given that they are animated by active members and volunteers. In this framework of action, two main types of coalitions can be observed: coalitions built on industry/sector-wide bases, aimed at sector-specific campaigns, and coalitions built for addressing the rights of self-employed workers in general.

Occupational/sectoral organizations often build partnerships with other associations in the same industry to jointly pursue sector-specific campaigns and policies. In Belgium, after a period of opposition with the journalists' trade unions, the AJP found a deal of reciprocal involvement thanks to a united front against bogus self-employment. In fact, the unions agreed to invite the AJP to the discussion table when major issues arise, while the AJP facilitates unions' access in workplaces where they are not present. Such collaboration turned out to be effective since it led to local gentlemen's agreements, regularly signed at company level. These agreements state that when one party starts a negotiation with a company, it invites the other party to participate and creates a common front; and that the agreements between the AJP and employers are transformed into regular collective agreements through the signature of official unions. The French AFD has established partnerships with several other design associations such as the Agence pour la création industrielle, Designers interactifs, Observatoire de l'EcoDesign, Fablab Woma, Shangaï Art, and design academy. The Dutch Kunstenbond association for artists collaborates with other associations, like ACT for actors, DuPho for photographers, and authors unions, as the Dutch association of writers and translators. These associations benefit from Kunstenbond's lobbying power and the tools and other services it provides for the self-employed. In turn, these associations bring in relevant professional knowledge and expertise regarding their sectors, hence facilitating the provision of tailored and specific services for their members. In the UK, both the MU and Equity, the trade union for actors and performers, are affiliated to the Federation of Entertainment Unions to improve the rights of workers in the creative industry. Moreover, the unions liaise with each other and with other unions like the Broadcasting, Entertainment, Communications and Theatre Union to lobby the government directly. For instance, in 2017 they successfully blocked an attempt to raise National Insurance contributions for self-employed workers by three percentage points, from 9 per cent to 12 per cent.

The second type of coalition is based on joining forces to lobby and campaign for the wider rights of self-employed workers, regardless of the economic sector or occupation involved. This second pattern of coalition-building can be traced back mainly in the organizations targeting a heterogeneous membership. The French FEDAE has established strong partnerships with a number of associations: Agence France Entrepreneur; Pôle Emploi (a French governmental agency which operates as an employment centre); Caisse interprofessionnelle de prévoyance et d'assurance; ACOSS/URSSAF (public agencies centralizing the collection of social contributions and ensuring their redistribution); the Régime social des indépendants; and Chambre nationale des professions liberals (Union of Liberal Professions). The British quasi-union IPSE works with other general professional associations such as the CBI and the REC to proactively campaign on issues that matter to businesses. The Italian quasi-union ACTA has successfully undertaken lobbying activities with a large coalition for approval of the Jobs Act for Autonomous Work (Law No. 81/2017). ACTA has also campaigned with trade union CGIL and vIVAce!, second level associations (ConfProfessioni), and movements (Coalition 27February, AltaPartecipazione) (for further details refer to Box 6.3). The French Business Cooperative has built partnerships with other cooperatives through the federation 'Integral Cooperative' that links different fields of the economic and social life, as well as with other organizations in autonomous workers' movements such as Bigre! that gathers together several organizations of the social economy (associations, cooperatives and mutuals). Partnerships around the cooperative organi-

---

BOX 6.3   COUNCIL OF PROFESSIONS (*CONSULTA DELLE PROFESSIONI*) (ITALY)

The Italian Council of Professions (*Consulta delle professioni*), coordinated by the union confederation CGIL (the Italian General Confederation of Labour) was created in 2009 with the aim of facilitating debate around professional self-employment among different organizations outside the union. It represents a permanent council at national level open to quasi-unions, professional associations, second-level associations (of both regulated and non-regulated professions) involved in self-employed representation. Specifically, the following organizations regularly take part: CoLAP (national umbrella organization for non-regulated professions); Confprofessioni (national umbrella organization for regulated professions); Strade, AITI and ANITI (three national organizations of translators); ANA and CIA (two national organizations of archaeologists); FEDERADIP (national association of tour guides); IVA sei Partita (association of architects and engineers); SINGEOP (national trade union of geologists); Inarcassa Insostenibile; MGA (lawyers), ACTA (quasi-union of freelancers in the advanced tertiary sector); CNA Professioni (umbrella organization); il Quinto Stato (think-tank of activists); and Coalizione 27 febbraio (movement).

The council operates on a national coordination level with scheduled meetings, while on a regional level the choice to activate a council is left to local organizations. National meetings foster dialogue among organizations on specific issues relating to the self-employed (legislative amendments, collective initiatives and proposals).

The Council of Professions is the result of a specific experience fostered by some union officials within the CGIL. It represents the first experiment in Italy of structured dialogue between a union and other organizations representing the self-employed, which evolved organization into a strategic context where the different actors coordinate and plan their lobbying activities to address ad hoc political battles (e.g. approval of the Jobs Act of Self-Employment: Law No. 81/2017). The council, by mediating among the different positions of organizations, can reach a unique political stance on disputed issues and, accordingly, advocate unitedly on behalf of the coalition.

zational model have contributed to diffuse new concepts of employment and enterprise. The Dutch PZO-ZZP closely lobbies with VNO-NCW, the employers' association: together they fight to halt emerging difficulties for self-employed professionals.

4.4   Collective Agreements for the Self-Employed: Hardly Negotiable

Our analysis confirms also that the traditional model based on collective bargaining of terms and conditions of employment is rarely applied as a strategy to recruit and organize self-employed workers. The negotiation of collective agreements for self-employed workers represents a tricky matter. The application of standard terms and conditions of employment to inherently individualistic and independent workers is not widely acknowledged as being an effective way of regulating the working conditions in self-employment. Some occupational unions in the creative industry in the UK, however, display a longstanding tradition of collective negotiation. The MU and Equity regularly negotiate and sign collective agreements, generally with individual employers and companies. The MU signs collective agreements with a large number of broadcasters, film producers and record companies, in particular in the recording and broadcasting department, hence for the music, film and television industries. The collective agreements apply to self-employed musicians engaged in recording music of all kinds, ranging from film soundtracks, to advertisement jingles, to soundtracks for TV shows. Unlike traditional agreements for salaried workers that set the hourly wage floor, the MU negotiates the minimum rate of pay based on three-hour sessions. Beyond setting the wage floor to be applied and the terms and conditions of work, the collective agreements establish the legal conditions applicable to the transfer of intellectual property rights. Hence musicians have some protection against their performances being recorded without their consent.

Consent is usually given through the use of MU standard agreements and consent forms, and the manner in which consent is given is important as it can affect payment for secondary and further uses. The agreements take into consideration also the qualifications of the musicians or, for instance, the number of instruments played. Likewise Equity, as a social partner, negotiates several collective agreements in all the main areas of the creative industry with diverse employers: single employers like the BBC, or trade bodies representing multiple employers in the same sector such as independent producers. The union involves in the negotiations its internal specialized committees representing occupations and groups who will be materially affected by the agreements. In some cases Equity also organizes ballots among workers potentially affected by an agreement before signing it. The collective agreement in particular sectors might also include new specific clauses: for instance, a special payment regime for auditions—so self-employed actors taking part in auditions, for example, get paid for their time. Equity has what are referred to as deputies in many workplaces, especially in casting and production centres. Despite not being fully trained like shop stewards, the deputies act as representatives of the union in the workplace and as a main point of contact between the union and workers.

4.5 Novel Ways of Connecting

Beyond the main patterns of organizational responses and strategies (servicing, lobbying and coalition-building), it is appropriate to mention some relevant novel practices as they shed light on the changing relationship between representative organizations and their members. First, most of the organizations analysed pointed out the increasing use of social networks, online forums, websites and digital tools to promote their services and campaigns, as well as to recruit and mobilize members. The large majority of cases regularly update their webpage, Facebook page and Twitter account. Second, much creative effort has been increasingly put into the promotion of new captivating and innovative campaigns. The British MU launched the campaigns #WorkNotPlay and 'Keep Music Live'; the Belgian AJP launched the campaign 'Freelancer not easily fooled (*pigiste pas pigeon*)'; and the Italian quasi-union ACTA launched campaigns on Twitter using word puns: #refurtIVA and #malusRenzi. Third, in various cases the organizations set up informal networking meetings in the forms of 'coffee break' or 'breakfast appointments': the French FEDAE organizes the '*café de l'entrepreneurs*'; the Dutch PZO-ZZP organizes 'knowledge cafés'; and the Belgian SmartBE sets up 'breakfast meetings'. These novel ways of connecting imply alternative definitions of different relevant audiences, addressing workers with varying levels of connectedness (e.g. members, registered users, relevant others/affected professionals, general public) and creating various opportunities for connecting (e.g. memberships, visiting events), but also using membership for creating legitimacy in different ways. When the number of consenting subscribers was greater than the number of engaged and committed members, this also affected the lobbying positions of organizations.

To sum up, the various organizational strategies (servicing, lobbying, coalition-building and novel ways of connecting) adopted by actors in the labour market addresses the strategies and ambitions of the organizations to collectively represent this segment of workers. The question of ambition for collective representation is not self-evident given the changing nature of the socio-economic context, with, on the one hand, fragmentation and individualization of the workforce, and on the other hand, the possibilities inherent in the rich institutional environment in most EU countries, capable of providing more ways to overcome individual vulnerability and address the collective challenges of workers than ever before.

We observed four main strategies in our study: (a) servicing (to clients/ members) where the organizations' responsibilities are limited to the provided services (this is true more so for LMIs with clients—cooperatives might think of more services to offer, but their service strategy may preclude offering them); (b) lobbying (generalized for all self-employed or for specific occupational groups), where actors need to be responsive and engage with a full breadth of challenges in the field and go along with new developments as they apply to the constituency for which they are responsible; (c) coalition-building, which could be based on broad activities (e.g. lobbying for a broader constituency), but also able to differentiate and focus on specific sets of activities and working with other organizations that cover alternative aspects where the self-employed need support; (d) novel ways of connecting, implying a varying definition of relevant audiences, addressing needs differently and using the organization's legitimating effect in various ways.

5. WHAT DOES ORGANIZING FOR SELF-EMPLOYMENT MEAN? CONCLUDING REMARKS

The comparative analysis of the organizational experiences in Europe sheds new light on our understanding of the collective representation of workers in a rapidly changing socio-economic landscape. In particular, the chapter has investigated two interrelated puzzles: first, what does it mean to organize in the light of the evolving characteristics of the labour market? And second, what are the strategies and ambitions of organizations to collectively represent the self-employed worker segment?

5.1 Organizational Structure: Trajectories of Creation and Organizational Embedding

In terms of organizational structure, interesting common trends have emerged across European countries, providing clear indications about the trajectories of transformation of the structures of the collective representation in new and unorganized segments of the labour market. First, novel innovative organizational structures have emerged: quasi-unions, labour market intermediaries and new forms of cooperativism have been launched across Europe. These new experiences, often created bottom-up by the autonomous initiative of groups of workers looking for collective visibility and voice, have gradually become institutionalized and are relevant interlocutors when the interests and the rights of self-employed workers are at stake in the public debate as well as in the political agenda. Created ad hoc to target the demands of this group of workers, they have quickly and flexibly responded to the new exigencies raised by self-employed workers in the labour market. Interestingly, these innovative organizational forms have in several cases preceded the action of the traditional trade unions. Most of these early new organizations built their membership on representing a specific economic occupational sector, addressing the specific challenges of their members. However, over time some of these organizations have broadened their constituency to take into greater account the distinctive interests of self-employed as such, but most remain focused on their core membership or client base.

Trade unions were less responsive to these new developments, focusing on protecting and advocating for their traditional constituency of salaried employees. When the group of precarious self-employed started to expand in the early 2000s, trade unions in Europe adjusted their structures to build membership among them. This process of adaptation and revitalization occurred at difference paces and followed diverse configurations. The dominant pattern, however, was the creation of ad hoc structures, separate from the core union structure. This strategy may be the outcome of two opposing objectives. On the one hand, the ad hoc structure might more flexibly accommodate the specific interests of this segment of the labour market, inherently different from the demands of the subordinated workforce. This is in line with the choices of several unions serving many self-employed, who became independent and thus better able to handle the specific requests of their constituency. On the other hand, however, 'this may also be seen as a means of marginalising such workers, rather than mainstreaming their organization within the core sectoral union structure' (Bernaciak et al. 2014, p. 4).

5.2 Strategies for Engaging in Support and Representation

Considering the strategies of all organizations engaged in supporting and representing self-employed workers, three main models emerged, alternative to the traditional approach of collective bargaining: servicing, lobbying and coalition-building. The collective negotiation of terms and conditions of employment in fact proved not to represent a widely used approach to organize the population of inherently individualistic and geographically dispersed workers with different requirements, and whose legal status also complicated their inclusion in the traditional institutional configurations of employment relations. Besides these main approaches, some novel mechanisms, such as social networks and online forums, were used to establish and maintain relationships with the membership, partly because of their technical availability, partly because of the nature of their constituencies.

Servicing, lobbying and coalition-building have proven to be effective in starting to build support and a collective identity. The provision of professional services dedicated to self-employed members represents the dominant focus of many organizations: legal advice, fiscal support, training and administrative services are the most widespread. However, some innovative cooperatives have set up also forms of mutualism for their members, in the form of mutual guarantee funds, customized insurance packages, leasing for professional equipment, microcredit for the development of professional activities, and subsidies. Such experimental solutions can be interpreted as a 'functional equivalent' (Marsden 2004) to the social protections that could be found in a standard employment relationship. In the words of these cooperatives, their goals are to 'smooth out the individual job transitions via transitional rights', trying to disconnect access to social rights from professional and employment status, hence minimizing risks for the workers. In other cases, service provision represents the first phase in the setting up of organizations, an effective and continuous recruitment tool for members, but that prefaces and complements a lobbying action.

The lobbying model embodies a second organizational strategy. Lobbying and campaigning for the rights of self-employed workers, for a better acknowledgement of their specific status to which the social and employment protections are attached, represent the core goal of some organizations. Advocacy and lobby actions are carried out towards governments, parliaments, public administrative bodies, local policymakers, and institutionalized consultative bodies. This is the case for quasi-unions, auto-entrepreneurs' associations and professional associations for self-employed workers, which concentrate their strategic actions in pursuing the approval of ad hoc measures and regulatory interventions that improve the condition of self-employed workers as a whole, beyond occupational and sectoral segmentations. Interestingly, some of the organizations following the lobbying model have investigated the possibility of developing services to strengthen their relationship with their constituency.

The third approach focuses on the construction of coalitions and partnerships with various actors operating in the same field. The large majority of the organizations belonged to at least one more or less formalized network/partnership/coalition. This reflects the complex inter-relatedness of the issues around representation of self-employed workers.

Beyond differences between sector-/occupation-based coalitions and those partnerships grounded in the wider issue of self-employment rights, the establishment of new alliances and coalition-building represents an attractive and effective strategy.

To conclude, what can we learn from these experiences? What are the lessons for a renewed and more encompassing social dialogue? The new demand of collective representation raised by the self-employed segment of the labour market has certainly challenged the theoretical categories of mobilization and unionization, which can hardly be applied in such a socio-economic landscape (Heckscher and McCarthy 2014). However, the notion of solidarity-building can more suitably fit the efforts made by traditional and new actors representing this peculiar labour market segment. Our findings show that solidarity was built from below, following a bottom-up trajectory triggered by groups of workers themselves who felt not to be otherwise represented. Hence solidarity mostly started from the under-represented or from the un-organized who autonomously decided to set up their own structures of collective representation, looking then for an institutional acknowledgement.

For an effective collective representation of new labour market segments, what seems to be needed is also the creation of a class consciousness that starts from a shared collective understanding of the phenomenon and from the acknowledgement of the relatively common challenges that workers have to cope with. With the growing share of self-employment and the long duration of self-employment for individual workers, there is a growing need to build a sound and lasting solidarity for this segment, if possible beyond occupational or sectoral-based segmentations. The collective identity of this population of workers seems to dismantle the basis for industrial solidarity, paving instead the way to a different exploration of complex identities grounded on the acknowledgement of having in common the status and accordingly the characteristics of self-employed. However, a common understanding then should be backed by new shared narratives and languages to address their specific demands. These are easier to develop bottom-up, from practice, and for specific groups. While some representative organizations, such as journalist unions, have been doing this effectively for a long time already, we found that only recently are unions and some of the new representative organizations broadening their scope to address the more generic group of self-employed workers.

Moreover a high degree of transnational emulation shows the relevance of learning from other cases of 'good practice'. Through affiliation to international federations, networking occasions and a wider access to digital tools, organizations have the opportunity to mutually learn from each other across national borders. Throughout European countries, similar organizational responses to common supranational challenges have emerged, although their prevalence and institutional embedding varied due to different national institutional contexts. Regardless, the geographical scale of collective representation seems to overcome national boundaries, to trespass in forms of international transfer of good practices of a new solidarity.

The different organizations have to act together within their national labour markets and political frameworks in order to be heard. In search for coalitions, our organizations show that it is not easy to develop effective alliances based on mutual acknowledgement beyond their own autonomy. The sharing of common visions and prospects should overcome the different logics of actions and of organizing that each association follows, but it is often hindered by the complexity and ambiguity of the phenomenon of the independent self-employed in the context of existing organizations of work and employment. The findings from this study show the variety of possible ways forward.

REFERENCES

Autor, D. H. (2008), *The Economics of Labor Market Intermediation: An Analytic Framework*, Working Paper 14348, National Bureau of Economic Research, September, accessed at http://www.nber.org/papers/w14348.

Banfi, D. and S. Bologna (2011), *Vita da freelance: i lavoratori della conoscenza e il loro futuro*, Milan: Feltrinelli Editore.

Bernaciak, M., R. Gumbrell-McCormick and R. Hyman (2014), *European Trade Unionism: From Crisis to Renewal?*, ETUI Report 133, Brussels, accessed at https://www.etui.org/Publications2/Reports/European-trade-unionism-from-cri sis-to-renewal.

Bieler, A. and I. Lindberg (eds) (2011), *Global Restructuring, Labour and the Challenges for Transnational Solidarity*, London: Routledge.

Crouch, C. (2012), 'Il declino delle relazioni industriali nell'odierno capitalismo', *Stato e Mercato*, **94** (1), 55–75.

Dølvik, J. E. and J. Waddington (2002), 'Private Sector Services: Challenges to European Trade Unions', *Transfer: European Review of Labour and Research*, **3** (2), 356–76.

Drahokoupil, J. (ed.) (2015), *The Outsourcing Challenge: Organizing Workers across Fragmented Production Networks*, Brussels: European Trade Union Institute (ETUI).

Frege, C. M. and J. Kelly (2003), 'Union Revitalization Strategies in Comparative Perspective', *European Journal of Industrial Relations*, **9** (1), 7–24.

Gottschall, K. and D. Kroos (2003), *Self-Employment in Germany and the UK: Labor Market Regulation, Risk-Management and Gender in Comparative Perspective*, 13/2003, University of Bremen, Centre for Social Policy Research (ZeS).

Gumbrell-McCormick, R. (2011), 'European Trade Unions and "Atypical" Workers', *Industrial Relations Journal*, **42** (3), 293–310.

Gumbrell-McCormick, R. and R. Hyman (2013), *Trade Unions in Western Europe: Hard Times, Hard Choices*, Oxford and New York: Oxford University Press.

Heckscher, C. and F. Carré (2006), 'Strength in Networks: Employment Rights Organizations and the Problem of Co-Ordination', *British Journal of Industrial Relations*, **44** (4), 605–28.

Heckscher, C. and J. McCarthy (2014), 'Transient Solidarities: Commitment and Collective Action in Post-Industrial Societies', *British Journal of Industrial Relations*, **52** (4), 627–57.

Koene, B., N. Galais and C. Garsten (2014), 'Management and Organization of Temporary Work', in B. Koene, N. Galais, and C. Garsten (eds), *Management and Organization of Temporary Agency Work*, London: Routledge, pp. 1–20.

Malone, T. W., R. J. Laubacher and T. Johns (2011), 'The Big Idea: The Age of Hyperspecialization', *Harvard Business Review*, July–August.

Marsden, D. (2004), 'The "Network Economy" and Models of the Employment Contract', *British Journal of Industrial Relations*, **42** (4), 659–84.

Martin, A. and G. Ross (eds) (1999), *The Brave New World of European Labor: European Trade Unions at the Millennium*, New York: Berghahn Books.

Pernicka, S. (2006), 'Organizing the Self-Employed: Theoretical Considerations and Empirical Findings', *European Journal of Industrial Relations*, **12** (2), 125–42.

Regini, P. M. (1992), *The Future of Labour Movements*, London: Sage.

Waddington, J. and R. Hoffman (2000), 'Trade Unions in Europe: Reform, Organization and Restructuring', in *Trade Unions In Europe: Facing Challenges and Searching for Solutions*, Brussels: European Trade Union Institute (ETUI), pp. 27–79.

Wood, A. J., V. Lehdonvirta and M. Graham (2018), 'Workers of the Internet Unite? Online Freelancer Organization among Remote Gig Economy Workers in Six Asian and African Countries', *New Technology, Work and Employment*, **33** (2), 95–112.

APPENDIX

Table 6.1a   List of organizations investigated, their organizational form, the year of establishment and country

Name of organization	Organizational form	Year of creation	Country
CSC: Christian Trade Union	Trade union	2015	Belgium
SmartBE	LMI	1998	Belgium
AJP: Association of Professional Journalists	Professional association		Belgium
FEDAE: Fédération des auto-entrepreneurs	Quasi-union	2009	France
Coopname (a business employment cooperative)	LMI	2003	France
AFD: Alliance française des designers	Professional association	2003	France
CGT: Confédération nationale du travail	Trade union	2017	Trade union
Platform Union (F3C-CFDT)	Trade union	2016	France
Ver.di Selbstständige	Trade union	2001	Germany
SmartDE	LMI	2013	Germany
Supermarkt	Platform cooperativism	2012	Germany
BDÜ: Federal Association of Interpreters and Translators	Professional association	1955	Germany
ACTA: Association of Consultants in the Advanced Tertiary Sector	Quasi-union	2004	Italy
vIVAce! the community (CISL)	Trade union	2015	Italy
CLAP: Chambers for Independent and Precarious Workers	Movement	2013	Italy
Kunstenbond	Trade union	1977	Netherlands
Yacht	LMI	1999	Netherlands
PZO-ZZP	Quasi-union	2002	Netherlands
Movement for Decent Work and Welfare Society	Movement	2011	Slovenia
Trade Union of Precarious Workers	Trade union	2016	Slovenia

CTAC: Confederació de Treballadors Autònoms de Catalunya	Trade union	2001	Spain
Autònoms PIMEC	Employer association	1999	Spain
UATAE Catalunya: Union of Associations of Autonomous and Entrepreneurial Workers of Catalonia	Professional association	2011	Spain
SEC: Self-Employment Company	LMI		Sweden
JU: Journalist Union	Trade union	1960	Sweden
Job Security Foundation	LMI		Sweden
MU: Musicians' Union	Trade union	1921	UK
IPSE: Association of Independent Professionals and the Self-Employed	Quasi-union	1999	UK
Equity	Trade union	1930	UK

7. Conclusions: perspectives on self-employment in Europe

Manuela Samek Lodovici, François Pichault and Renata Semenza

The proliferation of new forms of self-employment investigated in this book has highlighted some important developments in the labour market and some new crucial challenges for regulatory frameworks within European countries which to reflect the structural changes in production and consumption patterns resulting from technological innovation and modification of preferences and lifestyles.

As discussed in the theoretical framework by Semenza and Mori (Chapter 2), the growth of these forms of employment is questioning the theories of dualism and labour market segmentation, in particular the dichotomy between insider/outsider and dependent/independent work. Workers are increasingly involved in multiple jobs and fluid employment relationships often combining both forms of employment, and experiencing frequent transitions from one status to the other during their working lives. The social paradox we are witnessing is that higher educational qualifications and professional specialization are no longer a guarantee of high levels of income and social status and this has repercussions on class structures, until now identified according to the classification of occupations (Crompton 2010). We have underlined the contradiction between the consolidation of a 'professional work model' within companies and in the market—sustained by a growing demand for specialization—and high levels of social risks and income volatility due to the intermittent nature of work. Although, on the one hand, changes in the labour market open new potential employment opportunities, on the other hand, they are producing new employment and social risks that ask for a revision of social protection schemes, as well as of the social dialogue and industrial relations systems.

Focused on self-employed professionals and freelance workers, the studies presented in the previous chapters contribute to a better understanding of the types of gaps these new forms of work are opening up for social organizations—referring especially to legal status definitions, social protection schemes and collective representation—and the different approaches adopted across Europe in dealing with these gaps.

New opportunities for self-employed professionals relate mainly to the greater degree of autonomy in performing work, to the possibility of expanding the market for their services thanks to global platforms, and to a greater flexibility in the use of time and place of work, which could facilitate the work–life balance. However, these opportunities come at the price of job insecurity, and specific employment and social risks.

The European cross-country survey presented in Chapter 3 shows that, even though there is some heterogeneity in the income and working conditions among self-employed professionals, they are increasingly facing low and insecure income levels. This is due to the difficulty in obtaining fair compensation for their work and long delays in payments; multitasking and long working hours (including time allocated to unpaid administrative tasks, promotion, and training activities); blurred boundaries between work and family life; and very limited access to social security. Moreover, these self-employed workers underline the professional isolation they face and the difficulty in securing professional development and career upgrades.

Similar social challenges are addressed in different way across European countries, as the regulatory and policy frameworks are strongly embedded in existing national institutional and regulatory models that have become entrenched over the years.

The analysis of the national institutional regimes in the nine country case studies (Belgium, France, Germany, Italy, the Netherlands, Slovenia, Spain, Sweden and the UK) reported in Chapter 4, transversally compared by Pichault and Beuker in Chapter 5, underlines that the rise in the share of self-employed professionals has not yet been accompanied by a structural revision of the regulatory framework. There is a lack of a comprehensive reform design regarding legal recognition and regulation, social protection systems and industrial relations models, which still need to be adapted to the new emerging demands for employment rights and social protection of self-employed workers, as well as other non-standard workers and workers in the platform-mediated labour market.

The scenario emerging from case studies is of small reforms at the margin and great fragmentation of the measures implemented. In fact, the study shows a variety of legal distinctions on self-employment status adopted in European countries, and the regulatory approach is reflected in the degree of inclusiveness of the social security system. The institutional framework ranges from a universalistic model prevalent in Scandinavian countries, where no legal distinction is made between self-employed and employees (although fiscal and social protection legislation is differentiated according to the work status), to the binary regulative approach adopted in most continental countries (e.g. Belgium, France, Holland), where workers are either self-employed or employees. In other countries a third hybrid status has been defined, midway between dependent and independent employment with access to certain social protection rights, as in Germany, Italy, Slovenia, Spain and the UK.

Except in countries with a universalistic approach (e.g. Sweden), access to social protection remains generally limited for the self-employed, compared to standard permanent employees. In most countries, favourable fiscal regimes (e.g. financial incentives, tax exemptions, access to loans at preferential rates) in part compensate for the lack of social protection, although this contributes to the fragmentation of employment and favours socio-economic inequalities in the labour market. Social security schemes vary significantly across countries also in terms of their funding (general taxation versus social contributions, compulsory versus voluntary-based system, universal coverage versus contribution-based) and type of support, resulting in different degrees of social protection. For example, in social protection systems with variable or voluntary contributions, there is a risk that the self-employed with low and irregular income opt out or pay the lowest level of contributions, leading to under-insurance against social and health risks; while the lowering of tax rates for professionals might encourage companies to use freelancers in service contracts, instead of hiring workers. However, the study shows that in the European political debate of recent years there are signs of a greater awareness of the fragmentation of employment contracts and strong inequalities in employment conditions and incomes. The need to extend (selectively) social protection to the self-employed is today more evident. In some countries (like Italy and Spain), new legislation has been implemented in order to extend access to specific employment rights (such as rules and penalties on payment times, tax deductions on training costs) and selective eligibility to some universal social guarantees, such as maternity and sickness subsidies.

Moreover, European institutions are recently bringing the issue of employment rights and social protection for self-employment up front in the political agenda, and this move is likely to affect national regulations. The 'European Pillar of Social Rights' proclaimed jointly by the European Parliament, the Council, and the European Commission in November 2017,[1] is a first important step in in this direction.[2] Among its principles,

---

[1]   European Parliament, Council and European Commission (2017).
[2]   Although the Social Pillar is not a binding legislative tool, it provides a framework for the revision of EU intervention in the social and employment policy fields, including working conditions, social protection and quality of work.

it includes the need to ensure better working conditions and access to minimum employment and social rights for all workers, whatever their employment status. However, attention to the self-employed is still limited. While the social protection principle explicitly mentions the self-employed, the fair working conditions principle does not explicitly mention them and appears to be confined to employees.

This book has also focused on the new forms of collective representation and organization through which self-employed professionals articulate and defend their interests. This is a specific topic in the broader debate on non-standard and precarious work (Kalleberg and Dunn 2016).

The in-depth analysis of innovative forms of collective interest representation, carried out by Mori and Koene in Chapter 6, provides a picture of the proliferation of new actors and bottom-up organizations, besides (or beyond?) traditional unions, aimed at collectively representing this growing unorganized segment of the labour market. The study outlines how quasi-unions, LMIs and new cooperation practices have emerged across Europe and the way in which they are able to convey self-employed professionals' voices, operating transversally across occupations, economic sectors and professions. Rising from the erosion of the basis for traditional collective representation and the 'hard times' of trade unionism (Gumbrell McCormick and Hyman 2013), these organizations have gradually become institutionalized, becoming relevant interlocutors in the public debate and in policymaking. Interestingly, these new industrial relations actors have in several cases pre-dated classical trade unions in the collective representation of these non-standard workers. Conversely, trade unions and professional associations show some difficulty in adjusting their consolidated mission and organizational configuration to those emerging needs. Their adjusting process has followed diverse trajectories in European countries, with the dominant pattern being the creation of ad hoc structures (through a top-down approach), representing also other non-standard workers, and often separate from the core union structure in order to allow greater flexibility.

Based on twenty-nine collective organizations investigated across Europe, the study individuates three main organizational strategies for engaging in the support and representation of the self-employed: the provision of services, as neo-mutual organizations; the fulfillment of an advocacy, lobbying and political role; and building coalitions and new alliances in order to reinforce their legitimacy. A combination of strategies and the different capacity to create partnerships and coalitions characterize each national context or cluster of countries.

The servicing model, as organizational logic of action, is the most widespread. All the surveyed organizations provide professional services to reduce the administrative burden on their affiliates and to provide legal advice, fiscal support, training, and some forms of mutualism, including social and health insurance packages, leasing and access to (micro) credit. Support to community creation, often through the provision of virtual or physical spaces for aggregation and self-help in order to reduce the sense of isolation felt by the majority of freelance workers, is another common type of service provided.

The second recurrent strategy is lobbying and campaigning for the rights of self-employed workers, with a focus on fair remuneration and access to social protection. In the case of unions, even if some form of negotiation is implemented to improve the working conditions of freelancers in strongly unionized occupations (e.g. journalists, media workers), collective agreements for the self-employed are rarely feasible.

Coalition-building is the third dominant organizational strategy adopted to give a collective voice to these dispersed and fragmented segments of the labour market, through the creation of more or less structured and formalized partnership coalitions often involving both unions and other representative bodies. The coalitions can facilitate access to new constituencies of workers, particularly important when the recruitment of unorganized segments of the labour market is at stake, as in the case of the self-employed.

Beyond these three main patterns of organizational responses and strategies towards the collective representation of the self-employed, some innovative practices are spreading rapidly and shed light on the changing relationship of representative organizations with their members. Most of the organizations analysed pointed out the increasing role of social networks, online forums, websites and digital tools in promoting their services and campaigns, as well as for recruiting and mobilizing members.

The new needs of collective organization arising from dispersed segments of workers in the labour market, namely the increasing number of self-employed professionals, have certainly challenged the classical categories of mobilization and unionization that have adapted badly to a socio-economic context revolutionized by information technology and changed working relations. The research results indicate that solidarity and new organizational forms arise from the bottom, following non-conventional models, which combine different strategies and are recurring in different European contexts.

POLICY RESPONSES

The challenges posed to employment and social rights by new employment trends ask for new tailored and focused policy responses to support the equal treatment of workers, whatever their status, a level playing field across the EU, and upward convergence in working conditions and social protection. The existing European and member state legislation and policies need to be revised in order to address these challenges, avoiding labour market segmentation and growing inequalities in employment and social rights across workers and countries.

This asks for a rethinking of the regulatory framework on employment relations, the extension of welfare and social protection models towards a universalistic approach, and the recognition of new forms of industrial relations and social dialogue mechanisms both at European and national level.

The velocity and complexity of current and expected changes in employment patterns require the capacity to learn from institutional experimentation (Malsch and Gendron 2013) in order to explore new ways to face these changes. Switching from a rigid 'regulatory paradigm' (normative/legal) to a trial and error approach and a 'representative paradigm' of (self-)employment in Europe could support higher flexibility and rapidity in addressing changing employment conditions. We can expect that a stronger involvement of representative bodies in the provision of employment rights and social protection services will have a feedback on both the legal status and social protection sides. Comparative research on the pros and cons of different regulatory and policy models, and the exchange of experience among policymakers, regulators and representative workers' organizations, could also support the identification of new ways for ensuring fair working conditions and social protection to self-employed professionals and other categories of non-standard workers. The examples of good practices reported in this book (Chapter 6) provide already some interesting experiences that have to be evaluated in order to assess what works, how and where. European institutions could have an important role in supporting research and capacity-building through the exchange of experiences and practices among organizations, policymakers and regulators.

Rethinking the Regulatory Framework

As noted above, the evolution in the nature of work with the diffusion of new forms of employment relations and working conditions is challenging the traditional dichotomy between dependent and independent work, and generating new employment and social risks. The regulatory framework of employment relations has to evolve in order to address a number of issues emerging with the proliferation of these new forms of employment and to support a better quality of work for all workers, whatever their employment relationship.

A first issue is related to the legal status of new independent workers, which is defined in different ways in European countries. As shown in Chapter 5, these workers are usually considered as independent contractors or entrepreneurs, so that any attempt to structure collective demands risks breaching antitrust legislation and trade practices. On the other hand, semi-dependent freelancers who only work for a single employer might achieve an employee or 'worker' status.

The blurring boundary between self-employed workers and employees jeopardizes the effectiveness of employment and social rights, which depend on the workers' legal status. To the extent that workers are wrongly categorized as self-employed, they are removed from the protection of the European standards to which they should in fact be subject. The case of platform workers is emblematic in this respect. The status of these workers has not yet been clearly defined at European and national level. Platform workers in most member states are treated as self-employed providers of services (to whom collective agreements do not apply), although the platform's owners generally dictate all the contractual details (such as pay, working conditions and intellectual property). Another case is that of labour market intermediaries (LMIs), increasingly involved in the provision of services to self-employed workers (such as insurance packages, training, financial support), either considering them as quasi employees or quasi self-employed (Lorquet et al. 2018). In all these cases, where legislation does not define clear criteria, the role of court judgement becomes particularly relevant. Court judgement is indeed becoming an increasingly important source of employment and social rights protection for the self-employed, as it is crucial for qualifying ambiguous employment relationships particularly in those countries where there is no statutory definition of dependent employment. However, recourse to court judgement is usually difficult for freelance workers given the risks it involves for future work opportunities, the long procedures usually required, and the need to involve collective representative bodies.

In the current debate, there is an increasing awareness of the need to overcome the traditional paradigms of rigidly separated employment statuses. New approaches and criteria are needed to equip policymakers with guidelines for their regulative actions in this field. Among the many options assessed in the recent debate,[3] the adoption of a universal rights approach, whatever the workers' status and employment relationship, appears the

---

[3] Steward and Stanford (2017) list five options to re-regulate employment conditions in the gig economy: (1) confirm and enforce existing laws, (2) clarify and expand the definitions of employment, (3) create a new category of independent workers, (4) create rights for workers, not employees, (5) reconsider the concept of an employer.

most appropriate to address current and future trends in employment patterns. Fair working and payment conditions, standardized access to social rights (maternity and parental leaves, health insurance, safety at work, etc.), professional recognition and lifelong learning should transcend the employment status and relationships with particular employers. While for some rights, such as protection from discrimination, this option can be easily extended to all workers, for others, such as the definition of fair pay or paid leave, a minimum protection framework applicable to all workers has to be designed.

Another option could be to maintain the current dichotomy between dependent and independent work and expand the existing protection rules to cover at least those contractors that can be considered as 'dependent' and thus closer to a salaried status. However, the rapid evolution of new forms of employment midway between dependent and independent status makes it difficult to clearly identify these workers and their 'employers', as in the case of platform workers. As shown in the comparative assessment of nine European countries (Chapters 4 and 5) and in the case of platform workers, the blurring differences between dependent and independent work make the attribution very complex and discretionary, while the creation of a third status in the regulative framework further increases the fragmentation of employment patterns and cannot be considered as a solution in improving the working conditions and social protection of freelance workers.

A step in the direction of a more universalistic approach is the European Commission's (2017) proposal for a Directive on transparent and predictable working conditions released in December of that year as a direct follow-up to the proclamation of the European Pillar of Social Rights in December of that year.[4] Although self-employed workers are outside the scope of the proposed directive, some of the rights envisaged can be extended to them, as has been done in some countries, like Italy with the Jobs Act for autonomous workers, approved in May 2017.

Another important issue regarding the need to reconsider the concept and regulation of the 'employer' status is the introduction of advanced technology and platform work, which is creating new forms of intermediation difficult to regulate compared to previous temporary agency work. Online platforms are not considered traditional employers, but only intermediaries between the users and the 'service providers'. Therefore, platform owners are currently not responsible for paying social security contributions, although they often set prices and working conditions.

---

[4]   European Commission (2017).

Platform owners avoid transforming the relationship with service providers into an employment one, in order to avoid a host of legal regulations to conform with. The transnational dimension of digital platforms, however, calls for European action in order to avoid the risk of further fragmentation in member states' reactions to the need for regulation of new emerging problems and social risk within the European common market.

The growing role of LMIs, which are increasingly involved in the employment of self-employed workers, must also be taken into account. While some LMIs aim to assist freelance workers by providing them with supportive services, others instead contribute to the spreading of fragmented work relationships. It is thus necessary to determine the conditions under which these organizations support the working conditions of autonomous workers, either directly or by developing relations with other representative actors (e.g. unions and quasi-unions).

The role of public administrations as users and/or employers of freelance workers is another aspect to be considered when dealing with their legal status. Public administrations are increasingly outsourcing their activities to independent contractors and/or to private companies or third-sector organizations, often employing freelance workers as service providers. In this role, public administrations may support good working conditions and employment status via specific contractual clauses, avoiding tendering only on the basis of lowest price and requiring that all service providers respect basic employment and social rights.

Extending Social Protection

The issue of social protection against unemployment, sickness, accidental and occupational injuries, maternity benefits, and old age is particularly important for the self-employed, platform workers, and workers with discontinuous employment histories. Recent legislative developments have tried to extend some social protection rights to all workers, including solo self-employed workers, but still they do not seem sufficient, especially when considering the actual access to social protection.

As underlined in a recent European Commission's analytical document,[5] the main shortcomings of current social protection systems in the majority of member states concern the lack of coverage, transferability and transparency. Self-employed professionals have usually limited or no access to public social protection schemes. They generally have only a formal

---

[5]   Commission Staff Working Document (2017).

coverage of healthcare, maternity/paternity benefits, invalidity, old-age and survivors' pension schemes, but in several countries they are excluded from statutory access, or may only be able to opt in on a voluntary basis to key insurance-based schemes such as sickness, unemployment and occupational/injury benefit schemes (ESPN 2017). Effective coverage is usually very low, due to low take-up rates and hard to meet eligibility requirements, often based on rules valid for dependent workers but not for self-employed workers. There is also a wide variation in formal coverage both between and within countries across different schemes, and among categories of self-employed within the same scheme. Unemployment benefits, accidental and occupational injuries, sickness and maternity benefits are the areas of social protections where the self-employed are less covered.

Welfare and social protection models thus need to be revised in order to ensure a social safety net to all workers. Access to social protection, unemployment benefits, healthcare, maternity and sickness leave for all workers should transcend employment status and relationships with particular employers. A new social protection system should ensure full coverage for workers, whatever their status; the transferability of social protection entitlements across different schemes and employment statuses, as well as across countries; and the transparency of social protection schemes and rights, in order to ensure that workers are able to make informed choices by having the necessary information and awareness on how social insurance contributions affect their pension and benefit entitlements.

Among the possible options to ensure full coverage of social protection to all workers, a system based on a combination of mandatory and voluntary public and private schemes appears the most appropriate and financially feasible. A universal public scheme for all workers, whatever their employment status, financed through general taxation would provide a minimum level of social protection to all. The public scheme could be supplemented by mandatory occupational schemes managed by representative bodies (as in Nordic countries) and funded through social contributions paid by employers and workers with and opt-in or, better, opt-out clauses for the self-employed, and managed by representative bodies (as in social partners in Nordic countries). Voluntary integrative private schemes could represent a third component, provided by workers' representative bodies (unions, quasi-unions, associations, LMIs) through mutualization. Mutualization by representative associations may reduce the individual costs of private schemes, thanks to economies of scale and greater bargaining power with insurance companies, as exemplified by the experience of the Freelancers' Union in the United States. Voluntary access could be enhanced by adopting opt-out clauses and income-based contributions.[6] To support the take-up of occupational and private schemes fiscal incentives may also be provided.

This mixed system extends social coverage to those workers (dependent or independent) with a discontinuous employment history or unable to pay social contributions. Two main issues must however be addressed. The first is how to make companies, and in particular platform owners, contribute when they employ freelance workers. The second is how to remove barriers to access when setting entitlements, e.g. the level of social contributions to be paid by self-employed workers and the other obligations necessary to get access to benefits, in order to increase take-up and avoid opportunistic behaviours. Access and take-up of social protection could be increased by better tailoring social protection systems to the work realities of self-employed people (including the simplification of administrative procedures).

European institutions are already moving in this direction. In 2013 the European Parliament approved the resolution 'Social protection for all, including self-employed workers',[7] inviting member states to guarantee social protection to all workers including the self-employed; to provide mutual assistance to cover accidents, illnesses and pensions; to allow for continuous training for all workers; and to oppose 'bogus' self-employment. The specific reference to the category of self-employed workers represents a significant step towards the recognition of the peculiar identity and status of independent workers.

The European Commission released a Proposal for a Council Recommendation on access to social protection for workers and the self-employed in March 2018,[8] within the framework of the Social Pillar. Although the decisions on the protection levels to be guaranteed to workers (including the self-employed), remain under the responsibility of member states, the Commission's proposal for a Council Recommendation could provide guidance and support to member states on ensuring that

---

[6] As underlined in the cited Commission's Impact Assessment report: '*Opt-in clauses* require potential beneficiaries to take action to choose coverage whereas *opt-out designs* imply being covered is the default option, with action needed to avoid being covered. [. . .] Experiments and observational studies show that making an option a default increases the likelihood that it is chosen (default effect). [. . .] A large empirical literature shows the importance of default options in shaping decisions about retirement savings including savings plan participation and levels of contributions. [. . .] setting defaults can be an effective way of influencing behaviour also in a context of providing social security coverage' (Commission Staff Working Document (2018), Annex 10, p. 115).

[7] European Parliament (2014): *Resolution of 14 January 2014 on Social Protection for All, Including Self-Employed Workers (2013/2111(INI))*.

[8] European Commission (2018).

all workers and the self-employed: (1) through a combination of public, occupational or private schemes have full mandatory coverage in social security insurance for sickness and healthcare, maternity or paternity, accidents at work and occupational diseases, disability and old age. In the case of unemployment benefits the self-employed may adhere on a voluntary basis; (2) can accrue and take up adequate entitlements; (3) can transfer social security entitlements between schemes and employment statuses; (4) have transparent information on their social security entitlements and obligations.

The Commission's proposal also includes a provision asking for a commitment to collect and publish reliable statistics on access to social protection by type of employment relationships and individual characteristics, and for reinforced cooperation with Eurostat for the creation of appropriate indicators to monitor progress towards full coverage.

The support of European institutions towards a similar universally based social protection framework across European countries is relevant also to enhance labour mobility and avoid social dumping, especially in the case of international players, e.g. digital platforms that could choose to hire service providers in those countries where labour costs/social security are lower.

1.3 The Relevance of Collective Representation

Collective representation is a third crucial dimension for the protection of workers' rights with important repercussions and effects on their legal status and social protection.

The traditional recruiting, representation and collective agreements models do not work for independent and other non-standard workers, due to the growing individualization and fragmentation of employment relations over time, space and clients. In addition, European legislation and the legal frameworks in many countries do not allow collective bargaining over pay and working conditions for self-employed workers (due to antitrust regulations).

In this field too there is space for innovation and the experimentation with new forms of representation that could also support other non-standard workers. The country experiences and good practices presented in Chapter 6 illustrate the innovative ways adopted by new representative actors and associations to support networking and coalition-building strategies and the use of the Internet and virtual communities for recruitment, mobilization, and application of political pressure. These new actors are also increasingly relevant in the provision of support services, community-building and social protection schemes to self-employed workers, acting as functional equivalents to the range of social protection and employment rights generally guaranteed to subordinated workers by standard employment relations.

These new representation actors and strategies are becoming increasingly relevant not only for professional freelance workers but also for other non-standard workers and should be recognized and supported by public institutions as important drivers for the renewal/transformation of industrial relations and social dialogue models.

As discussed in detail by Gazier in the Afterword, there is indeed a need for revision of the traditional representation and industrial relation/social dialogue models. New negotiating frameworks have to be created and new actors have to be involved through both a revision of the industrial relations framework and social dialogue mechanisms, as well as capacity-building and funding mechanisms, so that the voices and needs of solo self-employed and other non-standard workers are heard in the policy-making process. Recent cases in the gig economy for consumption services demonstrate the capacity of new forms of collective organization and representation at territorial level to produce positive outcomes, at least with regard to insurance against accidents at work and minimum pay, when supported by local institutions and the involvement of final consumers.[9]

This revision also requires finding new ways of measuring workers' representation, as well as new ways of structuring the social dialogue. Again, different options are available in this respect. One is the creation of a parallel channel of dialogue between representative organizations and the government on issues relevant for autonomous workers, as in Spain with the creation of the Autonomous Work Council. Another option is to directly include representative freelance organizations in the social dialogue, as experienced in the journalism sector in Belgium. A third option could be to open membership of conventional unions to self-employed workers. All solutions have pros and cons that largely depend on the specific institutional and industrial relations framework present in each country.

Whatever the option adopted, the involvement of institutions representing the solo self-employed and other non-standard workers in the social dialogue is likely to generate greater attention on the social and employment rights of these workers, not only in labour law and in social protection, but also in active labour market policies, work–life balance measures and labour taxation all policy areas where the tripartite co-decision and/or consultation mechanisms are usually strongest.

Here too European institutions could play an important role, starting with a revision of the European Social Dialogue as envisaged in the

---

[9]   See Charhon and Murphy (2016); Johnston and Land-Kazlauskas (2018).

Commission Initiative for a New Start for Social Dialogue.[10] Although the Initiative does not explicitly mention self-employed workers and their organizations, EU institutions could encourage coalition-building between unions, quasi-unions and umbrella organizations, and support capacity-building through the exchange of experiences and practices.

Finally, further research is needed on new trends in employment relations and working patterns (Valenduc and Vendramin 2016). A revision of the conceptual approach on work statuses is necessary, to take into account the evolution towards new and mixed forms of work and the role of new technologies in changing work relationships. To this end, it is important to study how companies are changing their work organization patterns, with a focus on platform companies that 'exclusively' use self-employed service providers rather than employees.[11]

In order to develop a more evidence-based understanding of these changes, it is also necessary to improve data collection, facilitate the use of new data sources, tools and methods, and support data access for the research community, as also suggested by a recent US report (National Academies of Sciences, Engineering and Medicine 2017).

European institutions and Member States could also strengthen the knowledge base by supporting comparative research on the pros and cons of different institutional and industrial relations models in ensuring employment and social rights to all workers, as well as strengthening data collection and harmonization (Degryse 2016).

The authors hope that this book has paved the way to a better understanding of such complex evolutions and to broadening the usual conceptual frameworks relating to new forms of employment in order to support the development of more appropriate policy responses at European and national levels.

REFERENCES

Charhon, P. and D. Murphy (2016), *The Future of Work in the Media, Arts & Entertainment Sector: Meeting the Challenge of Atypical Working*, accessed at https://www.fim-musicians.org/wp-content/uploads/atypical-work-handbook-en.pdf.

---

[10] The Initiative provides milestones for supporting capacity-building among national social partners; a greater involvement of the social partners in EU policy- and law-making, including in the European Semester; and a clearer relationship between social partners' agreements and a Better Regulation Agenda. On this, see European Commission (2016) (Chapter 5: 'Capacity Building for Social Dialogue').
[11] Eurofound (2018).

Commission Staff Working Document (2017), *Analytical Document Accompanying the Consultation Document on the Second Phase Consultation of Social Partners under Article 154 TFEU on a Possible Action Addressing the Challenges of Access to Social Protection for People in All Forms of Employment in the Framework of the European Pillar of Social Rights*, SWD(2017) 381 final, 20 November, Brussels.

Commission Staff Working Document (2018), *Impact Assessment Accompanying the Document Proposal for a Council Recommendation on Access to Social Protection for Workers and the Self-Employed*, {COM(2018) 132 final}-{SWD(2018) 71 final}, 13 March, Brussels.

Crompton, R. (2010), 'Class and Employment', *Work, Employment and Society*, **24** (1), 9–26.

Degryse, C. (2016), *Digitalisation of the Economy and Its Impact on Labour Markets*, Working Paper 2016.02, European Trade Union Institute (ETUI).

ESPN (2017), *Synthesis Report on 'Access to Social Protection for People Working on Non-Standard Contracts and as Self-Employed in Europe'*: A Study of National Policies, accessed at http://ec.europa.eu/social/main.jsp?langId=en&catId=1135&newsId=2798&furtherNews=yes.

Eurofound (2018), *Automation, Digitalisation and Platforms: Implications for Work and Employment*, Luxembourg: Publications Office of the European Union.

European Commission (2016), *Employment and Social Development in Europe 2016*, Luxembourg: Publications Office of the European Union.

European Commission (2017), *Proposal for a Directive of the European Parliament and of the Council on Transparent and Predictable Working Conditions in the European Union*, COM/2017/0797 final-2017/0355 (COD), accessed at https://eur-lex.europa.eu/legal-content/EN/TXT/?uri=CELEX%3A52017PC0797.

European Commission (2018), *Access to Social Protection for All Forms of Employment: Assessing the Options for a Possible EU Initiative*, report prepared by Fondazione G. Brodolini, accessed at http://ec.europa.eu/social/main.jsp?catId=738&langId=en&pubId=8067.

European Parliament (2014), *Resolution of 14 January 2014 on Social Protection for All, Including Self-Employed Workers (2013/2111(INI))*, P7_TA(2014)0014, 14 January, Strasbourg, accessed at http://www.europarl.europa.eu/sides/getDoc.do?type=TA&reference=P7-TA-2014-0014&language=GA&ring=A7-2013-0459.

European Parliament, Council and European Commission (2017), *European Pillar of Social Rights*, accessed at https://ec.europa.eu/commission/sites/beta-political/files/social-summit-european-pillar-social-rights-booklet_en.pdf.

Gumbrell-McCormick, R. and R. Hyman (2013), *Trade Unions in Western Europe: Hard Times, Hard Choices*, Oxford and New York: Oxford University Press.

Johnston, H. and C. Land-Kazlauskas (2018), *Organizing On-Demand: Representation, Voice, and Collective Bargaining in the Gig Economy*, ILO Conditions of Work and Employment Series No. 94, 29 March, Geneva, accessed at https://www.ilo.org/wcmsp5/groups/public/---ed_protect/---protrav/--travail/documents/publication/wcms_624286.pdf.

Kalleberg, A. L. and M. Dunn (2016), 'Good Jobs, Bad Jobs in the Gig Economy', *Perspectives on Work*, **20**, 10–74.

Lorquet, N., J.-F. Orianne and F. Pichault (2018), 'Who Takes Care of Non-Standard Career Paths? The Role of Labour Market Intermediaries', *European Journal of Industrial Relations*, **24** (3), 279–95.

Malsch, B. and Y. Gendron (2013), 'Re-Theorizing Change: Institutional

Experimentation and the Struggle for Domination in the Field of Public Accounting', *Journal of Management Studies*, **50** (5), 870–99.

National Academies of Sciences, Engineering and Medicine (2017), *Information Technology and the U.S. Workforce: Where Are We and Where Do We Go from Here?*, Washington DC: National Academies Press.

Stewart, A. and J. Stanford (2017), 'Regulating Work in the Gig Economy: What are the Options?', *Economic and Labour Relations Review*, **28** (3), 420–37.

Valenduc, G. and P. Vendramin (2016), *Work in the Digital Economy: Sorting the Old from the New*, Working Paper 2016.03, European Trade Union Institute (ETUI).

Afterword: conditions for a new social dialogue in Europe

Bernard Gazier

Entitling independent workers to social rights and social protection, and ensuring that they earn decent incomes and have some control over their personal and professional lives, has become a major challenge of our time. Self-employed professionals represent here a key stake, because they are skilled, they are mere workers and do not possess the traditional capital and assets of entrepreneurs, and they have been the most dynamic part of the workforce since the beginning of the century. They represent, in a context of enduring unemployment and precarity in the European Union, one central way of developing employment and diversifying careers.

However, they do not fit into the classical processes of social dialogue, which were devised and implemented for salaried workers many years ago. The classical rationale for organizing salaried workers is that they suffer from a pervasive and structural inferiority versus employers, and then should benefit from a counteracting set of institutions, through labour law and collective negotiation. While employers, organized too, may find advantages in these collective arrangements (through a more stable, productive and predictable workforce), independent workers have been largely left out.

This situation is now increasingly regarded as unsatisfactory, not only because the number of these workers is increasing, but also because the classical salaried workers group now is at best stable and more often shrinking and undergoing profound transformations. New risks are appearing in the labour market, most of them related to the increased discontinuity of work trajectories. Stability for independent professional workers could be achieved through management of the increasingly discontinuous careers of many different types of workers: salaried workers looking for a more independent way of working and living; unemployed persons looking for alternatives, either temporary or permanent; purely independent, benevolent workers in non-profit projects; classical salaried workers or retired workers looking for an income complement, and so on. The debate narrows down to supporting diversified and even 'oblique careers', of which one central part is independent work.

The challenges and possible action fields for the European Union will be discussed in two steps. First, using the traditional definition of social dialogue, trends and challenges affecting this norm in the European Union will be examined briefly. The specific needs of these new workers will also be considered, connected to the rich potential resources they could provide. However, exploitation of these resources can only be achieved if one goes beyond the traditional social dialogue, and an enlarged version is considered. Second, three main strategies for bringing more rights and protection to these workers have been distinguished in the previous chapters. These will be examined in the context of such a renewed social dialogue and shown that they should act as complements rather than competing or substitute strategies. The possible roles of member states and the European Union in favouring this new social dialogue will be sketched, mainly through support for a positive interplay between the three strategies.

1. FROM A CLASSICAL VERSION TO AN ENLARGED VERSION OF SOCIAL DIALOGUE

Social dialogue has four components and begins with (i) information sharing and is mainly (ii) centred on negotiating wages, working time and working conditions. It also may include (iii) participation in the management of social security organizations, and ends in (iv) participation in the management of firms. Components (i) and (ii) are universal and without them there is no social dialogue. These cases, dialogue containing only the first two components, are typical of Anglo-Saxon countries. In other countries and especially in the European Union, one finds cases with three or four components. The differences across countries arise from the importance and intensity of each component, and from the way they may interact. In a nutshell, Nordic and Germanic countries have developed social dialogue with all four components, in an intensive way. Information sharing leads then to concertation, and negotiating occurs with strong, centralized and representative partners. Participation in the management of social security organizations and firms, through 'co-determination', is unevenly but usually well developed. In other countries, mainly in Southern Europe, a less intense and more sketchy set of institutions and practices can be observed: information remains asymmetric and does not lead to concertation, and negotiations are more decentralized and are led by less structured and less coherent partners. Participation in management presents a very uneven picture. In some countries, social partners really participate and in others they have only a minority position, sometimes only symbolic, decisions being taken without them (Gazier and Bruggeman 2016).

This complex and uneven architecture has been and is under pressure since the beginning of the century. Among the main trends and challenges, one can mention the strong tendency, encouraged by the European Union, towards more decentralized bargaining, and a strong tendency, here also reinforced by the European Union, towards less binding labour law arrangements and towards deregulation. While in many countries collective agreements have been extended to firms and workers of a whole branch or sector, sometimes automatically, these 'covering' practices have been lessened or made optional. Another source of weakness of European social dialogue lies in the social partners themselves, especially in the shrinking demography of unions: their membership is declining and militants are often ageing men in industrial sectors, in a world where services, women and young workers are becoming more important. However, it should be observed that this tendency mainly affects unions in the south of Europe.

Against this rather gloomy picture, one can easily insist on the needs and potential of independent professionals. While traditional salaried workers may feel that they are well protected (as long as they do not suffer from unemployment) and then become less militant and even passive in one way or another, these workers may feel that they have to build a new world to represent and protect them. They are, to some extent, in the same position as the 'Sublimes' were in nineteenth-century French social history: highly skilled, independent workers, at the same time individualistic and solidary. During the 1860s and 1870s, these Parisian workers were precisely at the very origin of mutual help institutions and funds, and at the origin of French unions.

Let us be precise in discussing the context of current action for the self-employed professionals of today. While independent and sometimes isolated, they face networks of firms and may build networks of workers, working spaces, mutual help funds and co-working spaces. They can, and many of them effectively do, combine individualistic traits with collective engagement.

However, it is quite clear that the traditional social dialogue can neither integrate nor support their action. What is needed is a renewed form of social dialogue—it already exists, but in a patchy way. Let us start from the three basic functions performed by social dialogue: ensuring social integration, balancing the diverging interests of social partners and distributing income and resources, and coordinating projects. While the second function has been and remains the main one, the other two are of prominent importance and now become central. For example, if one considers the fate of precarious workers and subcontracting firms in a context of restructuring, the representation of the interests of such actors is mainly absent from classical negotiations over the restructuring process. A renewed version of social dialogue should integrate them, probably mainly on a territorial basis. The process then is an enlarged version of collective negotiation, with new actors and new objects. The new actors' list comprises territorial actors such as municipalities, regions, professional networks and associations. The new objects of negotiation add to the traditional agenda project initiatives such as creating additional and specific social protection devices, intensive training and re-training, social follow-up, and so on.

In this enlarged landscape, the emerging collective actors of independent professionals should play an important role through diversified practices which have been presented in Chapter 6, such as offering services, lobbying, and taking part in negotiations over income guarantees, holidays, training rights, and so on. One can understand the emerging enlarged social dialogue as an integration of the four components presented above, either on a territorial basis or on a branch/sector basis. The tendency towards more decentralized negotiations noted above has then to be reconsidered, leading not only to plant by plant negotiations over wages and working conditions, but also to territorial and branch-wide negotiations—a recomposed, intermediate level of dialogue and coordination.

2. THE EU IN FRONT OF THREE COMPLEMENTARY STRATEGIES

What could the role of the European Union be in such a complex and emerging process? What kind of social dialogue could be adopted and what would it contain? Of course, current practices in EU member states are highly diverse and there is no 'one-size-fits-all' perspective here.

One may start from one of the main results of the study: the identification of three main national strategies aiming at better protecting independent workers, all of them being present in each member state to some extent, and all of them with advantages and limits. We will see that these strategies may justify European Union interventions, but involve very different modalities.

The first strategy consists in exploiting the stabilization potential of a salaried relationship for at least some independent workers. It entails two very different versions. The first one is the 'reclassification' strategy, used in some sectors for protecting 'economically dependent' independent workers, transforming them into salaried workers. As has been seen in 2017 for Uber drivers in California, this version concerns the so-called 'bogus' independents, because in fact their employment situation is very close to that of salaried workers. Two limits are observed here. First, this strategy cannot concern 'real' independent workers, but only a quite small fraction of them (say, less than 6 per cent). Second, some of these workers may not be willing to be considered as salaried workers, and may prefer to be considered as independent, and protected in another manner. However, a second version exists, more successful at least in some countries. It is opening access, to some groups of independent workers, to the social protection advantages of salaried workers. This technique of partial assimilation may concern independent workers in the entertainment and art sectors, but also workers acting as managers and entrepreneurs inside firms. It has also been developed for skilled workers delivering intellectual services, for example in the case of 'portage salarial'. The survey presented in Chapter 3 has shown that such arrangements, if not easily readable for other workers, do bring objective and subjective protection to the workers concerned. The arrangements' limits are easy to acknowledge: these workers are effectively protected if they succeed in getting enough hours of work, either beyond an official threshold (as is the case of the French 'intermittents du spectacle' regime) or simply for earning sufficient income from fragmented and unstable work opportunities. So there is a double risk of segmentation: first, for the workers in such sectors unable to get enough hours, who may be left out or left with insufficient income and protection, and second, for the independent workers in other sectors, operating under less favourable schemes. Such strategies can be extended only if they are combined with other, more general strategies, entitling non-covered independent workers to substantial inclusion and guarantees.

The second strategy is the reverse of the first one. It is a general and 'universal' strategy: developing a basis for social rights for every member of the workforce. This can be achieved in two ways. First, by setting a universal social protection scheme, either ambitious (as is the case in Nordic countries, cf. the case of Sweden presented in Chapter 4, Section 9) or more limited (as is the case in transitioning and less advanced countries, such as Slovenia, as we can see in Chapter 4, Section 7). A second way is to develop some enabling transversal rights, such as training rights or unemployment insurance rights, which can be granted to several categories of workers beyond salaried workers. A technique for developing such rights is to implement 'social drawing rights', rights that can be activated under some circumstances or at some period of the life course. Such strategies may be very costly because their intent is to cover a very large population with very different needs and contributory capacities. If governments choose to limit their costs by limiting their extent and intensity, they could become more cosmetic than real or result in a minimal form of safety net.

Here again, segmentation is a serious concern. While the most skilled may take advantage of transversal rights, less-equipped and less-skilled workers may simply not make use of their rights.

The last strategy is a bottom-up one and relies more directly on social dialogue: organizing independent professionals through organizations. Through networks, mutual funds, services and lobbying at different levels, and unions and quasi-unions, one can improve the living conditions and social protection of diverse groups of independent workers. This strategy and its ramifications have been explained in Chapter 6. Among the main results, it has been shown that it will necessarily remain unevenly implemented but is always relevant because it fosters autonomy and collective self-management. One interesting trait here is the diversity of application fields, from additional social protection to negotiations, aiming at ensuring a minimal price for services delivered through platforms. The stake here for the EU and its member states is developing a rich ecosystem of agile collective actors, able to perceive and elaborate the needs of these workers and to integrate isolated professional workers into groups of peers. The networking of these heterogeneous actors is an obvious way to improve their influence and legitimacy.

These three strategies are present, in a way or another, in all the national cases which have been studied in the I-WIRE project. Each strategy has strengths and drawbacks, and the view emerging from the book is that they should be more deliberately combined in order to reinforce each other and to act as complements rather than competing options. The risk of transversal rights remaining symbolic only can be overcome if two conditions are met: first, these rights should be effectively connected to other securing guarantees. As these guarantees may remain closed to workers not enrolled in the schemes or not fulfilling all the required conditions for being integrated, one needs to develop general protections and transversal rights to be given to any kind of worker in any kind of situation. Second, national and European interventions should fight against the abuses of subcontracting and restore the responsibility of principal firms and platforms. There is here ample room and need for political choices beyond the technical ones.

In order to develop the new social dialogue, policymakers in the European Union should take seriously two challenges which should be transformed into opportunities. The first one is the long-term consequences of the tendency towards decentralizing collective bargaining. As we have seen, the emerging new economy is one of networks and collaborative actors, and in this context the decentralization process is not a simple and univocal one. It should be reinterpreted as not only the priority of connecting the needs and resources of individual actors and firms in local contexts, but also the creation of new fields of solidarity and co-decision in branches and territories. The second challenge is the current state of slow growth in Europe as well as in most of the developed world. While things seem to have improved ten years after the global financial crisis in 2008, mid-term and long-term prospects remain modest. If so, and whatever the causes may be (ecological concerns as well as ill-explained productivity slowdown), economies and societies have to adapt. Accordingly, in a context where the creation of additional hours of paid work seems hampered, the idea of a work-sharing process through the whole life course is gaining momentum. It should be a flexible and even reversible one, for example through parental or training leaves.

In both domains, the needs and experience accumulated by self-employed professionals are central. The new social dialogue is a necessity not only for them but for all other workers and for society as a whole.

REFERENCE

Gazier, B. and F. Bruggeman (2016), 'Dialogue social et dialogue social territorial au début du XXIe siècle. Un essai de théorisation', *Négociations*, **2**, 55–72.

Index

on-demand service economy 1
Online Labour Index (OLI) 22, 28
Organisation for Economic Cooperation and Development
(OECD) 32, 148
organizational embedding 184–8
organizational logic of action 209
organizational strategies 14, 188–98,
209
coalition-building model 193–6
collective agreements, self-employed
196–7
connecting, novel ways 197–8
lobbying model 189–93
servicing model 189
organizational structure 184–8
creation trajectory, bottom-up and
top-down 186
mixed and heterogeneous
membership 186–8
timeframe 184–6
Osborne, C. 53, 54

parental leave 162
pension insurance 162
Perkin, H. J. 30, 31
pigistes 154
Piore, M. J. 26
policy responses 210–14
collective representation relevance
217–19
regulatory framework, rethinking
211–14
social protection, extending 214–17
portage salarial company 87
post-Fordism 21
post-Fordism paradigm 23
professional work model 31, 206
professionalism 29–31, 37
proliferation, self-employment forms
206
proto-union 40

quasi-unions 10, 40, 79, 182, 183

Rapelli, S. 3, 49, 50, 111, 140
recognition gap 32–3
recurrent strategy 210
*Regimen Especial de Trabajadores
Autonomos* (RETA) 163

Régime social des indépendants (RSI)
88, 165
regulatory frameworks 141–7
binary approach 141–3
hybrid approach 144–7
representation gap 33
Ribó, J. 118
Riesco-Sanz, A. 117, 118, 120
The Rise of Professional Society 30

salaried-entrepreneurs 87
Sarkozy, Nicolas 193
Schmidt, C. 8
Schulze Buschoff, K. 8
Sciberras, J.-C. 89
second-generation autonomous work
47
*The Second Generation of Self-
Employment* 24
self-determination 2
self-employed population, data analysis
48
self-employed professionals 1–15
in knowledge/skill-based activities
3
self-employed workers 28, 84
self-employment status 207
Sennett, R. 21
Simmel, G. 31
slash worker generation 65
Slovenia
collective representation 114–15
legal and institutional framework
111–13
national framework 110–11
new autonomous workers, public
policy 113–14
self-employed professionals,
precarious nature 110–16
social dialogue 114–15
SmartBE 189
SmartDE 189
Snowball sampling 12
social dialogue 77, 222–8
social paradox 206
social protection 215
binary approach 168
collective bargaining coverage
172–3
degrees of 168–70